THE PRACTICE OF POLITICAL THEORY

NEW DIRECTIONS IN CRITICAL THEORY

Amy Allen, General Editor

New Directions in Critical Theory presents outstanding classic and contemporary texts in the tradition of critical social theory, broadly construed. The series aims to renew and advance the program of critical social theory, with a particular focus on theorizing contemporary struggles around gender, race, sexuality, class, and globalization and their complex interconnections.

Narrating Evil: A Postmetaphysical Theory of Reflective Judgment, María Pía Lara

The Politics of Our Selves: Power, Autonomy, and Gender in Contemporary Critical Theory, Amy Allen

Democracy and the Political Unconscious, Noëlle McAfee

The Force of the Example: Explorations in the Paradigm of Judgment, Alessandro Ferrara

Horrorism: Naming Contemporary Violence, Adriana Cavarero

Scales of Justice: Reimagining Political Space in a Globalizing World, Nancy Fraser

Pathologies of Reason: On the Legacy of Critical Theory, Axel Honneth

States Without Nations: Citizenship for Mortals, Jacqueline Stevens

The Racial Discourses of Life Philosophy: Négritude, Vitalism, and Modernity, Donna V. Jones

Democracy in What State?, Giorgio Agamben, Alain Badiou, Daniel Bensaïd, Wendy Brown, Jean-Luc Nancy, Jacques Rancière, Kristin Ross, Slavoj Žižek

Politics of Culture and the Spirit of Critique: Dialogues, edited by Gabriel Rockhill and Alfredo Gomez-Muller

Mute Speech: Literature, Critical Theory, and Politics, Jacques Rancière

The Right to Justification: Elements of Constructivist Theory of Justice, Rainer Forst

The Scandal of Reason: A Critical Theory of Political Judgment, Albena Azmanova

For a complete list of books in this series, see page 295

THE PRACTICE OF POLITICAL THEORY

RORTY AND CONTINENTAL THOUGHT

CLAYTON CHIN

Columbia University Press
New York

Columbia University Press
Publishers Since 1893
New York   Chichester, West Sussex
cup.columbia.edu
Copyright © 2018 Columbia University Press
Paperback edition, 2021
All rights reserved

Library of Congress Cataloging-in-Publication Data
available from the Library of Congress
ISBN 978-0-231-17398-8 (cloth)
ISBN 978-0-231-17399-5 (pbk.)
ISBN 978-0-231-54799-4 (e-book)

Cover design: Lisa Hamm
Cover image: © CC BY-SA 4.0

TO ANA, FOR ALL THE STRENGTH AND
SUPPORT THAT MADE THIS POSSIBLE.

CONTENTS

Acknowledgments ix
List of Abbreviations xi

I. RORTY AND POLITICAL THINKING

INTRODUCTION. THEORY AND METHOD: RECONSTRUCTING RORTY 3

1. THE AUTHORITY OF THE SOCIAL: A PRAGMATIC ETHOS OF INQUIRY 22

II. RORTY AND CONTINENTAL POLITICAL THOUGHT: ONTOLOGY, NATURALISM, AND HISTORY

2. THEORIZING AFTER FOUNDATIONS: ONTOLOGY, LANGUAGE, AND HEIDEGGER 65

3. RECONSTRUCTING NATURALISM: PRAGMATIC OR ONTOLOGICAL? 98

4. HISTORY AND MODERNITY: SELF-ASSERTION AND CRITICAL REFLEXIVITY 127

PART III: RORTY AND CONTEMPORARY POLITICAL THEORY: PRAGMATIC SOCIOPOLITICAL CRITICISM

5. PRAGMATIC POLITICAL THINKING AND CONTEMPORARY CRITICAL SOCIAL THEORY 155

6. HOW PRAGMATISM CONSTRAINS AND ENABLES POLITICAL THINKING 202

Notes 247
References 259
Index 275

ACKNOWLEDGMENTS

There are many people I am indebted to for aiding me in the completion of this book. I would like to thank the School of Social and Political Science at the University of Melbourne for graciously allowing me a semester free from teaching in 2016 during which time I completed the bulk of the book. This much-needed space can claim much of the credit for whatever is of value here. Similarly, I would like to thank the good people at RIPPLE, KU Leuven. The short time I spent there in 2015 as a visiting postdoctoral fellow was a rich and challenging time during which many of the broad ideas of this project were set down. More personally, I would like to thank Caroline Williams, Matteo Mandarini, Nathan Widder, Michael Bacon, Stephen White, Annabelle Lever, and Lasse Thomassen all of whom provided deeply valuable and insightful advice about both the intellectual content here and the always-fraught publishing process. Michael, in particular, deserves my thanks not only for the continual insights into pragmatism and Rorty but for suggesting Columbia University Press as an ideal destination. I must also thank Wendy Lochner at Columbia, whose patience and support has often surprised me, and the anonymous reviewers of the manuscript, whose generous comments have seen this project through. It is also very important to acknowledge the contemplative labor expended in the development of this work. Daniel McCarthy, Tara Mulqueen, Simon Kaye, and Ana Estefanía Carballo all willingly sacrificed hours of their lives to read chapter drafts. They have thereby incurred responsibility for any errors here. Finally, and most significantly, I want to thank my partner, Ana Estefanía Carballo, who, quite literally, is responsible for the completion of this book. Her help, support, encouragement, and affection have been the motivation to always keep poking that bubble.

ABBREVIATIONS

Works by Richard Rorty

CIS	*Contingency, Irony and Solidarity* (1989)
CP	*Consequences of Pragmatism* (1982)
EHO	*Essays on Heidegger and Others* (1991)
ORT	*Objectivity, Relativism, and Truth* (1991)
PCP	*Philosophy as Cultural Politics* (2007)
PMN	*Philosophy and the Mirror of Nature* (1979)
PSH	*Philosophy and Social Hope* (1999)
TP	*Truth and Progress* (1998)

THE PRACTICE OF POLITICAL THEORY

I

RORTY AND POLITICAL THINKING

INTRODUCTION

THEORY AND METHOD

Reconstructing Rorty

The value of Rorty's contribution . . . resides in his attentiveness to the potential for philosophy in its role of gathering up the threads of new knowledge and perspectives into a central tendency to exclude, overlook, and distort the range of meaning inherent in the diverse social experiences of different individuals and groups.

—CHRISTOPHER VOPARIL, "PRAGMATIST PHILOSOPHY AND ENLARGING HUMAN FREEDOM"

QUESTIONING RORTY

Newcomers to political theory are often struck by its diversity of traditions, approaches, and projects. The discipline pulls in many directions: from continental criticisms of the biopolitical controls of neoliberal governmentality to normative frameworks for linguistic justice in federated democracies. Surprisingly, this diversity is characterized by high degrees of mutual suspicion and misrepresentation, as if the presence of difference compromised others' aims and projects. Lacking an adequate meta-account of its own practice—a result of foundational crises only partially addressed—the only point of commonality is an unwillingness to accept that political theory can serve multiple purposes.

Richard Rorty directly addressed this deep disagreement on the metalevel, providing the frame of a mode of intellectual and political engagement that allows critical and normative political thinking to proceed from within these conditions. He directly responded to the crisis in philosophical foundations, the problem of justification it elicits in inquiry, and the problem of pluralism that follows in political argument. To do this, he dramatically redescribed the practice of human inquiry and the role of political thinking in sociopolitical life in a manner still not appreciated within political theory. Rather than establishing foundational principles for or critical unveilings of politics, Rorty conceives political theory as a form of situated sociopolitical criticism attuned to the problems of internormative engagement, one that intervenes using the public language of its day to reconstruct problematic practices across difference. However, this potential was not immediately apparent in his writings, only emerging in concrete form in his final volume of philosophical papers on "cultural politics" (Rorty 2007h). It has thus been ignored by much of the critical literature. Further, this method and model, drawn out throughout this analysis, is not free of implicit challenges. His work (and pragmatism generally) still sits underneath the charge of "acquiescence": that it lacks sufficient theoretical resources for political criticism, methods to identify practices as harmful, *and* normative resources to transform them. This criticism still dominates his reception in political theory.

To test this charge and alternative possibilities, my rereading of Rorty makes two incursions into contemporary debates. First, it engages the ontological turn in political theory, "weak ontology," stemming from continental philosophy. As discussed below, Rorty's relation to these approaches has never been thoroughly examined, and an engagement between these two perspectives, in terms of their responses to the crisis in foundations, promises to clarify the possibilities and problems facing contemporary critical and normative political inquiry. My analysis argues that there are good reasons to doubt the strengths attributed to ontology for sociopolitical criticism assumed by much of continental political theory, particularly among radical agonistic approaches to democracy. Second, never attempted before, it offers a meta-account of Rorty's relation to continental political thought, reconstructing his reading strategy for his key continental sources. Tracking this strategy across his accounts of hermeneutics, Heidegger, Nietzsche, Hegel, and Foucault reveals the shape of his relation to this tradition *and* the rationale of his selective appropriation and critique. Further, as this is the main context of its development, this enables the explication of his theory of sociopolitical criticism.

In this introduction, I situate Rorty within the theoretical matrix surrounding the metatheoretical question of the nature of political theorizing. I then examine Rorty's problematic through the shape of pragmatist political thought before illustrating his critical reception and its failure to examine the methodological injunctions of his work and how they manifest in his later sociopolitical approach. Finally, I outline why contemporary ontological political theory is ideal both to draw out this reconstruction and expose his relation to continental political thought.

RORTY'S PROBLEMATIC: METAPOLITICAL TRENDS IN POLITICAL THEORY

The present discussion focuses on the trends in political thought that structured Rorty's work: those that confronted the problem of the foundations/grounds/metaphysics. While such groupings are always problematic impositions, three principal clusters are significant: pragmatism, (Habermasian) critical theory, and postfoundational (ontological) thought.[1] Rorty engaged all these positions. This section establishes their parameters. Subsequent discussion will illustrate his problematic and the critical framework for this analysis, outlining the scope of the present study and its significance for the possibility of a critical political methodology.

It is necessary to comment on analytical political theory. While Rorty often engaged this tradition (e.g., in his noted embrace of Rawls; see chapter 5), this literature is not the frame for several reasons. First, a substantial portion of its criticism on Rorty focuses on his relation to liberal theory. This is true even of recent trends that, as discussed below, offer new opportunities (e.g., Curtis 2015). While this literature still has its gaps, his relation to continental thought and what that indicates about his work and political theory are where the significant lacunae remain.

Second, this debate has not focused on his *method* for internormative engagement and resources for sociopolitical criticism as much as the traditions discussed below. This is simply because these are not as central projects in liberalism and because Rorty's engagements with liberalism focus elsewhere: on a postmetaphysical vocabulary for liberalism. As a result, while I draw upon liberal analytical analyses, they do not frame this study.

In contrast, pragmatism, critical theory, and postfoundational thought engage these questions in general (often in debate with Rorty). Further, they are linked by a common rejection of what is called "foundationalism": the idea that society and politics are somehow grounded by principles that are undeniable and immune to revision (i.e., universal) and exterior to the realms of society and politics (i.e., transcendent). These foundations assure stability in sociopolitical structures built on their principles (Marchart 2007, 11; Rajchman 1985, x). Unfortunately, the problem of foundations is both one of the most widely accepted *and* insufficiently examined aspects of contemporary political thought. It has been articulated within a variety of contexts in different terms but is avoided by many thinkers. Further, few explicit connections have been drawn among its various iterations, and often there is the problematic assumption that all articulate the same issues.[2] However, the general idea is that we lack the philosophical (i.e., epistemological, ontological, and metaphysical) grounds to make political imperatives flow from philosophical conclusions. In political theory, this is the problem of justifying normative claims within a plural public sphere.

While these clusters all denounce foundationalism in different terms, they all frame it in relation to the "linguistic turn": the idea that all knowledge and validity are linguistically mediated, conditioned by history and the presence of embodied subjects in determinate contexts. This has led to a common *problem of justification* in the realm of sociopolitical criticism. How do we justify the explicit normative claims and implicit normative assumptions that guide sociopolitical criticism and reconstruction? On the one hand, we must recognize the historicity of knowledge and normative claims. On the other, we need political action in an increasingly globalized and interwoven world; this requires raising claims to the validity of decisions and the critical and normative frameworks that serve them. In this manner, the problem of justification represents the high-theoretical form of the central problem of postwar twentieth-century political thought: *the problem of political pluralism* (e.g., Berlin 1999). This is the problem, increasingly refined in recent years, of how to organize democratic engagement across substantive cultural-political differences. Such a project requires a framework that appreciates

> the limits of theory, just because it begins with the need to listen and respond to the plurality of voices we actually confront in a concrete setting, and not transcending them in a projection of its own account of what is right or true. Such a political theory can exhibit the range of disagreement, of contestation in political life, and so keep alive the possibilities that are excluded when we work and think only within a particular framework as, to a large extent, we must.
>
> (Moon 2004, 25)

These two tensions structure these clusters in political theory today and have been inadequately examined in their mutual relations.

While I examine the shape of pragmatist political thought in more detail later, its history is centrally concerned with the foundations of human thought and the political consequences thereof. Beginning in the late nineteenth century, pragmatism is associated with Charles Sanders Peirce, William James, and John Dewey. These three were united by a focus on inquiry, a reorientation of thought to human action, and a rejection of idealisms (Bernstein 2010, 1–25; 1995). After pragmatism fell out of fashion in the 1930s with the rise of analytic philosophy, *neo*pragmatism revived in the 1960s and 1970s around three basic issues: First, the aforementioned crises in the traditional image of philosophy as a transcendental mode of inquiry capable of grounding claims to "Truth, Goodness, and Beauty" (West 1989, 3). Second, this disenchantment led to a concern with the relation between knowledge and power. Pragmatism repoliticized American philosophy by emphasizing the role of knowledge in our social practices and political organization. Third, these changes reemphasized human agency. The humanist assumption of an autonomous unencumbered agent is not revived, but neither is the poststructuralist death of the subject assumed. Human desires and values are primary. As Cornel West argues, contemporary pragmatism is defined by an opening of Anglo-American philosophy to alternative traditions of Marxism, structuralism, and poststructuralism (among others) *and* by the need to situate its examinations within its context and its existing languages and practices (West 1989, 4). This is a product of its distinctive focus on social practices as a strategy to address foundationalism.

The differences between pragmatists and continentals are clearly illustrated in the points about human agency and context. While receptive to contingency, pragmatists generally retain some commitment to objectivity. Our knowledge and our norms may be embedded in social practices, but those practices (say, for inquiry or democratic society) are oriented toward the world and our actions, and so theoretical reflection must support inquiry. For example, while Rorty is in the minority of pragmatists in his views on truth for inquiry (Misak 2007, 2), he still reconstructs truth to support inquiry (see chapter 1). As a result, pragmatists have often allied themselves more with critical theory than with continental philosophy.[3]

Critical theory refers to the school dominated by Karl-Otto Apel, Jürgen Habermas, Hans Joas, and Axel Honneth. These thinkers extensively connected the intersubjective model of communicative action to pragmatist theories of inquiry (Bernstein 2010, x, 23–25; Rehg and Bohman 2001; Hoy and McCarthy 1994). Habermas has been especially significant regarding foundations. Similar to pragmatism, he argues for regrounding our thinking in a procedural rationality. While foundationalisms depend on an intrinsically rational world, his postmetaphysical thinking constricts rationality to approaches and procedures. Now, "what counts as rational is solving problems successfully through procedurally suitable dealings with reality" (Habermas 1992, 35). This response to the issue of philosophical foundations is key to both Rorty's own response (as examined in chapter 5) and his relation to continental thought.

Postfoundational philosophy, in contrast, confronted the crisis of foundations by turning to ontology and contingency. While a problematic grouping, it centers on postwar French philosophy working within Heidegger's legacy: a "Heideggerianism of the Left" that has emerged since poststructuralism. This, perhaps more than the others, is a wide cluster of perspectives, mostly associated with self-declared "continental" forms of political thought. However, it goes well beyond continental Europe, including a variety of figures within contemporary political thought that, in some manner, employ an ontological approach in the analysis of politics

(Marchart 2007; White 2000; Silverman 1993). While it has often been marginalized as the self-declared "critical" approach, it is a major voice on the question of foundations.

Its response to the crisis in philosophical foundations is characterized by continual engagement. It does not merely reject foundations, as it accuses pragmatism and critical theory of doing; this assumes the possibility of eclipsing the foundationalist issue. Rather, this cluster defines itself against antifoundationalisms, which in totally rejecting the notion of foundations remain within the foundationalist logic (Bernstein 1991, 8; see also Fairlamb 1994, 7–13). Instead, postfoundational thought grapples with the simultaneous necessity and contingency of foundations in political philosophy. Instead of attacking "metaphysics," it subverts the terrain on which foundationalism operates. Foundations cannot simply be negated; we must understand how foundations are erected and what they authorize, and we must also question their ontological status (Butler 1992, 7). This "quasi-transcendental" move depends upon Heidegger's notion of ontological difference and the associated distinction between *politics* and *the political* (Mouffe 2005, 8–9). The latter is an ontological dimension to politics that necessitates an understanding of contingency. The ultimate impossibility of a final ground makes all political forms necessarily contingent for postfoundational thinkers (Marchart 2007, 15, 25–26). In this analysis, this position is represented by Martin Heidegger, William E. Connolly, new materialisms, and variants of agonistic democracy. Their versions are the main voice in dialogue with Rorty's pragmatism in this assessment of his reconstruction of political thought.

These three clusters structured Rorty's response and his implicit alternative model of sociopolitical criticism that manifests in his late concept of "cultural politics." While pragmatism sets the intellectual strategies, from critical theory (particularly Habermas) he derived a critique of continental philosophy and a justification of cosmopolitan democracy. Finally, from postfoundational thought, Rorty gained an ally in undermining the foundationalist project of Western philosophy. He selectively drew on elements from all, but only to serve his reconstruction of theoretical practice and political engagement.

With this frame in mind, it is necessary to draw a little more shape around pragmatist political thought. As discussed in chapter 1, Rorty's transformation of political thinking and his engagement of alternative traditions (like continental thought) occurs within his reading of pragmatism. However, two difficulties (and potentials) emerge when examining this influence. First, internally, it is a divided tradition (Bernstein 1995; Rescher 2000; Mounce 1997). This makes identifying its themes difficult, especially as Rorty was rejected by many pragmatists. Second, externally, pragmatism has had a contentious history and stands at the brink of a unique theoretical potential today. In terms of the former, the dominant narrative has been one of cycles of eclipse and resurgence. Against this, Richard Bernstein has argued for the gradual growth and "mainstreaming" of pragmatist ideas throughout the last hundred years, the "Pragmatic Century" (Bernstein 2006, 3).[4] This is not an argument for direct influence but a nuanced illustration of pragmatic themes becoming increasingly central within analytic and continental thinking. For Bernstein, pragmatism's nonfoundational conception of human inquiry, focusing on how humans are shaped by *and* shape normative social practices, has strong resonances in both (Bernstein 2010, ix–x, 17–19). Its key themes (fallibilism, critical communities of inquiry, sensitivity to radical contingency, and the irreducible plurality of perspectives) amount to a shift to human practices as the primary context of thought (Green 2013, 6; Bernstein 2006, 3).

This focus on social practices is a critical and substantive project of antifoundationalism that links pragmatism with recent trends across the analytic-continental divide (Chin 2016a, forthcoming; Chin and Thomassen 2015). It reveals that the central question of pragmatism is the theoretical significance of antifoundationalism. This goes beyond a critical, negative point to ask about positive transformation. Its core component is a critical conception of *reflexivity*. While the modern project of science (and the values associated with it) is commended as valuable for gaining knowledge, it is tempered by an attempt to maintain a reflexive critical understanding of its own status (Volbers 2014). As argued here, this double movement characterizes Rorty's antiauthoritarianism, which offers a metavocabulary of vocabularies, a sociological perspective on language use, normativity, and authority, to maintain this relation.

Despite their divisions, pragmatists share this twin emphasis on reflexivity and social practice. As Bernstein notes, pragmatism approaches ideas, theories, and concepts as tools to do this. This is not a representational claim; it is the notion that this framing highlights their social and practical aspects while offering a reflexive agency in relation to their use (Bernstein 2010, 10). Dewey notes, "All intelligent thinking means an increment of freedom in action . . . conceptions, theories, and systems of thought are always open to development through use. . . . They are tools. As in the case of all tools, their value resides not in themselves but in their capacity to work shown in the consequence of their use" (Dewey 2008a, 163). This point repeats West's argument that while pragmatism shares continental thought's skepticism toward foundationalism, it is committed to nonreductive senses of objectivity and human agency.

As a result, pragmatic political thinking circles several concerns. Principally, it rejects any metaphysical realism about moral and political value. Such a realism can be constituted by any claim to a "determinate way the world is," whether that be a fundamental human nature or the inherently conflictual or cooperative nature of political life, and would extend to any articulation of such a claim (epistemological, ontological, metaphysical, etc.). However, equally, pragmatist political thought rejects skepticism/subjectivism about normativity. These views assume that without a neutral framework for inquiry, conflict about values will persist and there will be no rational way to resolve disputes; this would mean that no claims about the better or worse nature of values or actions could be substantiated. Pragmatism rejects this for four reasons. First, both belief and doubt require justification. Radical doubt, for the pragmatist, is neither possible nor desirable; we always need a reason to doubt a belief. Second, fallibilism: our knowledge is always open to revision and critical reflexive development. Third, concepts and attitudes are historical, and theoretical reflection must be an active agent willing to eliminate and create ideas. Fourth, reasoning is a collective and social activity. It involves dialogical forms of interaction between individuals and groups.[5] The latter are the ultimate context of validity. Finally, all of these claims are framed within a horizontal and reciprocal understanding of the theory-praxis nexus. Rorty makes all these claims in one form or another.

As a result, the pragmatist political project focuses on the values, principles, and norms implicit within an existing form of sociopolitical life as objects for elucidation, critical clarification, and melioristic reconstruction. Importantly, and this is contentious with respect to Rorty and is the subject of the critical clarification here, disagreement provides the impetus and fertile soil of such actions. All of this is an important starting point for thinking about pragmatism's relation to other traditions, its ultimate theoretical potential and significance for various disciplines (political theory included), *and* Rorty's contribution to the question of sociopolitical criticism within political theory.

DIVIDING METHOD AND POLITICS: RORTY'S CRITICAL RECEPTIONS

Political theorists generally ignore this pragmatic project when confronting pragmatism and Rorty. Neopragmatism in the 1970s and 1980s was followed by a perception that pragmatism entailed a "politics of acquiescence" unable to distinguish good from bad political consequences. This charge, originally made against classical pragmatism, was redeployed against neopragmatism in general and Rorty specifically (MacGilvray 2000; Festenstein 2003; Shapiro 1990). It initially made Rorty an object of controversy at the center of many debates in political theory. Neil Gross, his unofficial academic biographer, claims that "one could not be taken seriously as an intellectual in the 1990s without forming some kind of opinion as to Rorty's views" (Gross 2008, 336).[6] Of the more than 1,200 entries in a comprehensive bibliography of secondary literature on his work compiled in 2002, only a handful are classed as "friendly to Rorty" (Rumana 2002, ix). This resulted in a consensus, prominent in the 1990s, that he had little to contribute to political theory. Consequently, his critical role shifted. No longer a foil, Rorty is now casually dismissed and, outside pragmatism, ignored. Alan Malachowski notes that there is the perception now that Rorty was "insufficiently provocative." Here, his supposed destruction of philosophy "lays down nothing more dangerous than some damp intellectual squibs" (Malachowski 2011, 87). This critical tendency is not the product of a deep understanding of his work.

Readings of Rorty in political theory suffer from several problematic tendencies. First, *superficiality*: they generally ignore the detailed theoretical and methodological justifications of his political approaches. Second, *selectivity*: they are overly focused on a limited number of sources (e.g., *CIS*) and ignore later developments in his thought. Finally, *partisanship*: they usually focus on saving a figure or tradition (e.g., Derrida or liberalism) from Rorty's "unjust appropriation." This section briefly addresses the critical literature on Rorty from within political theory to demonstrate his place and clarify these problems. Subsequently, it turns to these recent pragmatist rereadings in order to illustrate their potential and relevance to these questions.

Communitarians critiqued Rorty's alleged misunderstanding of the community, the nature of justification therein, and the effect on individuals. For Alasdair MacIntyre, Rorty ignores how the nature of communities allows for rational progress (MacIntyre 1985, 223).[7] Critical theorists repeated this focus. Habermas lumped Rorty in with other "postmodernists" in their common emphasis on the world-disclosive function of language (Habermas 1987, 205–7). Thomas McCarthy similarly criticized Rorty, along with poststructuralists, for only seeing reason as a negative lack. For both of these theorists, it is not contingency but the universality of reason and validity claims that provides for social critique (McCarthy 1991, 5). However, some critical theorists attempted more detailed analyses of the consequences of Rorty's antitheory. Continuing, McCarthy rightly sought the consequences of Rorty's "depoliticized theory and detheorized politics." However, he failed to develop this connection in any detail (McCarthy 1991, 25–26). Nancy Fraser repeats this emphasis, contending that Rorty builds his public/private divide atop a division between theory and politics. The former is relegated to the solely poetic function of self-creation and the latter to homogenized solidarity. This leads to a strict dichotomy between a romantic, antisocial private sphere and a totalitarian political "we" (Fraser 1990, 314–15; 1995). In both of these examples, however, the connection is only nascent. Neither relates these points to substantial analyses of how Rorty reconceives theoretical and political practice, ignoring his method and its political consequences.

Postfoundational theorists share these deficiencies, offering a political critique that ignores the details of Rorty's method. They read his work through a division between his "good philosophy" and his "problematic politics," consequently misunderstanding both. On the one hand, they embrace his critiques of foundationalism and Enlightenment rationalism, positing substantial theoretical agreement. Ernesto Laclau notes, "though I certainly agree with most of Rorty's philosophical arguments and positions, his notion of 'liberal utopia' presents a series of shortcomings which can only be superseded if the liberal features of Rorty's utopia are reinscribed in the wider framework of what we have called 'radical democracy'" (Laclau 1996b, 105; see also Mouffe 1996b). This does not preclude *some* political overlap. Chantal Mouffe, for example, applauds Rorty's attempt to separate liberalism from that rationalism and acknowledges his important contributions to shifting the literature from trying to underpin liberal-democratic principles rationally to creating an ethos that sustains and motivates them (Mouffe 1996b, 5; Laclau 1996a, 60; 1996b, 105).

On the other hand, postfoundationalists and the agonistic democratic subcluster reject his democratic politics. As discussed in chapters 2, 3, and 4, Connolly charges Rorty with a social foundationalism that emerges from his failure to carry through on his critique of foundationalism to see the necessity of ontology and the violence of all socialization. The result is an ontology of mastery and an apology for status quo liberalism (Connolly 1987, chap. 8; 1990, 105-8). Similarly, for Stephen White, Rorty misunderstands the nuance of weak-ontological approaches and how they disrupt traditional metaphysics within liberalism (White 2000, 15-17). For Laclau, there is an "internal inconsistency" in Rorty's liberal utopia (i.e., his normative ideal), which relies on a series of conceptual distinctions (force/persuasion, reform/revolution) that are essentially impure (e.g., there is no persuasion without force). As a result, he assumes a simplistic version of social conflict and power and mistakenly thinks a society of persuasion, without force, is either desirable or possible. "Thus, the radical democratic 'utopia' that I would like to counterpose to Rorty's liberal one does not preclude antagonisms and social division but, on the contrary, considers them as *constitutive* of the social" (Laclau 1996b, 114-15, my emphasis). Similarly, Mouffe laments that Rorty does not go further in his criticisms of Habermas, sharing an ignorance of the "central integrative function" of conflict in pluralist democracies. As a result, Rorty overvalues consensus as an ideal of democratic engagement, not realizing that democratic engagement is better served by agonistic relations. In this manner, he is incapable of appreciating the complexity of the political, the inadequacy of consensus to it, or the nature of contemporary pluralism, which is *constitutive* of political life (Mouffe 1996b, 7-8, 10-11).

Consequently, postfoundational thinkers focus more on dissociating themselves from Rorty's politics than on examining, in depth, his methods, their justifications, and their possibilities for political reconstruction.[8] They broadly identify the limits in his thought but fail to expose their potential. Why does Rorty reject ontology? How do we understand his argument for a social-practice-based understanding of theory and politics? Postfoundational theorists repeat the aforementioned tendency to superficial, selective, and partisan readings, ignoring the detailed connections between his methods and model of political thinking.

NORMATIVITY WITHOUT FOUNDATIONS: REFLEXIVITY IN POLITICAL THEORY

There is a "third wave" of pragmatist scholarship offering new resources for alternative uses of Rorty and pragmatism (B. Allen 2004; Green 2008; Koopman 2007; Rogers 2009a; Voparil 2006; Bacon 2007; Curtis 2015; Chin and Bacon 2015). Colin Koopman's reinterpretation of Rorty is particularly illustrative of this rereading and its potential. He remains critical but utilizes Rorty's largely ignored later writings to develop a situated cultural-political theory that is transformative and not acquiescent. For Koopman, Rorty's philosophy offers a political ethos of hopeful meliorism and a reconstructive method of narrative redescription, which together constitute a form of "transitionalism," a method of political engagement designed to shift problematic practices and understandings in ways essential to any democratic politics (Koopman 2009). In this way, Koopman and others highlight Rorty's key methodological contributions to allowing political theory to transition toward particular problems and situations by theorizing forms of democratic politics oriented to the reconstruction of current practices. Importantly, this raises the possibility of directly responding to the acquiescence charge.

These readings, which are ongoing yet ignored within the conversation of political theory, inform my reconstruction of Rorty. Through this study, I further these interpretations and their insights for a critical political methodology. To do this, I engage Rorty with ontological approaches to political theory, particularly that of William E. Connolly, which are ideally suited to clarify the theoretical significance and difference of his sociopolitical method. However, this analysis will not only examine Rorty but also employ the emerging method to reflect back critically on these ontological approaches.

As a submovement of postfoundationalism that significantly crosses over with agonistic democracy, ontological political theories are at the center of contemporary debates in methodology and democracy, ideally situated to bring out this reconstruction of Rorty. First, much of this group operates in the Anglo-American world and is similarly situated in contemporary debates to Rorty, not least of all in their theoretical sources, also drawing on both the continental and analytical traditions in political thought. Second, they directly confront the problems of justification and pluralism and the need to maintain normative stances. Third, as discussed later, they similarly approach this balancing act through the lens of reflexivity, differing in where they place it and how they operationalize it. Finally, there is little literature examining pragmatism and weak ontology and their different solutions to common problems.

Stephen K. White has dubbed the ontological turn in political theory "weak ontology." Here, ontology is both fundamental and contestable, both unavoidable and ungrounded. As in postfoundationalism, this paradox requires a twofold approach. Political philosophy must simultaneously think from two different perspectives. Confronting radical contingency and the impossibility of a final ground, it must gesture beyond our particular moment to think an impossibility and necessity that exceeds particular determinations. However, it must also realize that this external moment can only occur within a particular historical constellation, and it must also engage that constellation, establishing its limits and borders (Marchart 2007, 31–32). However, unlike Rorty's pragmatism, the situated nature of thinking does not necessitate a social-practice-based model. Rather, as that thinking gestures further, we must think current assumptions while projecting cautious alternatives.

> The fundamental conceptualizations such an ontology provides can, at most, prefigure practical insight or judgment, in the sense of providing broad cognitive and affective orientation. Practice draws sustenance from an ontology in the sense of both a reflective bearing upon possibilities for action and a mobilizing of motivational force.
>
> (White 2000, 11)

While weak ontology shirks the foundational project of making political forms flow from ontological analyses, it is concerned to make positive political claims, distinguishing it from postfoundationalism, which emphasizes critique over normative reconstruction.

In this emphasis on normative construction, weak ontology and recent pragmatism meet. For pragmatism, political inquiry seeks "normativity without foundations," to make political claims without reference to foundations. It must be critical and prescriptive without absolute grounds (Koopman 2011a, 537). This framing illuminates considerable crossover, although specific differences remain. Placing ontology to one side momentarily, both reject strong ontologies while retaining affirmation to some ideal. Both understand all claims as contestable without not only critiquing foundationalism but also addressing "what must be articulated, cultivated, and affirmed in its wake" (White 2000, 8). Further, contestability, the claim of necessary pluralism, structures both of their articulations of politics, which requires that each build reflexively into any positive politics. Contestability must "in some sense fold back upon itself, disrupting its own smooth constitution of a unity. In a way, its contestability will thus be enacted rather than just announced" (White 2000, 8). The difference is how they articulate that positive and weave in reflexivity. Weak ontology resorts to the level of ontological analysis in order to integrate contestability into its presuppositions. It seeks to break with the existing set of ontological presuppositions, to varying degrees, in modernity. Pragmatism, in contrast, *does not integrate reflexivity at that level, nor does it attempt such a break*. Rather, as illustrated in Rorty, it reconstructs modern understandings of inquiry and political practice by focusing on the level of linguistic social practice both to explain pluralism and to provide the possibility of normative engagement. These differences structure the relationship between ontological approaches and pragmatism, which otherwise overlap considerably in their critiques of and responses to philosophical foundationalism.

Pairing these approaches reflects the current tension within critical political thought between now-established ontological methods and the emerging *situated* approaches of recent pragmatism (and others).[9] While these perspectives share criticisms of ideal liberal theory, rejecting its abstract approach to normative political theorizing, their shifts to social practice and ontological approaches, respectively for pragmatism and weak ontology, represent two contending pathways, competing options never sufficiently engaged.[10] A conversation examining this tension promises uniquely significant results.

The particularities of Rorty's thinking make him an ideal interlocutor for weak ontology. While the third wave of pragmatism certainly goes well beyond his work, involving reconstructions of Dewey (Rogers 2009a, 2009b), James (Livingston 2012), and Peirce (Misak 2000; Talisse 2007), there are two reasons for choosing Rorty. First, he directly engaged the issues of ontology and foundations. His notable critique of foundations and his assessment of the ontological alternative place him in a unique position for dialogue with that now-established approach. Second, flowing from this, his reconstructionist method directly addresses a lack in weak ontology around how to change institutions and practices once they have been critiqued. This makes the depth of comparison available in Rorty unique and needful.

The center of all these features is Rorty's direct examination, similar in detail and scope to the ontological alternative, of the *problem of metatheoretical difference*. Under the problems of justification and pluralism, engagement at the metalevel of competing frameworks for inquiry and competing normative traditions for politics becomes deeply difficult. It is inquiry in the absence of shared criteria. This study argues that this comparison with ontology illustrates that Rorty's theory offers a framework for opposing the usual strategies by which metatheories justify themselves and disallow competitors. It is thus an effective metatheory for enabling linguistic engagement at the level of normative difference, promising significant results for both the method of political theory and questions of democratic pluralism.

The comparison with ontological theory also enables this study to respond to the charge of acquiescence. As discussed above, postfoundationalists and agonists charge Rorty with lacking critical and normative resources in a similar manner to the previous charge of acquiescence against all pragmatism. To examine this I turn to Connolly, employing the latter's ontological method and his assertion of a series of ontological assumptions behind Rorty's nonfoundational method. For him, Rorty assumes an ontology of *mastery*, a common set of assumptions in modernity that approach the world as something to be bent to human agency and assume that it is predisposed to such a relationship. My reading counters this by arguing for another dynamic, one that culminates in his late concept of cultural politics. Throughout Rorty's work there is the subterranean development of a cultural-critical method for political theory that, in turn, exposes the covert authoritarianism and normative confusion of ontological methods like Connolly's. First, Connolly fails to weave contestability and reflexivity into his ontological model and ends up treating its figuration of being as foundational. Second, and consequently, Connolly's politics are overly dependent on this ontological base and insufficiently argued for without it. The result is that his political imperatives end up carrying little weight. Thus, while weak ontology may link Rorty's thought to an ontology not otherwise apparent, my analysis exposes how as a basis for understanding and modeling political action it is Connolly's ontological method that reduces politics to a series of perspectives and theory to a means of normative articulation (rather than transformation). While not without weaknesses,[11] Rorty's cultural-political method of criticism and reconstruction contains more fecund methodological insights for contemporary political thought.

Finally, beyond aiding the explication of Rorty's model of sociopolitical criticism and resources for reflexivity, ontological political theory enables the second incursion of this study into continental political theory: systematizing Rorty's reading strategy for, use of, and relation to continental thought. By connecting his accounts of hermeneutics, Heidegger, Nietzsche, Hegel, and Foucault (among others), this study reveals the shape of and rationale behind his oft-noted counterintuitive approaches to central figures in that tradition.[12] Linking these back to the aims and method of his emergent model of sociopolitical criticism clarifies the coherence of his readings with his political method.

CHARTING THE WAY

My argument will proceed as follows. Chapter 1 situates Rorty within his early metaphilosophy, critique of epistemology, brief turn to hermeneutics, and subsequent reading of pragmatism and Dewey. It argues that these reveal the problem at the heart of all Rorty's thought, that of normative difference at the metatheoretical level, and his unified strategy of resorting to the level of social practices. This "turn to the social" further entailed a politicization of thinking and a transformation of theory to a situated form of sociopolitical criticism.

This analysis continues, in chapters 2–4's analyses of language, naturalism/holism, and history, respectively, examining Rorty's positive pragmatic method in dialogue with Connolly's ontological method. Chapter 2 contrasts his rejection of ontology with Connolly's explicit use of it, exposing how those positions are rooted in contrasting readings of language, contingency, and continental philosophy (specifically, Heidegger). Chapter 3 extends this analysis, contrasting Rorty's conception of naturalism with recent trends toward "new materialism" in continental political thought. Finally, in chapter 4, the analysis turns to historicism as the key approach to normative transformation for Rorty and contrasts his reading of modernity with the ontological critique thereof.

In chapter 5, I pick up the explicit thread of Rorty's sociopolitical criticism, engaging him with debates around universality and critique in contemporary social theory. Illustrating his mutual critique of Habermasian critical theory and radical continental criticism, I examine the central ethos of inclusivity at the heart of his politics. Finally, I systematize his varied interpretations of Foucault. Chapter 6 closes the study with my examination of his late conception of cultural politics and its basis for a form of situated sociopolitical criticism. By engaging Rorty with the question of intermethodological work in political theory and contemporary agonistic democracy, I draw out potentials for future political thinking.

All of this places this reconstruction in the aforementioned trend in third-wave Rorty scholarship that reads Rorty less as a negative skeptic and more as a positive theorist of transformation. These readings reveal that the central guiding thread of Rorty's politics is not a problematic liberalism or a regressive public-private divide but an ethos for contemporary pluralistic democracy that takes inclusion beyond the quasi-foundational approaches of liberal proceduralism and radical ontological thought.

This is reading Rorty by his own method, *redescriptively/reconstructively*, in light of current debates, such as the ontological turn in recent continental political thought. It is reading him *holistically* by seeing how all the aspects of his thinking hang together, in the broadest sense. This is the key methodological structure of his positive philosophy.

Further, it is the approach of the "first-rate critic" that examines "an optimal version of the philosopher's position—one in which the holes in the arguments are plugged or politely ignored, and the unfortunate side-effects of his work, or the side-issues she discussed, are trimmed away" (Rorty 1987, 11–12). Finally, it is reading him *metatheoretically*. Throughout its development, the metaquestions of the nature of linguistic and normative change and engagement are the central struts of Rorty's thought. Such is also the case in his politics, where his ultimate concern is our dispositional relation to the status of our own claims and norms and the task of creating a framework for political thinking that is more inclusive yet reflexive, less foundational without being relativistic, more critical without losing normative force. It is the enduring value of Rorty's thinking to have confronted unhesitatingly the conditions of political inquiry that make this project our best response (so far) to the problems of justification and pluralism.

1

THE AUTHORITY OF THE SOCIAL

A Pragmatic Ethos of Inquiry

I am a hedgehog who, despite showering my reader with allusions and dropping lots of names, has really only one idea: the need to get beyond representationalism, and thus into an intellectual world in which human beings are responsible only to each other.

—RICHARD RORTY, "PHILOSOPHY AS A TRANSITIONAL GENRE"

THE QUESTION OF PRAGMATISM

Contemporary political theory turns. There are the ontological, situated, and methodological turns. There are postsecular, practice, and realist turns. The entire discipline is constantly turning, and Rorty is no different. However, the premise of this critical reconstruction is that Rorty turned once and spent a career examining the implications. This is his oft-noted though often poorly understood turn toward pragmatism and away from analytic philosophy of mind/language. There are several falsities in this simple narrative; Rorty, for one, did not turn away from analytical thought in any substantive way, as it continued to preoccupy large sections of his published works.[1] However, he did turn toward the use of pragmatic thinkers and the metaphilosophical consequences of their work for theoretical practice. As I will argue, this pragmatic turn entailed shifting away from asking certain types of questions (epistemological, ontological) to others (sociopolitical) and shifting away from analytic thought and to traditions more deeply concerned with sociopolitical criticism (hermeneutics, critical theory, and continental philosophy).

This chapter examines Rorty's early pragmatist turn and how it frames his model of sociopolitical thinking. Set in his initial contributions to the philosophy of mind and his critique of analytic epistemology in *Philosophy and the Mirror of Nature* (*PMN*), it illustrates his continuing concerns with the nature of normative authority and linguistic change and his strategy of *sociological circumvention* when confronting epistemic/ontological figurations of these issues. In this account, this strategy frames his subsequent turn to pragmatist sources and their metaphilosophical understandings of the nature of theorizing and its relation to human inquiry. Focusing both on Rorty's general articulation of the pragmatist framework and on his specific use of Dewey, it distills a series of themes Rorty deploys to shift theoretical practice toward an embedded form of sociocultural criticism of the linguistic practices of human communities. Using this emerging model, in this chapter I also compare Rorty's accounts of two literatures that explicitly consider the method of sociopolitical criticism: hermeneutics and pragmatism. Rorty turned to these traditions to refine and distinguish his model. These engagements illuminate its significance for the contemporary sociopolitical sciences and political theory.

Throughout this discussion, two key claims emerge: the necessity of a public model of philosophy and the priority of the social. First, contra the theoretical critique that Rorty's work is an end-of-philosophy argument and the political critique that it is a privatization of theoretical reason, Rorty's turn to pragmatism inaugurates a reconstruction of theoretical practice as a public, political activity. Second, his early critiques of epistemology and ontology employ a methodological prioritization of the social that does the work of this publicization by leveling theoretical practice with other forms of sociopolitical thinking. Specifically, he publicizes philosophy through a methodological argument to focus on the linguistic social practices of contemporary democracies as the primary site of normative critique and reconstruction. Together, these two moves inaugurate Rorty's pragmatic account of the problem of justification.

ANALYTIC PHILOSOPHY AND THE SOCIAL TURN

Analytic philosophy, epistemology, and the philosophies of language and mind frame Rorty's early contributions to the metaphilosophical questions this study elucidates. It is within these contributions that his critique of ontology and epistemology and his turn to social practice originate.[2] While Rorty began as a rising star within analytic thought, this section illustrates the unity of this early phase with his turn to pragmatism and a social-practice-based model of sociopolitical criticism. Rorty's work in the philosophy of mind, particularly the mind-body problem, and eliminative materialism illustrates the original framing of his rejection of ontology and epistemology for understanding normativity.

THE EARLY RORTY: STRATEGIC ELIMINATION

Rorty's philosophy of mind occurred within the widespread linguistic turn of analytic philosophy in the 1960s. He outlined this metaphilosophical context in an introduction to an edited volume on the turn. This text betrays a clear concern with methods, the claim to being "presuppositionless," and the question of the linguistic relation to the world. "The history of philosophy is punctuated by revolts against the practices of previous philosophers and by attempts to transform philosophy into a science—a discipline in which universally recognized decision-procedures are available for testing philosophical theses" (Rorty 1967, 1). These revolts typically take the form of a new method that allows philosophy to break out of whatever stale set of discussions it is stagnating in. In this way, true knowledge will emerge, and philosophy will achieve the secure path of a science; that is, it will be in a relation of correspondence with the world.[3]

The concern behind this is methodological diversity—how should we account for it, and is the linguistic turn just another iteration in the train of "presuppositionless one-upmanship," or does it eclipse this tendency? Rorty's answer is that the linguistic turn is best seen not as one united methodological development but as a diverse set of motivations, approaches, and goals (Bernstein and Voparil 2010, 15–19). It is a series of turns he makes no effort to reconcile.[4] This diversity is not reducible to a core. His point is metaphilosophical (and methodological): "The most important thing that has happened in philosophy during the last thirty years is not the linguistic turn itself, but rather the beginning of a thoroughgoing rethinking of certain epistemological difficulties which have troubled philosophers since Plato and Aristotle" (Rorty 1967, 39). The linguistic turn's significance is the manner in which it reveals the problems with the traditional epistemological project. Specifically, the focus on linguistic practice reveals the contingent nature of both those practices and the "traditional problems of philosophy" our current ways of speaking have engendered.[5]

Rorty's essays in the philosophy of mind provide important context on this rejection of ontology and epistemology. In the 1960s and 1970s, parallel to his metaphilosophical concerns, he offered a striking response to the traditional mind-body problem he called *eliminative materialism* (Rorty 1965, 1970a, 1970b). Importantly, this response is characterized by a prioritization of sociolinguistic practices. Within this debate, the "mind" concerns the specifically nonphysical aspect of humanity, the part that thinks and has "mental" states. Delineating its nature has been one of the central problems of modern philosophy since Descartes, who begins with the question of mind-body relations. In twentieth-century analytic linguistic philosophy, this problem concerns a distinction between sentences that utilize "mentalistic" or psychological terms and those that deploy physical terms to explain the mental. This is the context of Rorty's eliminative materialism, which is a theory of language and its status. His concern is with the nature of concept change and its implications for the mind-body problem (Gascoigne 2008, 19).

Rorty begins his account of eliminative materialism with an analogy between the contemporary language of "sensations" and "demons" in a hypothetical "primitive" community. Both terms function to explain reality and allow individuals to report mental states (e.g., I am in pain/I am possessed by a demon). Importantly, both are in principle eliminable. He argues it would do no harm to our understanding of persons if we stopped thinking of them as things having sensations (or demons). Sensations are not a necessary part of our conceptual scheme. Additionally, getting rid of mental/demon talk would not impair our ability to describe and predict the world. The key point is that changing our vocabulary about mental states is not about reduction but elimination, that is, swapping the use of one vocabulary for another (Rorty 1965, 28–41). This means that no actual ontological claim (no claim about the existence of particular objects in the world) is made in the process of linguistic change, which only involves using different explanatory frameworks through the elimination of a vocabulary, not its reduction. Rather, Rorty opposes the claim that there are, in principle, concepts (e.g., "sensations") that are *ineliminable* parts of language. However, if sensation talk is, in principle, eliminable, and if the future does contain the elimination of that vocabulary, as Rorty claims, why are those who speak of sensations not presently guilty of false beliefs?

The answer is found in the *status* of Rorty's argument. His theory of eliminative materialism is not arguing for the superiority of the materialist position (or any position) but the in-principle eliminability of all vocabularies and the necessity of alternative vocabularies (Hiley 2002, 108–9). However, the temporal dimension of this argument (i.e., the, in principle, future eliminability of sensation talk) reveals a fundamental condition of language use: the social origin of linguistic norms. The idea of temporality assumes that in concept change, and specifically in the future, certain descriptions can become pragmatically *needful*. Suggesting change involves comparing present language with a hypothetical future. This stands in complete opposition to the dominant (modern) desire to judge our understandings against the antecedently real. By focusing on the level of linguistic description, Rorty naturalizes the mental "by construing the normativity of the reporting of sensations in terms of social practices" (Gascoigne 2008, 30).

In fact, Rorty's distinctiveness in this literature is in how he builds this into two distinct claims. First, the assertion that mental states (for example, "incorrigible first-person reports") are normative phenomena: they concern the *authority* of certain types of reports. Second, authority is always instituted by linguistic social practices, that is, ways of speaking that give those claims. Here, the social practice of treating certain reports as authoritative is the source of their authority, not an ontological or epistemic relation.

The consequences are fundamental. "Once ontological distinctions have been drawn in normative terms of *authority* and *responsibility*, social pragmatism about norms means according a certain substantial categorical privilege to the ontological category of the social" (Brandom 2013, 26).

The rules and practices for making and contesting various claims reside within the linguistic communities that employ the vocabularies being used, and, as a result, authority remains, from a metaphilosophical perspective, ultimately social. This has dramatic results for the two other ontological categories usually ascribed with authority: subjectivity, which concerns things over which individual subjects are given incontestable authority; and objectivity, which are those things not to be susceptible to the authority of individuals or communities but which exercise normative authority to make us responsible *to them*. Rorty's claim is that this is not an equal three-part division between the subjective, objective, and social but that the former two fall under the normative authority of the latter. For him, "ontology can only be done by examining the normatively governed linguistic practices by which we detail our view of reality" (Levine 2010, 573). This is an antiontological point in the sense that our access to the social is the linguistic practices of a community. Consequently, each ontological realm is instituted on sociopragmatic grounds, on the sociolinguistic practices taken as authoritative in each sphere. This does not deny the reality of subjective and objective but only argues that their authority will depend upon socially articulated categories.

This is a creative response. Intervening in a fairly specific debate in the philosophy of mind, Rorty elides the entire question through a metaphilosophical claim about the priority of the social in conceptual-linguistic change. This pairing is important. As his reflections on the linguistic turn indicated, and which others have argued,[6] these inventive contributions to one of the central problems of the philosophy of mind take place within a set of metaphilosophical concerns about the role and significance of a focus on language for the philosophical project. This illustrates the first iteration of a recurring Rortian strategy. By resorting to the social origin of the authority of our various practices, Rorty *sociologically circumvents* a philosophical problem blocking theoretical inquiry. In doing so, he reveals this barrier as optional (though not false) and better elided by adopting alternative ways of speaking. To assess the strength of this strategy, we must turn to its fuller manifestation in Rorty's *PMN*.

For the present purposes, it is important to emphasize that this is a distinctly antiontological and antiepistemological move. It is an understanding of concept change, where explanatory frameworks are eliminated rather than reduced; for Rorty, while these frameworks may make ontological claims about the world, his understanding of concept change does not. Rather, it deflates the philosophical and ontological significance of our diverse linguistic practices at the metatheoretical level to avoid the problems ascribing that authority entails. In *PMN*, this develops into a critical account of ontology as an arbiter of human culture. While such privilege may be important and useful within particular vocabularies, it is inappropriate on the metalevel of linguistic difference.

EPISTEMOLOGICAL BEHAVIORISM: A SOCIOLOGICAL CRITIQUE OF PHILOSOPHY

PMN significantly develops this social turn in its critical strategy and alternative vision of a postepistemological form of philosophical practice. Rorty's focus remains the "mind" as a standard of philosophical knowledge. He begins this work with a statement of how philosophy understands itself and its project:

> Philosophy can be foundational in respect to the rest of culture because culture is the assemblage of claims to knowledge, and philosophy adjudicates such claims.... To know is to represent accurately what is outside the mind; so to understand the possibility and nature of knowledge is to understand the way in which the mind is able to construct such representations.
>
> (Rorty [1979] 2009, 3)

Rorty connects his work on the philosophy of mind to a general critique of the foundational epistemological project of analytic and modern Western philosophy. For him, the concept of the mind and the dualism between it and the body have maintained the idea that philosophy, exclusive of other disciplines, has unique access to the foundations of knowledge. It is the continued assumption that the mind alone "represents" the external world that supports this claim. On this understanding, the mind, and philosophy as our unique access to it, is the mirror of nature: the single neutral method for judging the accuracy of our representations. For Rorty, this image of the mind containing representations, which philosophy judges, captivates the discipline and incorrectly assumes the possibility of a *neutral, permanent framework for all inquiry* (and culture). This representationalist assumption is the main target of this work and philosophy as a whole, as he suggests in this chapter's epigraph. Instead, he offers a behavioral and pragmatic account of epistemology.

There is a fundamental undercurrent of antiauthoritarianism in Rorty's thought and in his specific critique of epistemology. It is also one of the most misunderstood aspects of his thinking. For Rorty, the demand for a theory of knowledge is "the desire for a constraint—a desire to find 'foundations' to which one might cling, frameworks beyond which one must not stray, objects which impose themselves, representations which cannot be gainsaid" (Rorty [1979] 2009, 315). The attempt to oppose the epistemic authority of the mind, and of extrasocial structures in general, is what unites *PMN* and Rorty's earlier work on eliminative materialism.

In chapters 1 and 3 of *PMN*, Rorty narrates the development of this authority structure, and the desire for authority in general, in the history of Western philosophy. Philosophy, as a distinct discipline, arose with the idea that its main task was a "theory of knowledge." Such a theory was intended to provide foundations to the sciences and all other forms of inquiry. As such, philosophy, a recent, modern invention, is a continuation of a longstanding quest for certainty in Western thought. Rorty's claim is that this epistemological view of philosophy depends upon seeing knowledge as a problem about which we might have a theory. This, in turn, depends on seeing knowledge as an assemblage of representations that correspond to the world (Rorty [1979] 2009, 131–32, 136; Gutting 2003, 43). Importantly, this conception (which culminates in modernity) is based upon a series of perceptual metaphors that link the Platonic and modern projects of philosophy (in the quest for certainty) and are the main objects of Rorty's critique of epistemology.

Three figures are especially important in this project. Descartes is its modern inaugurator in inventing the metaphor of the mind as an inner theater of various contents. This offers the first prospect of foundation: the idea of a mental realm distinct from the physical both provided a field of inquiry somehow prior to all discourse and created the possibility of certainty. Such an inner-outer distinction also created the problem of whether inner representations match outer reality *and* its solution, a discipline and method for certain knowledge. Locke, the second, rejects Descartes's rationalism while attempting to fulfill his promise. Instead of focusing on innate ideas, sense experience provides the foundation. For him, sensations cause simple ideas in the mind. Since such simple ideas are the result of solely causal processes, they link our beliefs with the outside world. We can achieve rational relations between our beliefs by focusing on the origin of those ideas; that is, by giving a causal account of how ideas are formed in the mind through the external world impacting our senses, we acquire an epistemological account of certain knowledge (Rorty [1979] 2009, 141–43).

The fundamental addition here is making *causation* the key element of justification. This assumption is one of the main support struts of the modern image of the mind as a representing entity that represents through ideas. It is crucial to the view that this is the basis of knowing, that "a quasi-mechanical account of the way in which our immaterial tablets are dented by the material world will help us know what we are entitled to believe" (Rorty [1979] 2009, 143). In this manner, we assume that accuracy of representation depends upon the manner of its causal production. Importantly, this whole history is simply a string of footnotes to the original Platonic project, revealing the larger object of his criticism. This is the "Platonic Principle," the idea that "differences in *certainty* must correspond to differences in the objects known" (Rorty [1979] 2009, 156). This principle follows from modeling knowledge on perception and attempting to ground that knowledge. It assumes that we need different faculties to attain certainty with different types of objects (e.g., numbers versus physical reality). "The theory of knowledge will be the search for that which compels the mind to belief as soon as it is unveiled" (Rorty [1979] 2009, 163). For Rorty, there is a continuing neo-Kantian consensus[7] that philosophy-as-epistemology must be concerned with these immutable structures that contain knowledge, life, and culture.

This frames Rorty's metaphilosophical project in *PMN* and his strategies for overcoming representationalism. Following this narrative, Rorty attacks the root: the premise that causation and justification are interrelated. In chapter 4 of *PMN*, he illustrates the crucial error of this empiricist foundationalism by combining two arguments from Wilfrid Sellars and W. V. O. Quine, which invalidate the epistemological and ontological projects while inaugurating his behavioral and linguistic alternative.

Sellars argues that a belief can only be justified (or not) on the basis of another belief or set of beliefs. "The essential point is that in characterizing an episode or a state as that of *knowing*, we are not giving an empirical description of that episode or state; we are placing it in the logical space of reasons, of justifying and being able to justify what one says" (Sellars 1997, sec. 36). He claims that there is no way to connect the supposedly nonconceptual material of perception (the given) from the filtered, conceptual, products of knowledge. This means that everything that acts as a justification must already be within "the logical space of reasons." As Colin Koopman notes, this is in fact a modest claim that "every conclusion in belief stands in need of reasons as supporting premises," but one with significant consequences (Koopman 2011b, 65). For him, our unconceptualized experiences of the world cannot play a justificatory role in our practices (Rorty [1979] 2009, 182–92).

Quine illustrates that perceptions and sensations are insufficient for the purpose of *certain* justification. This in no way denies that they cannot be fit into a particular conceptual classification but only that they cannot justify any particular conceptual system over against others. Instead, on Quine's thesis of ontological relativity, any experience is always amenable to a variety of conceptual appropriations. As a result, concepts, *on their own*, do not justify. Rorty takes this claim to mean that there is no way to link up particular conceptual understandings or claims with specific bits of the world because we do not encounter perceptions in such a manner. Rather, we encounter them as part of complex webs of theory and practice. In this manner, they are always bundled together with a "general scheme of belief" (Rorty [1979] 2009, 202).

Part of the impact of *PMN* was Rorty's insight that, when combined, these two claims drastically challenge the epistemological and ontological projects. Sellars illustrates that there are no epistemic givens, no awareness not already within linguistic/conceptual forms. Consequently, only a conceptually articulated belief can justify another belief; only concepts can justify. This rejects the distinction between "the given" and "the postulated." Quine illustrates how no concept, on its own, can determine the correct usage of another concept. This means that our being caused to believe something does not on its own justify it because causes will always be inserted into general schemes of belief as particular claims.

Consequently, he rejects distinguishing between the "necessary" and the "contingent" (and associated dualisms between the empirical and the structural). Together these two claims break the link between cause and justification that modern philosophy assumes.[8]

The main methodological insight that results, for Rorty, is an imperative to theoretical *holism*. This holism claims that justification is always a relation among concepts; however, it is never a relation among individual concepts but among *webs of concepts*. Thus, holism represents not just an antifoundational rejection but the basis of his sociopragmatic alternative. In *PMN*, this is his "epistemological behaviorism," the alternative justificatory model he offers in place of representationalist epistemology and ontology. It holds that "justification is not a matter of a special relation between ideas (or words) and objects, but of conversation, of social practice" (Rorty [1979] 2009, 170). Human knowledge can be entirely understood, and deployed in all the ways we have, when we frame it within the social justification of belief. Consequently, there is no *need* to see it as accuracy of representation or inquire into how to assess representation on the metaphilosophical level.

In the absence of representation (the attempt to mirror nature) and the resulting attempt to ground knowledge, the premise of a metadiscourse capable of arbitrating the knowledge claims of all human practices disappears. Epistemological behaviorism thus destroys the quest for certainty. Quine's and Sellars's works raise behaviorist questions about the epistemic privilege that logical empiricism claims for certain "privileged representations." They suggest, in different ways, that assertions are justified by linguistic practice rather than by the nature of the inner representations they express. For Rorty, this invalidates the project of attempting to identify such privileged representations and, in turn, explains rationality and epistemic authority by social norms of justification. This holist behaviorism claims "that if we understand the rules of a language-game, we understand all that there is to understand about why moves in that language-game are made" (Rorty [1979] 2009, 174).

At this point, we must ask why a behavioral explanation of epistemic norms is desirable.[9] Quine and Sellars may drastically undermine the possibility of representationalist epistemologies, but they don't necessarily prove the superiority of a sociopragmatic account. Does philosophy as a metadiscipline not require an account of knowledge that connects the real world up with beliefs? The real division here is between two fundamentally different approaches to truth as "what is good to believe" and as "correspondence with reality." Endorsing the former, Rorty is emphasizing the *status* of his claim. Epistemological behaviorism does not assert the truth of behavioral explanations of knowledge claims or mental states. Rather, it is an assertion of the limits of theoretical practice to arbitrate diverse systems of knowledge and a refusal to attempt a certain sort of explanation: one that judges the absolute reliability of human reports about their environment. Causal reports of the world and its events and conceptual breakdowns of the structure of the mind, neither of which are rejected, are only problematic if they are taken as necessary premises for grounded knowledge and master discourses for all languages. "Behaviorism in epistemology is a matter not of metaphysical parsimony, but of whether authority can attach to assertions by virtue of relations of 'acquaintance' between persons and, for example, thoughts, impressions, universals, and propositions" (Rorty [1979] 2009, 177). Rorty's concern is with the authority we attach to knowledge claims. He claims that a relation of correspondence between people and reality, mind and world, mental states and sense impressions, is not the source of justification within our social world. In this manner, he extends the claims and shape of eliminative materialism, not making an actual ontological claim about knowledge but only a social claim about the origin of authority.

The power of this criticism is its approach. It goes behind specific claims to or about knowledge and correspondence to challenge its very logic. The issue behaviorism raises in epistemology is not "the adequacy of explanation of fact but rather whether a practice of justification can be given a 'grounding' in fact" (Rorty [1979] 2009, 178). Rorty does not question whether knowledge has foundations but whether the claim that it does is coherent. In response to the kneejerk charge of relativism he argues that this charge assumes the existence of a permanent neutral matrix for inquiry. Without this assumption, the idea of reconciling, of providing a master set of criteria for, different explanatory frameworks and methodologies dissolves. It is the basic assumption of the quest for certainty and the image of the mirror of nature that sustains that quest. Rorty emphasizes that his intent is only to cultivate a "distrust of the Platonic quest for that special sort of certainty associated with visual perception. The image of the Mirror of Nature—a mirror more easily and certainly seen than that which it mirrors—suggests, and is suggested by, the image of philosophy as such a quest" (Rorty [1979] 2009, 181). He shifts our demands away from the project of such an account of human knowledge, of the attempt to *reduce* (which, contra elimination, *is* an ontological claim) norms to facts. In this, it is specifically anti- or nonontological. Given that, it asks what the possibilities and constraints on speaking about the correctness of our various practices are. As we will see, this maneuver forms the basis of Rorty's political turn to the question of the *normative* correctness of various critical and political discourses.

The question now is how justification is situated within social practice. This is a larger question for this critical reconstruction of Rorty's sociopragmatic method. The language of coherence in *PMN* indicates Rorty's framework for justification. As our beliefs and norms (even for knowing) in society are a dynamic intersubjective body, justification is a process of relating one bit of language with another, and languages must "cohere" to some degree. "Nothing counts as justification unless by reference to what we already accept, and that there is no way to get outside our beliefs and our language so as to find some test other than coherence" (Rorty [1979] 2009, 178). This is not a strong claim for coherence as the single universal standard but a social observation that the only way to justify or disallow claims will be through their relation to other claims.[10] Justification is about the interaction of a belief with a whole host of other claims. Its primary relation is between assertions rather than between assertions and the world.

This coherentist model of justification requires a certain disposition to inquiry. While this model of inquiry and its ramifications for sociopolitical thinking are further developed in his pragmatist turn and discussion of hermeneutics, in *PMN* he does note that this model of justification makes all inquiry reformist. In the absence of a neutral framework, "criticism of one's culture can only ever be piecemeal and partial—never 'by reference to eternal standards'" (Rorty [1979] 2009, 179). The lack of neutral standards external to our practices and languages entails an antirevolutionary conception of inquiry. It is important to note, though, that for Rorty this means only that the changes in language and practice we advocate are constrained by the need to speak to our present practices in some discernible manner. They cannot simply derive their justification from external theoretical standards. As we will discuss, this has often been interpreted as the methodological form of Rorty's "complacent liberalism" (Bacon 2006, 865–66). The argument here, in contrast, is that the critique that Rorty lacks any critical and normative resources in his thought fails to understand that one of the key functions of his model of justification and inquiry, and his model of sociopolitical criticism, is the invention of new languages.

METAPHILOSOPHY AND METHODOLOGY

For Rorty, this reconceptualization of justification as behavioral, holistic, and separate from causation leaves epistemology without a project. It invalidates the assumption of a permanent neutral framework for inquiry that ensures correspondence with the world and the hope of a philosophical method of accessing that framework. The point of the previous argument has been to illustrate the original development of this antiepistemological and antiontological turn in Rorty's work and situate it within a strategic prioritization of the social that structures both his critical strategy and his positive alternative. The priority of the social makes privileging ontology and epistemology fallacious; they are continued desires for authority, compulsion, and certainty.

Several questions remain. Foremost is what this category of "vocabularies" means and does. The idiom of vocabularies, what Brandom calls Rorty's "vocabulary of vocabularies," is the central device of Rorty's metaphilosophical project. Operationally, it catches all aspects of linguistic practice (e.g., both meaning and belief) and denotes a loose whole over sets of practices that are interrelated. In this, it is a way of designating discursive bodies that does not encourage the "ontological urge" to engage in ontological legitimation. It achieves this by not making any ontologically specific distinction between what we talk about and how we talk about it. This is because, as I will discuss in chapters 2, 3, and 4, vocabularies are relative to specific purposes and goals. Importantly, such purposes can also only be understood from within the vocabulary—this is no neutral utilitarianism (Ramberg 2004, 14).[11]

The result is Rorty's "pragmatism about norms," the previously discussed claim of the social origin of the authority of our linguistic practices. It is "the thought that any normative matter of epistemic authority or privilege—even the sort of authority exercised on what we say by what we talk about—is ultimately intelligible only in terms of social practices that involve implicitly recognizing or acknowledging such authority" (Brandom 2000, 159). It is only in the context of a set of social practices and a vocabulary that something can have authority, carry responsibility, or have any normative significance. This is not the idealism that the world has no contact with our beliefs. It does causally act on us. However, only concepts can justify other concepts, and concepts always exist within vocabularies. This means that normative authority is exclusively an intra- rather than intervocabulary relation (Brandom 2000, 160–61). The justification of a claim within a vocabulary will always depend on how that claim can be related to other claims in the vocabulary and not on the basis of some external standard (truth, god, reason, etc.).

A question of implications and scope naturally follows. Is Rorty invalidating any vocabulary that justifies with reference to external criteria? Must all languages relate to authority along the lines he draws? This is a deep concern not only for the philosophies of science, mind, and language but also for sociopolitical thought, in terms of the nature of moral and political, critical and normative discourses and the claims they make in public. The latter are our primary object, and this issue will not be fully clarified until later chapters. However, the direction of this critical reconstruction of Rorty can be found even at this stage. Brandom notes an ambiguity within Rorty's work in the consequences of this account on the normative authority for discourses of objectivity. This is a tension between a strong or weak reading. On the strong reading, Rorty's account of normative authority entirely undermines any attempt to invest authority in anything external to social consensus. The world is absolutely the wrong thing to understand as bearing any kind of authority; this is only something we, as language users, do to one another. This absolutely invalidates standards like objectivity.

There is a weaker, more nuanced reading that argues that investing authority in extrasocial entities, such as placing subjective authority in the incorrigible subject or objective authority in the languages of the natural sciences, is not unintelligible; it is *only* optional and contingent. This allows that such structures of authority may have good reasons behind them and good purposes they fulfill *but* that we may find better reasons and purposes for advocating a different structure of authority. The key point is, as Brandom argues, that the sociopragmatic conception of normative authority "does not entail that only the humans who institute those statuses can exhibit or possess them. The notion of responsibility to some non-human authority is not in principle undercut by the Enlightenment pragmatist insight that any such status depends on human attitudes of taking or treating something *as* authoritative" (Brandom 2013, 28–29). Rorty has suggested this reading (Rorty 1998e, 44).

The point is that there is an important difference between the things we appeal to in the act of justification and the manner in which justifications are given normative authority. We will of course refer to the world, representations, demons, etc. in justifying, *but* those justifications will only have normative force socially because to justify is to give and ask for reasons. On this reading, then, there is no de facto problem with investing normative authority in external sources (e.g., the environment) as long as we understand that it is we who do this, which makes it contingent and optional, and that it is we who must change them when they become problematic.[12]

To understand this point fully we must return to the metaphilosophical context of Rorty's work. He followed Sellars in arguing that "philosophy is an attempt to see how 'things, in the largest sense of the term, hang together, in the largest sense of the term'" (Rorty [1979] 2009, 114; Sellars 1963a, 1). He offers a *framework for speaking about the diversity of languages and their relations*, one that replaces the dominant representationalism. Its virtue is what it allows us to do while avoiding the problematic foundationalism of external standards engendered by the quest for certainty and the epistemological and ontological projects. In this manner, Rorty's vocabulary of vocabularies is exactly the sort of move within language he is describing: it seeks to change our relation to the authority of claims by shifting our vocabularies and thereby shifting our way of relating to other languages. It is a pragmatic assessment of what can overcome present difficulties. "The only way out of moribund foundationalism, Rorty argued, would be to undertake a methodological shift in philosophical orientation . . . toward the metaphor of our beliefs as aspects of the vocabularies in which we justify ourselves to one another" (Koopman 2011b, 64). In this manner, the vocabulary of vocabularies is crucial to his positive antiauthoritarian alternative. This is principally because it allows us to do three things: speak about the diversity of ways of speaking in the world; understand the presence of and deploy normative claims from within vocabularies; and, perhaps most importantly, change our linguistic practices.

This alternative, though underemphasized by Rorty, is fundamental to his methodological potential. As Koopman has argued, Rorty is often overly associated with antifoundationalism, which is indeed important in his thought, to the point where his antirelativism is forgotten. However, he is dedicated to the question of how we can have normative correctness in our practices. Already in *PMN*, he is clear that his epistemological behaviorism is not a relativism but a project of "clearing the ground" for a pragmatic theory of normative practice (Koopman 2011b, 68; Rorty [1979] 2009, 193).

I will argue in subsequent chapters that this antirelativist project goes further than even Rorty's sympathetic critics usually think because it contains the possibility of a kind of reconstruction of rationality as a guide for normative critique. The gradual softening of his oft-noted rejection of this concept has been observed by several commentators and by Rorty (Ramberg 2004, 2; Cooke 2006, 34; Rorty 2000g, 2). However, its origins are apparent in this stage of his work. Rorty often quoted, with great approval, the following passage from Sellars: "Science is rational not because it has a *foundation*, but because it is a self-correcting enterprise which can put *any* claim in jeopardy, though not *all* at once" (Rorty [1979] 2009, 180–81; Sellars 1963b, 170). This raises the possibility that there are better and worse ways to relate to our languages and practices from the perspective of a critical social theory. Essentially: there is a way of relating to our own ways of speaking and acting that allows for more reflective forms of control. In this manner, antifoundationalism could lead to an expansion of agency, rather than a contraction.

Developing this resource as a way of accepting the human responsibility for normativity is the crux of Rorty's project. It is in this sense that he calls for "an intellectual world in which human beings are responsible only to each other" (Rorty 2004, 4). This is Rorty's "second Enlightenment," where we fully take responsibility for the norms we enact and the places we institute authority. Such a project requires a mode of assessing and weighing where we put such authority. It is thus, explicitly, a metaphilosophical project of the most difficult kind. The argument here is that this purpose is the central structuring imperative of Rorty's thought and that it bears a series of methodological insights that require development in contemporary sociopolitical thinking. To explicate this, we must turn to his treatment of pragmatism and hermeneutics, where he initially looked for the resources to fulfill these ambitions.

HERMENEUTICS AND THE QUESTION OF INQUIRY

In the final part of *PMN*, Rorty focuses on hermeneutics to sketch out the beginnings of a postcertainty theoretical frame. This section addresses this brief turn; the next addresses his enduring turn to pragmatism. This roughly follows their chronology.[13] Rorty's hermeneutics burned bright and burned fast. Confined to a limited set of writings (Rorty [1979] 2009, pt. 3; 1980; 2000a), it has been the subject of comparatively sparse critical reflection.[14] However, his discussion of hermeneutics raises key concerns about inquiry and the project of theoretical reflection that continue into his writings on pragmatism and that flow from his reflections on the social origin of authority. The turn to hermeneutics is the first step in questioning how human inquiry proceeds in the vocabulary of vocabularies. It is the initial frame of Rorty's positive antirelativist project to offer a new way of speaking and relating to the diversity and temporality of human thought. It concerns how we can have critical reflection and normative prescription after certainty and constraint, and it is crucial to his model of sociopolitical criticism.

HERMENEUTICS AS ATTITUDE

Rorty's hermeneutics is a social and antiessentialist image of philosophical practice and an antiauthoritarian method of sociolinguistic change and inquiry. It is a way of thinking inquiry on the metaphilosophical level of vocabularies. Importantly, this use of hermeneutics raises several themes of Rorty's positive method. However, it is not an approach in the traditional (epistemological) sense. It has no clear precepts, methods, or techniques.[15] Rather, it rejects the task of commensuration, of bringing all thought under one rational standard. It rejects the notion that rationality imposes methodological rules on inquiry. Thus, it is not another method. "On the contrary, hermeneutics is an expression of hope that the cultural space left by the demise of epistemology will not be filled—that our culture should become one in which the demand for constraint and confrontation is no longer felt" (Rorty [1979] 2009, 315; see also 1980a, 39). Hermeneutics is an antimetaphysical disposition more properly conceived as an *ethos* specifically oriented against the authoritarian desire for constraint that stands behind this demand. It is an attitude to both knowledge and wider culture.

In hermeneutics, Rorty's target is the assumption of commensurability that flows from desires for constraint and external authority.

> The notion that there is a permanent neutral framework whose "structure" philosophy can display is the notion that the objects to be confronted by the mind, or the rules which constrain inquiry, are common to all discourse, *or at least to every discourse on a given topic*. Thus epistemology proceeds on the assumption that all contributions to a given discourse are commensurable.
>
> (Rorty [1979] 2009, 315–16, my emphasis)

Commensurability assumes that inquiry can be brought under one set of rules that can tell us how and when rational agreement has been achieved, thereby settling any conflicting accounts. It is the assumption of the possibility of agreement and common ground. These assumptions have been construed in many ways in the history of thought; their absence has frequently been taken as an assault on rationality and prelude to relativism.

In contrast, hermeneutics "sees the relations between various discourses as those of strands in a possible conversation, a conversation which presupposes no disciplinary matrix which unites the speakers" (Rorty [1979] 2009, 318). It is an ethos of dialogue and engagement that may desire agreement but does not necessitate it. Rorty is clear that it is equally aimed at "fruitful disagreement." The language of conversation, which has caused much ire among critics, is purposely sociological. He is suggesting that we see inquiry and claims to knowledge from the external perspective of one examining the social interactions of a community. Inquiry is a social practice that must be interpreted hermeneutically and holistically, moving back and forth in a "hermeneutic circle" encountering as many particular aspects of the community as possible while interpretively weaving them into a greater unity.

This changes the end of inquiry. Rorty is emphatic that this is not another way of knowing but another way of *coping* (Rorty [1979] 2009, 356). This notion is one that Rorty does not ever fully clarify but that is part of his naturalistic frame, which is meant to catch the broadest sense of the human activity of adaptation and reaction. I link it in chapter 3 to a reflexive capacity for learning and reflective development. What is important now is that this *injunction to holism*, adumbrated in the previous discussion, is one of the central methodological imperatives of Rorty's model, and it is one carried forward after the demise of the language of hermeneutics. It arises, as a methodological imperative, first here and lays the basis of Rorty's mature conception of practice-based sociopolitical criticism.

This ethos depends on Thomas Kuhn's substantive account of scientific paradigms, which Rorty widens to language, culture, and inquiry. Here he finds confirmation of his sociological approach and a view of the natural sciences that seems to fit *within* his account of vocabularies and that is compatible with the metatheoretical hermeneutical ethos he is offering to govern various discourses, that is, one that subsumes even the most paradigmatically rational discourse within the vocabulary of vocabularies. This allows him to resolve one of the most important debates within the philosophy of science and the social sciences at this point, the debate between interpretive and empirical methods, which his endorsement of hermeneutics has already raised.

Rorty turns to Kuhn to undermine a series of distinctions that divides science from the humanities (*Natur-* and *Geisteswissenschaften*) and to recast those divisions within inquiry as merely the result of different moments. Thus, where epistemology and hermeneutics are usually distinguished by the disciplines and objects they are thought appropriate to, Rorty maps them onto Kuhn's division between normal and revolutionary science "'Normal' science is the practice of solving problems against the background of a consensus about what counts as a good explanation and what constitutes a solution. 'Revolutionary' science is the introduction of a new 'paradigm' of explanation, and thus of a new set of problems" (Rorty [1979] 2009, 320; see also Kuhn 1962, 10–12). Epistemology and hermeneutics correspond to normal and revolutionary discourse, respectively. This removes the epistemology-hermeneutics divide from its familiar dualisms (fact-value, objective-subjective, nature-spirit, natural sciences versus human sciences): these hierarchical distinctions of certainty construct the former epistemological term as superior to the latter hermeneutic one. In contrast, the normal-abnormal distinction concerns the state of inquiry in a community. In normal (epistemological) periods, the standards regarding defining and solving problems are established. Revolutionary (hermeneutic) or abnormal inquiry exists outside the dominant rules of a community and potentially destabilizes that matrix. This ends the pendulum swing between realism and idealism through a behavioral approach to the question of knowledge that offered a historical account of the development of scientific paradigms. By illustrating the dramatic shifts in basic science, Kuhn demonstrated the enclosed nature of theoretical paradigms and the lack of neutral criteria in these movements and invalidated algorithmic theory choice.

Rorty adopts Kuhn's distinction not to destroy scientific values or their place in Western culture. Rather, like Dewey, he wants to preserve those values without their metaphysical baggage. For him, the idea that science is only justified if it is not a value-based enterprise stands upon those aforementioned distinctions that divide inquiry into hard and soft varieties. These distinctions only function with the assumption of a neutral framework or language that assures correspondence with the world. For Rorty, assuming such a neutral language "blocks the road of inquiry" (Rorty [1979] 2009, 349).

Kuhn expands Rorty's strategic prioritization of the social as a way to encapsulate explanatory and normative difference. In a later essay, Rorty emphasizes the "morals" implicit within Kuhn's remapping of human culture. Its significance is metaphilosophical and not meant to undermine scientific practice, its claims to unique predictive success, or its "aesthetic and moral grandeur" (Rorty 1999d, 188). Rather, they are only about the *status* of the natural sciences, which have no "epistemico-ontological" priority that places them at the top of some "cultural pecking order" because of a unique ability to correspond, proceed rationally, or exhibit the scientific method (Rorty 1999d, 185–86). In fact, Kuhn undermines the idea that there is a distinctive method, in general, and thus that it can serve as a guide for the social sciences. Instead, he necessitates historicism and pluralism: his analysis of the development of paradigms within Western science illustrated how ontology is relative to historical period, while the effect of his sociological conception of science as primarily based within communities of inquiry has opened up methodologies in the social sciences.

Rorty took up and furthered these themes in several ways.[16] Kuhn's concepts of "disciplinary matrix" and "paradigm" expanded his notion of vocabularies to the parts of human culture engaged specifically in inquiry, suggesting that they suffered from similar constraints on explanatory and normative claims. Further, it led Rorty to argue that there can be no *single* set of criteria for judging the success of a discourse or the claims within it and that fields are contestatory sites of different goals and purposes with different propensities for agreement. Even when there is agreement about purposes, which will be temporary and never total, these will be different from other areas of human inquiry and culture. The powers of prediction and control and the goal of agreement, both of which seem unproblematic in the natural sciences, are simply unachievable and inappropriate in the social sciences (and wider human life), where our goals are different and our capacity for agreement less. Neither predictive accuracy nor any other criterion, as a result, is *a goal all vocabularies share*. Thus, no single method can claim a higher propensity for rationality or truth. In this, Rorty replaces hierarchical epistemic distinctions with horizontal social differences.

This understanding of inquiry informs Rorty's argument for the hermeneutic ethos as the governing metatheoretical frame for human inquiry. This ethos is not a set of precepts for conducting inquiry in any particular area. It is a metaphilosophical understanding of inquiry in its broadest sense as a social practice that necessitates both *holism* and *historicism*. For Rorty, at the widest level, the only viable understanding of inquiry is adaptive coping (Rorty 1980, 39). This entails the important caveat that hermeneutics is not a generalizable framework for inquiry appropriate at every given moment and in every sphere of thinking. However, neither is it confined to the softer, interpretive human sciences. The Kuhnian distinction illustrates that hermeneutics is properly applied to situations of vocabulary change or debate, when the framework itself is in question (Rorty [1979] 2009, 347). Hermeneutics is an ethos to govern only those moments when vocabularies have been significantly internally challenged or in the context of intravocabulary exchange. It is a metatheoretical strategy for contexts where justification has broken down.

THE REJECTION OF HERMENEUTICS AND METHOD

This account of Rorty's hermeneutics is selective. It focuses on the questions and themes that persist into his sociopolitical method and so are relevant to this reconstruction. This may seem capricious. As a reading strategy, it is one that Rorty endorsed and employed, and it is justified by his later rejection of hermeneutics. In "Intellectual Autobiography," written only a few months before his passing, Rorty describes part 3 of *PMN* as a "false start." His "invocation of Gadamerian hermeneutics was feeble and unproductive," and the distinction between systematic and edifying philosophy on which it depended was not the contrast he wanted (Rorty 2010, 13).[17]

This raises the question of why hermeneutics disappears and how pragmatism becomes the main theoretical frame of Rorty's positive thought. The decisive issue is method. When Rorty employed the term "hermeneutics" for his ethos of inquiry around the publication of *PMN*, he aimed to reject the general notion of a hard method that predominated in both the natural and social sciences of the day. However, he became uncomfortable with the term because of the assumption, held by many hermeneuts, that it constituted such a distinct method for the human sciences. These areas of inquiry were thought to be shot through with a phenomenon called "meaning," which arose because humans are beings constituted by language with which we exist in an "essential" relationship.

At the time of *PMN*, Rorty's strategy was to employ hermeneutics to mean what he wanted. This is the hermeneutical metatheoretical ethos of antiauthoritarianism and the injunctions to holism and historicism. However, already there he rejects a precept that is the main reason for his eclipse of hermeneutics. "We do not escape from Platonism by saying that 'our essence is to have no essence' if we then try to use this insight as the basis for a constructive and systematic attempt to find out further truths about human beings" (Rorty [1979] 2009, 378). For Rorty, the critique of foundationalism does not mean that antiauthoritarianism should be essentialized. We must resist going out into the world to discover fundamental aspects of it that either undermine or support epistemological forms of philosophy or positivistic social science. This merely changes the shape of authoritarianism while retaining the hierarchical relation it establishes with the rest of culture. That is, they remain claims to a neutral vocabulary. This means *we cannot essentialize or reify our lack of foundations.*

Rorty applied this criticism to hermeneutics and its understanding of the category of language. For him, hermeneuts are right to claim that narratives and descriptions are key elements of human inquiry that should not be ignored in favor of laws and predictions. This is a useful protest against behavioral social scientists and tendencies toward scientism. However, this claim is often expanded to the idea that there is a distinct task, "interpretation," which is the primary duty of the social sciences, in contrast to the natural sciences' "explanation." For Rorty, "this protest goes too far when it waxes philosophical and begins to draw a principled distinction between man and nature, announcing that the ontological difference dictates a methodological difference" (Rorty 1982d, 199). This amounts to the claim that language and meaning *constitute* human existence, as opposed to other objects of inquiry, and this ontological difference requires different methods of inquiry. For Rorty, this language of constitution is especially problematic. Once its sense is distinguished from the usual physical sense of the term (e.g., where buildings are constituted by various materials), there is no clear sense in which language constitutes our existence. Does this entail that it is somehow more essential to us than our physical embodiment? What kind of priority is being argued for, and how is it known? For Rorty, the only sense this claim has is that, as humans, we won't know a lot of the things there are to know about us if we ignore what we and others say. But this relational, holistic claim is no less true of physical objects. We would not know much about any particular object without knowing many specific things about its relations to other objects. Such relations are always only articulated in language and thus "*anything* is, for purposes of being inquired into, 'constituted' by a web of meanings" (Rorty 1982c, 199). For this reason, the claim that something constitutes our existence (i.e., that it is more essential to us than any other aspect) is as empty as "drawing a line around a vacant place in the middle of the web of words, and then claiming that there is something there rather than nothing" (Rorty 1982c, xxxvi). It is a rhetorical sleight-of-hand to argue that our favorite things have metaphysical priority over all other aspects and all the ways they could be articulated.

When language is the *essential* aspect of human existence, and meaning as that which *constitutes* our lives, it is a short jump to assuming that these structural features of humanity require a distinct method of study, entail a distinct object of inquiry, and require a distinct discipline of inquirers. All of this repeats the above claims that inquiry is something constrained by the external world, which seeks to render views of it that are commensurable with any perspective; that is, it repeats the logic of correspondence (Rorty 1980, 43). In light of this, Rorty ultimately rejected hermeneutics for the ethos and set of moral virtues for inquiry he advocates. For him, it shares with empiricism the problematic assumption that there are philosophical solutions to the methodological question of the correct shape and status of the human sciences (Festenstein 1997, 133). It retains the assumption that the object of inquiry dictates how to study it.[18]

This begins to illustrate the originality of Rorty's methodological project. His metatheory does not attempt to replace empiricism with hermeneutics (or any approach). This would continue presuppositionless one-upmanship. Instead, he formulates a different relation to inquiry, one appropriate to the metaphilosophical level. Empiricism and hermeneutics both export the values and aims of a particular discipline, with a particular object of inquiry and particular methods of justification, to all inquiry as such. For Rorty, in contrast, at the widest level of generalization, where we speak about all vocabularies, we need a different disposition. His ethos hopes

> that the very idea of hermeneutics should disappear, in the way in which old general ideas do disappear when they lose polemical and contrastive force—when they begin to have universal applicability. My fantasy is of a culture so deeply antiessentialist that it makes only a sociological distinction between sociologists and physicists, not a methodological or philosophical one.
>
> (Rorty 1991f, 103)

For this fallacy Rorty later included Gadamer and hermeneutics with those seeking a "post-Nietzschean" philosophical method (Rorty 1999d, xx). Similarly, in an obituary for Gadamer, Rorty makes the same methodological point, but in a rather more positive relation to Gadamer's work. Interestingly, he highlights a notable claim of Gadamer's that seems to focus directly on the constitutive role of language: "being that can be understood is language" (Gadamer 2004, 474). For him, this is not a metaphysical discovery about the intrinsic nature of being but a suggestion about how to redescribe the development of human reflection on ourselves. It is the claim that "the more descriptions that are available, and the more integration between these descriptions, the better is our understanding of the object identified by any of those descriptions" (Rorty 2000a, 4). This conception replaces metaphors of depth with one of breadth in conceiving human culture, its development, and its internal relations.

Importantly, this comment on post-Nietzschean method and the language of depth and breadth foreshadow Rorty's central criticism of continental philosophy and his rejection of post-Heideggerian thought, which he argues repeats this depth with ontology and contingency (this will be discussed in chapter 2). However, here too there is ambivalence between a positive relation to historicism (in Gadamer and Heidegger) and concerns over the assumption of methodism, that the nature of what we are studying constrains our descriptions of them.

Presently, what is important is how this shapes Rorty's pragmatist alternative. The argument is that hermeneutics sets several parameters for that method. He claims to be able to say everything hermeneutics can without "talking about anything being 'constituted by language'" (Rorty 1991f, 107). Ultimately for him, while hermeneutics valuably argues for the necessity of historical perspectives, it is not holistic or naturalistic enough. As a way of understanding the diversity of human practices and languages, hermeneutics suggests that these disciplines have different ways of "representing" or relating to the world. Instead Rorty eschews this notion and its implicit hierarchies. At the metaphilosophical level, he levels all vocabularies. The next section illustrates how Rorty's turn to pragmatism allows that.

THE PRAGMATIC TURN: THEORY AND PRAXIS AFTER FOUNDATIONS

Rorty's pragmatism is the subject of much commentary. Within the tradition, there was a strong rejection of his association. Externally, his faults were often reduced to pragmatism and its "soft" resources. Perhaps the latter explains the former. This discussion is not concerned with either of these trends but with the recent tendency to read Rorty and pragmatism reconstructively in relation to the metatheoretical projects of philosophy and political thought. Specifically, it will examine the intention and potential of his turn to pragmatism. Rorty undertook his (final) turn to pragmatism to theorize a mode of theoretical praxis as an embedded form of sociopolitical criticism. This more successful turn clarifies the ambitions and ultimate eclipse of hermeneutics previously discussed.

RORTY'S EARLY PRAGMATISM: ETHOS AND PLURALISM

Despite protests, Rorty falls squarely within the antimetaphysical and antirelativist pragmatist political project. While diversified, pragmatist political thought does cluster around a series of broad themes. Principally, it is focused on the primacy of social practices and the goal of a reflexive form of antifoundationalism. This entails that it is skeptical of metaphysical realism about values but rejects general skepticism about normativity. Instead it seeks a fallibilistic sense of agency with respect to the project of normative development. These priorities are clearly illustrated in several of Rorty's early essays in metaphilosophy, contemporaneous with those discussed earlier, which positively utilize pragmatist ideas for the first time. These sympathies are specifically with "metaphilosophical pragmatism" and its capacity to exit from the central paradox of metaphilosophy: its simultaneous aim for neutrality among philosophical systems even though each system generates metaphilosophical self-confirming criteria that disallow its competitors (Rorty 1961a, 1961b). Here, the social-practice-based conception of justification provides the possibility of managing this situation.

Chris Voparil has convincingly illustrated the significance of these pragmatic claims on Rorty's work, especially in terms of his later model of philosophy as cultural politics, which I will discuss in later chapters. What is presently important are the core features of this early pragmatism. Fundamentally, Rorty accepts the aforementioned paradox on thinking and its consequences for interframework engagement. At this level, theoretical practice cannot be about truth or agreement but about enabling productive communication and dialogue. In this protoconversational conception, the point at this level of engagement is not to overcome disagreement but to make it fruitful. This is achieved, Rorty suggests, by shifting the terms of focus to this level. In fact, this is the entire motivation for the focus on practices; "the appeal to practice transfers the question of the acceptability of a philosophical program out of metaphilosophy and into the realm of moral choice" (Rorty 1961b, 111). In this manner, the social-practice-based approach is both illuminating and enabling. It demonstrates how any theoretical framework is ultimately dependent on normative authority derived from the social; that is, it is a communal activity involving ethical values about individual interaction. This frames theoretical controversies in moral and relational terms. However, it also suggests a way to proceed through an appeal to moral virtues of engagement. As Voparil has suggested, this is the keystone of this phase of Rorty's work. He seeks to derive ethicopolitical insights only from the social and relational context of human life. He "locates philosophy in a space of contingency and choice. By situating epistemological issues in a moral and political context oriented toward our relations to others, Rorty is able to present an alternative picture of the social practice of justification that *takes other human beings seriously*" (Voparil 2014b, 87).

Rorty's antiauthoritarianism is tied to a positive ethicopolitical moral project, which is the origin of his central sociopolitical strategy. By framing epistemological and ontological debates in social terms, Rorty politicizes such questions. While this is more fully fleshed out subsequently, one of the strengths of this is a fundamental *leveling* of different descriptive and normative frameworks, so that they exist along a horizontal set of distinctions around purpose rather than a vertical one around certainty. However, such a leveling also raises a fundamental question: does a horizontal account of linguistic difference level all languages up to the authority of the natural sciences or down to the human (Rorty 1991o, 63)?

To clarify Rorty's moves here, it is necessary to turn to his contested relationship to Dewey, with whom he grapples on this issue. Importantly, this is the first step toward a general pragmatic strategy of politicizing theoretical practice that grows into Rorty's distinctive methodological contribution to contemporary political thought.

RORTY'S DEWEY: CRITICAL HISTORY

Rorty's relationship with Dewey is crucial to his pragmatism and the nature of this politicization.[19] However, it has also been highly controversial. Is the former's interpretation a reconstruction that updates Dewey in the pragmatist spirit? Or is he Dewey's "oedipal son," reading his philosophical father to destroy him? The highly polemical and alarmist nature of much of this criticism is prompted by the fact that Dewey was often an enigmatic influence on Rorty's philosophy, a pervasive yet elusive presence that he ambiguously drew on in accounts oriented to questions other than interpretation. Nonetheless, a relationship can be discerned. The following proceeds through an account of the literature on this question, Rorty's reading strategy, and his positive use of Dewey's thought. I argue that Rorty is aware of his selective reading and that this approach is both consistent with Dewey's own thought and illustrative of the aspect of Dewey most central to Rorty's pragmatism.

While three waves of Rorty-Dewey criticism have been identified, the first two tend to a similar form. Rorty, incorrectly and without rigor, subsumes Dewey within his own brand of neopragmatism. His reading is at best "selective" or at worst a misreading that ignores key elements of Dewey's philosophy, particularly his metaphysics. Further, he fails to see how method is central to Dewey's entire philosophy. His philosophy is integrated and holistic; it stands or falls together and cannot be selectively drawn upon. The explicit worry in this literature has been that Rorty fundamentally undermines Dewey's work in his appropriation, and so the resulting strategy has been to dissociate the two, by emphasizing the centrality of the elements of Dewey Rorty omits. This alarmism has characterized the two initial waves of Rorty-on-Dewey scholarship, which respectively focused on their philosophical and political relationships.[20]

A third wave of Rorty-Dewey scholarship has unsettled this narrative. Beyond rejecting the de facto defensive posture, it has situated Rorty's use and reading of Dewey within the former's larger theoretical project *and* current debates in philosophy and political theory.[21] As Voparil convincingly argues, the real weakness of these earlier periods was not their claims. They do correctly point out where Rorty omits and selectively reads Dewey. Rather, they fail to engage that reading in a productive way, assuming that "the mere fact of having departed from Dewey's positions is enough to discredit Rorty's perspective" (Voparil 2014a, 377). In this they assume that Rorty's project and the present debates they occur in have no insights for that reading.

THE LIVING AND THE DEAD: RORTY'S READING STRATEGY

In response to this hostile reception, Rorty clarified this approach. In "Dewey Between Hegel and Darwin," he discusses pragmatism and Dewey and how he seeks to develop their strengths while eliding their faults. He notes how both William James and Dewey were influenced by idealism and panpsychism (a view regarding the unity of experience in a mental aspect). In fact, Dewey draws his language of experience and its unity from these two sources. In contrast, Rorty situates Dewey between Hegel and Darwin in order to ignore the idealism and panpsychism in each:

> I shall be describing what Dewey might have and, in my view, should have said, rather than what he did say. I shall be constructing a hypothetical Dewey who was a pragmatist without being a radical empiricist, and a naturalist without being a panpsychist. The point in constructing such a Dewey is to separate what I think is living and what I think is dead in Dewey's thought, and thereby to clarify the difference between the state of philosophical play around 1900 and at the present time.
>
> (Rorty 2000b, 3)

This is one of Rorty's clearest statements on reading Dewey. He attempts to isolate the elements of Dewey's philosophy that speak to contemporary debates and problems. In this, he utilizes Dewey as a tool for his own "situation." He is much more interested in the philosophical question than the exegetical one regarding Dewey and in the wider spirit of Dewey's work and its continued relevance (Rorty 1995c, 52).

This approach is not confined to Dewey; it is Rorty's general reading strategy for theoretical sources. As will be discussed in chapter 2, he also selectively reads Heidegger (among many continental theorists). Similarly, his use of Wittgenstein is in no way concerned with what he meant but with his fruitful legacy (Rorty 2007l; Horwich 2010). The continuity and coherence of Rorty's reading strategy with his pragmatic turn should be coming into view. Rorty similarly foregrounds the role of contingent choice by reading figures in relation to present needs and debates. That is, he politicizes interpretation. Consequently, he was often confused by the hostile reaction to his use of Dewey. For him, his updating and utilizing of Dewey for the contemporary context was utterly Deweyan, or at least it resonates with the living, rather than dead, Dewey (Rorty 1995b, 99).

A DIVIDED DEWEY: THE QUESTION OF SOCIOPOLITICAL INQUIRY

This brings us to Rorty's actual interpretation of Dewey, which is crucial to the question of the social sciences and sociopolitical theory for Rorty. In fact, this issue frames most of his engagements with Dewey. As many third-wave commentators have observed, Dewey comes to eclipse the other central figures of Rorty's thinking in this period. As such, this interpretation is fundamental to the shift to the social central there.

Rorty identified two opposing currents within Dewey's thought, an essential tension around the question of neutrality. On the one hand, Dewey is an iconoclastic critic of the history of Western philosophy, undermining its oldest dualisms and reenvisioning its project away from foundational metaphysics and toward embedded social practice. On the other hand, Dewey succumbs to a desire for metaphysical grounds in his appeals to science, method, and "experience" (and the search for "generic traits of existence") to bolster his account of social practices. For Rorty, these are not merely different projects but contradictory images of the practice of philosophy:

> Between the image of the philosopher as social activist, concerned to keep the spirit of reform alive by constant criticism of the adequacy of current practices and institutions, and the philosopher as politically neutral theoretician—a specialist in, and authority upon, such peculiarly philosophical topics as the rules of logic, the nature of science, or the nature of thought.
>
> (Rorty 1986b, x)

The latter constitutes a commitment to objective truth. In "Dewey's Metaphysics," Rorty argues that Dewey was never satisfied with cultural criticism. The desire for more led to the category of experience, so central to Dewey's vocabulary. For Rorty, Dewey assumed that a critique of philosophical and metaphysical dualisms enabled a nondualistic account of experience. He assumed that "there must be a standpoint from which experience can be seen in terms of some 'generic traits'" and that this standpoint "would resemble traditional metaphysics in providing a permanent neutral matrix for further inquiry" (Rorty 1982b, 80). With this assumption, Dewey rejected the social nature of inquiry and claimed a foundational form of knowledge. He rejected his own historicist critique of philosophy and assumed an "integrated unity" behind philosophical thought.

For Rorty, Dewey confuses two approaches to opposing philosophical dualisms. The first is to indicate that the dualism was imposed by a tradition for specific cultural reasons but is now useless. The second is to describe the phenomenon in a nondualistic way that emphasizes "continuity between higher and lower processes." This confuses cause with justification by attributing a causal status to our claims, rather than a social one. "To say, as Dewey wants to, that to gain knowledge is to solve problems, one does not need to find 'continuities' between nervous systems and people, or between 'experience' and 'nature'" (Rorty 1982b, 82). That is, he assumes that normativity is a product of a worldly relation rather than a social one. The result is a metaphysical commitment to the reality of concepts. Dewey mistakenly believed that cultural criticism *requires* context-transcendent neutrality and that a naturalistic metaphysics of experience was the best way to achieve that.

This tension surrounding the status of cultural criticism and the necessity of metaphysics leads to an ambiguity within Dewey's method. At times he treated his method and its conclusions as contingent, while at others he assumed their neutrality. He struggled to find a "middle ground between a well-defined procedure—a method in the sense of a set of directions for what to do next, something like a recipe—and a mere recommendation to be open-minded, undogmatic, critical, and experimental" (Rorty 1986b). Is this method universally valid or merely better for modern secular cultures? Rorty is emphatic that Dewey did not provide a method. By attempting to abstract from the scientific method, in a manner applicable to all inquiry (sociopolitical included), he hit an ambiguous middle ground between actual techniques and virtuous habits. For Rorty, there is no generalizable method in this liminal space. As always, the question is about the *status* of these claims. It is not de facto illegitimate to attempt social reform through reference to the generic traits of existence but only to assume that such an account has priority over any other. For Rorty, Dewey struggled with this tension throughout his philosophy. His commitments to "the scientific method," "critical intelligence," and "reflective thinking" claim but never achieve a methodological neutrality he assumed was the basis of sociopolitical criticism. This led Rorty to a particular use of Dewey.

This is the (second) Deweyan image of the philosopher as social critic.[22] For Rorty, this antiauthoritarian Dewey is the living aspect:

> What seems to me most worth preserving in Dewey's work is his sense of the gradual change in human being's self-image which has taken place in recorded history—the change from a sense of their dependence upon something antecedently present to a sense of the utopian possibilities of the future, the growth of their ability to mitigate their finitude by a talent for self-creation.
>
> (Rorty 1991k, 17)

There are two important moves. First, Rorty foregrounds the antiauthoritarian metatheoretical project in Dewey. What is living is Dewey's overcoming of a series of philosophical dualisms that have structured philosophy's history in order explicitly to emphasize the human as the proper object of reflective development. That is, he offers a program for theoretical praxis that orients it to an embedded engagement in sociopolitical life. As Dewey notes, "Philosophy records itself when it ceases to be a device for dealing with the problems of philosophers and becomes a method, cultivated by philosophers, for dealing with the problems of men" (Dewey 2008b, 42). For Rorty, this is Dewey "overcoming the tradition" (Rorty 1982f, 49). Philosophy as a form of embedded social criticism, specifically oriented to contemporary problems. Thus, the sociopolitical model of theoretical praxis being distilled from Rorty's thought has its first mature articulation in an engagement with Dewey and pragmatism that flows from antiauthoritarianism.

Second, and perhaps more importantly, Rorty attempts this in a manner that does not fall into the problems of methodological neutrality. This involves two main issues. First, how does the theorist do this without running afoul of Rorty's metaphilosophical antiauthoritarianism? That is, with what criteria do we engage in the act of criticism? While Rorty is less overt at this stage, he does emphasize the theoretical contribution of a focus on linguistic social practices; this "is a study of the comparative advantages and disadvantages of the various ways of talking which our race has invented. It looks, in short, much like what is sometimes called 'cultural criticism'" (Rorty 1982c, xl). The distinct role for theory is to offer a synthetic vision of the cultural present. This is an overview of the normative linguistic practices deployed within a vocabulary, or across several, in a given moment. It is

> seeing similarities and differences between great big pictures, between attempts to see how things hang together. He [the social critic] is the person who tells you how all the ways of making things hang together hang together. But, since he does not tell you about how all possible ways of making things hang together must hang together—since he has no extra-historical Archimedean point of this sort—he is doomed to become outdated.
>
> (Rorty 1982c, xl)

This Sellarsian language emphasizes the metatheoretical role for sociopolitical thinking. It also reiterates Rorty's methodological imperative to sociopolitical holism. Along with the emphases on historicism and naturalism, holism is a key theme of his positive method.

Second, he pairs this conception of theoretical practice with a sense of the values that support the project of reflective self-creation (Dewey's legacy). In this way, Rorty's move in relation to Dewey is similar to what Voparil's is in Rorty: in both, *antiauthoritarianism is tied to an ethicopolitical project*. In terms of the former, this is centered on the status of the previously mentioned "methods" in Dewey's thought. Rorty purposefully (mis)reads them as "beyond method." "'Critical intelligence' is as good a name as any for being experimental, nondogmatic, inventive, and imaginative, and for ceasing to expect, or try for, certainty" (Rorty 1995b). Critical intelligence, Dewey's name for the mode of thought operative within his method, is a set of antiauthoritarian virtues rather than a pathway. This is an imperative to be "reflective but determined, open yet disciplined, tolerant but discriminating, bold but not too bold, imaginative yet not wild" (Rorty 1995b); these are *fallibilistic* virtues Dewey could have advocated without the language of scientific method. Consequently, he understands Dewey only as offering *social practices*. The dispositions that inform our inquiry and our approach to the world are social and behavioral. They stretch beyond specific disciplines, like the physical sciences, and affect whole cultures. Further, they are open to critical confrontation in practice. In this, Rorty draws from Dewey a much looser sense of method, as a general disposition to the development of our linguistic social practices; "an innovative and experimental attitude, a willingness to redescribe things in a new vocabulary and see what happens" (Rorty 1986b).

This reading of Dewey and Rorty's critique of epistemology share a logic. Rorty utilizes the same social circumvention to deabsolutize Dewey, to substitute "linguistic behavior for 'experience'" (Rorty 1995b). While his tendency to read Dewey in light of the linguistic turn has been the subject of criticism from within pragmatism,[23] he was explicit in justifying this approach. A focus on language and a construal of practice in those terms allows us to divide off the problematic radical empiricism of James and Dewey from the productive holism and historicism. This is a project of extending one bit while eclipsing another.

There are two key elements here. Both are well summarized in the claim that Dewey exasperated his opponents by trying to move out of the range of their vocabulary, by dissolving their problems rather than offering solutions to them, and by transferring issues to the fuzzy, hard-to-discuss area of conflicting values. That was because he thought it was those values which were at stake, and that the "more precise" issues which his critics raised were just ways of evading the important questions.

(Rorty 1991h, 110)

On the one hand, for Rorty, his own practice of reading Dewey is an exhibition of the Deweyan strategy of focusing on the conflicting values behind different approaches. Thus, as recent commentators have argued, this strategy of politicization in Rorty has Deweyan origins and constitutes the main theoretical link between the two thinkers (Voparil 2011b, 115). On the other hand, there are the particularities of Rorty's approach. Sociopolitical criticism is concerned with the metaengagement of normative difference, with the criteria by which we make determinate judgments. Broadly, this is a politicization of theoretical practice and method, shifting it into the realm of contestation. It is also a development of a general theoretical strategy. To shift issues to the level of linguistic social practice, Rorty reorients the discussion from the level of epistemology, ontology, and metaphysics to 'cultural politics" (Ramberg 2002, 1; Rorty 1999g, 57). This amounts to a reframing of issues in terms of the values they articulate and modes of human relation they suggest.

The role of values and ethos is important. The goal here is to switch our

> attention from "the demands of the object" to the demands of the purpose which a particular inquiry is supposed to serve. The effect is to modulate philosophical debate from a methodologico-ontological key into an ethico-political key. For now one is debating what purposes are worth bothering to fulfill, which are more worthwhile than others, rather than which purposes the nature of humanity or of reality obliges us to have. For antiessentialists, all possible purposes compete with one another on equal terms, since none are more "essentially human" than any others.
>
> (Rorty 1991f, 110)

This ethicization is both the goal and the means. As discussed previously, for Rorty, the notion of method is not appropriate to the metalevel of discourse where we encounter linguistic, and hence normative, diversity. The social nature of authority precludes the neutrality it posits. At this stage of Rorty's work, so concerned with the social sciences, this leads to the claim that method assumes that the object of inquiry constrains the way we talk about it (Rorty 1982d, 191). Instead, he highlights the role of ethical value through the concept of *purpose*. This is a tricky concept, with its connotations of a simple instrumentalism or utilitarianism. However, it must be interpreted widely as a social- and practice-based view that understands vocabularies as enabling and disabling of certain types of practices. This is a view focused on how linguistic practices affect the way we proceed and live in the world (our "purposes") and how we can utilize language to speak (and act) in new ways. Rorty follows Dewey in arguing that the role of sociopolitical inquiry, on this metalevel, is not to ground a purpose but to encourage a disposition that motivates reflective investigation into those purposes, and their fulfillment in practice, and to change them (Dewey 2008a, 182).

Rorty pairs the latter project, and the image of the social critic, to his distinct and developed account of the metatheoretical conditions of inquiry. This illustrates a concern with difference and the problem of inclusivity that was not present in Dewey (for good contextual reasons). Rorty is concerned with how discourses of inquiry and the scientific method can, equally to others, be used to marginalize (Voparil 2014a, 389). As a result, what he adds with his focus on the specifically linguistic origins of normative difference is a fallibilistic ethic of inquiry oriented to doubt and the abnormal (Ramberg 2013, 59). For him, this is the disposition most appropriate to the metalevel of normative and linguistic plurality. As I will illustrate in later chapters, Rorty's notion of cultural politics shares these Deweyan origins and extends this model and its pluralistic concerns to render more inclusive theoretical exchanges.

At this phase of his work, these concerns lead to a reconstruction of the notion of inquiry. This model rejects the goal of convergence assumed in other models, developing his anticommensuration view of language (Rorty 1991k, 38).[24] This involves two key moves. First, Rorty reconstructs inquiry as a process of "recontextualization." I read this as Rorty's reconstruction of Deweyan reconstruction. The latter is broad and often imprecisely delineated. In fact, it tends to be a term employed by Dewey (and Deweyans) rather than defined. This is perhaps fitting, as it is inherently processual, embedded in practice. For our purposes, Koopman's view of reconstruction as "meliorative transitioning" is particularly useful. Reconstruction is a mode of change that is inherently contextual; it arises out of a particular situation that is experienced and understood in particular ways, usually as problematic. Further, it can only draw on resources that are articulated and found within that context. No external standards are available. Finally, it is historical in its very occurrence. It is a "transitioning," an acting that moves from the past to the future (Koopman 2009, 197–98).

It is as contextual, embedded, and historical that we should understand Rortian recontextualization. Languages are self-reweaving webs of beliefs, desires, attitudes, and habits of action. Inquiry is a process of putting parts of these centerless webs in dialogue with others as well as with new ideas or tensions that arise. For Rorty, this is an antiessentialist and broad account of inquiry that can catch all the ways in which vocabularies develop themselves. Essentially, it is as holist, naturalist, and historicist as we can be about inquiry (Rorty 1991f, 93–99, 109).

Second, Rorty argues that the goal of recontextualization is not objectivity but solidarity. This language was the subject of great ire. However, it must be understood in terms of the metatheoretical concern with the status of claims. Objectivity posits the fundamental standards of inquiry as external to humans. Solidarity, in contrast, posits them as other humans with whom we exist in social relations (Rorty 1991r, 21–22). Given all the arguments about the source of normative authority, Rorty's mandate to aim inquiry at solidarity, to seek as much intersubjective agreement as possible, is the claim to subject our claims reflexively to as many linguistic challenges as possible. Importantly, when we do this, we *will* be speaking specific languages of inquiry (with all their relevant criteria). However, none will have metatheoretical priority. Objectivity may be a way we justify to each other, it may be a reason we give in the game of giving and asking for reasons, but it is not a metatheoretical standard for that practice, because objective reference only gains authority within a particular social-linguistic set of practices. Thus, the only common goal of inquiry among languages can be the metatheoretical virtue of solidarity. Once again Rorty is shifting to the language of a moral virtue. He substitutes an ethical foundation for reflective interaction and reciprocal loyalty for an epistemic claim. Importantly, he is not making the epistemic claim that there are no grounds and thereby stays true to his strategy of sociological circumvention (Rorty 1991r, 33; 1991k, 45).[25]

This account notably contrasts with the usual understanding of inquiry as aimed at the precise understanding of reality in terms of which we can make judgments. Whether conceived in terms of ideal categories, realist objects, or ontological conditions of impossibility, an external standard rules. Instead, Rorty desires the right ethical disposition (orientation) to the metatheoretical conditions of inquiry, backed up with a nonmetaphysical social-practice-based understanding of inquiry to act as a practice-guiding ethic under contemporary pluralistic conditions. This, he argues, will allow a critical form of inquiry into human culture.

CONCLUSION

A much clearer understanding of Rorty's thought is emerging in recent criticism and in light of his late work. Contrary to the usual end-of-philosophy rhetoric, his great achievement was an "internal critical challenge" of the practice of philosophy aimed at a fundamental transformation of the practice of the discipline (Koopman 2013a, 75; Ramberg 2002). For him, its greatest theoretical contribution is at the metalevel, concerned with the conditions of possibility of inquiry. Further, his social-practice-based account of justification offers a new way of thinking of the metaconditions of dialogue among diverse participants, which enables a new mode of sociopolitical criticism. After laying out the structure of normative authority, he argues that the main task of the theoretician is to negotiate between our various vocabularies. As he noted later, the theorist "is the most appropriate description for somebody who remaps culture—who suggests a new and promising way for us to think about the relation among various large areas of human activity" (Rorty 1999d, 175). Theory can structure interframework dialogue, as a shared linguistic practice, in a way that avoids presuming the standards of any particular perspective, while remaining reflective and critical.

This project, and its initial possibility, is the result of a unique pairing. Rorty links metaphilosophical analysis, and its implications for the philosophy of mind and the epistemological enterprise, with an interpretation of Dewey's work that emphasizes this linguistic focus, prioritizing intelligent and directed intervention in the historical development and creation of human values. The point is that the former enables a less problematic version of the latter, appropriate to contemporary conditions of plurality. The social lens and the strategies of circumvention are the most appropriate to the metalevel of inquiry where contrasting and partially overlapping clusters of normative authority exist without neutral standards or procedures for justification. For Rorty, this provides a new pathway for a positive project for theoretical practice, the task of sociopolitical criticism. Further, as has begun to emerge, the model of inquiry, as intersubjective solidarity, and the pragmatic virtues Rorty offers for this metalevel can encourage critical reflexivity in our political thinking. As introduced in the discussion of hermeneutics and further developed in the pragmatic turn, there is a weakened but distinct sense of the importance of the reflective, developmental capacities of humans as the basis of political thinking.

II

RORTY AND CONTINENTAL POLITICAL THOUGHT

Ontology, Naturalism, and History

2

THEORIZING AFTER FOUNDATIONS

Ontology, Language, and Heidegger

The most persistent issue facing critical interpretation today is the ironic relation it assumes to its own ontopolitical projections.... The sense that this ambiguous condition sets the terms within which thought necessarily proceeds today constitutes our reverence and spur simultaneously.

—WILLIAM CONNOLLY, THE ETHOS OF PLURALIZATION

What is the legacy of the crisis in foundations and metaphysics? Is it something to be overcome, or is it an immutable condition to be confronted continually in the theoretical analysis of politics? The epigraph sets this chapter's question: how can we acknowledge the impossibility of absolute justification yet retain critical resources for political thought? This lacuna in political thinking was exposed by the crisis in foundations. The task before contemporary political theory is over how we proceed. The debate between Rorty and Connolly, described in this chapter, asks how to maintain an ironic relation to our present interpretations in order to provide for critical reflexivity, for a perspective that undermines and interrogates any assumptions or privilege it might implicitly assume.

This chapter begins by examining Rorty's positive alternative to foundationalism. This builds on chapter 1, where we examined Rorty's critiques of analytic philosophy, his early turn to social-practice-based theories, and his general strategy of politicizing theory. These led him to the implicit project of reforming philosophy into a form of situated sociopolitical criticism. Here, we expand our scope by turning to Rorty's mature work (i.e., post *PMN* and *CP*) and its development of these themes. Specifically, I analyze his theories of language and contingency to begin illustrating the resources within his methodological linguistic turn. Chapters 3 and 4 will continue to address the sociopolitical method that came out of his early metaphilosophical reflections and turn to pragmatism and will engage the themes of naturalism and historicism.

To assess his potential, especially in relation to contemporary political thought, this discussion places Rorty's model in opposition to weak ontology, specifically the ontopolitical model of William E. Connolly. The ontological response to the crisis in foundations was a major twentieth-century alternative central to continental thought.[1] Further, it has become a dominant voice within self-declared "critical" forms of contemporary political thought, seeking a form of thinking that also mobilizes the ideas of contingency, language, naturalism, and historicism. Thus, this examination of Rorty's methodology and his theories of language and contingency will contrast Rorty's and Connolly's positions on ontology and close by turning to their readings of continental philosophy. Connolly's and Rorty's interpretations of the language and uses of continental philosophy inform their relationships to ontology and the pathways they chart away from foundations.[2] This approach allows us to consider one of the dominant continental critiques of Rorty: that in his rejection of ontology, Rorty reintroduces covert ontological assumptions that compromise the critical capacities of his thinking. In contrast, in this chapter I suggest that Rorty offers resources for a type of critical reflexivity that exceeds Connolly's own attempt at such resources, turning the earlier critique back on Connolly, ontological political theory, and continental philosophy.

AFTER FOUNDATIONS: CULTURAL POLITICS OR ONTOLOGICAL ANALYSIS

In chapter 1, we saw it was clear that a social turn had occurred within Rorty's early work, a turn that formed the basis of his subsequent critique of epistemology and foundationalism. His subsequent reworking of philosophy led him to rethink inquiry and the nature of concept change. I now look at how this opposition to ontology matured. In his theorizations of inquiry, social justification, and language, Rorty asserts the ontological priority of the social. It is the social practices we have, the languages we speak, and the communities that exist that determine our ontological reality. In contrast, Connolly posits the irreducibility of ontological presuppositions and the necessity of critically engaging ontology to assess the implicit assumptions of any politics.

RORTY AND THE ONTOLOGICAL PRIORITY OF THE SOCIAL

Rorty's context is important for his position on ontology. The single concern of Rorty's philosophy is to debunk the idea of a neutral or privileged framework for inquiry. This Archimedean point is the fundamental assumption of those positing the *commensurability* of all discourses. If all discourses are, in principle, commensurable, they are all subject to the same universal rules of inquiry. This certainty and uniformity is in fact a claim to authority, a claim that one sphere of culture is more primary than others. This concern forms the basis of Rorty's opposition to ontology. He rejects the use of ontology for philosophical and political reflection precisely because of his opposition to a neutral framework for inquiry within the representationalism of classical epistemology. For him, ontology is inevitably the search for the one correct view of reality, the neutral viewpoint against which all assertions are to be measured, a sort of metaphysical trump card.

While Rorty often reiterated his opposition to ontology, especially in relation to the emerging ontological turn in political thought, it was only in his final volume of papers, *Philosophy as Cultural Politics*, that he examined it in detail. This mature circumscription of ontology reveals both its persistence within his thinking but also its potential resources for a situated form of sociopolitical criticism.

For Rorty, ontology is a claim to privilege. "The reason why quarrels among metaphysicians about the nature of Reality seem so ludicrous is that each of them feels free to pick a few of her favorite things and to claim ontological privilege for them" (Rorty 2007i, 106). Ontology inevitably assumes the existence of a correct view of reality from which to build a self-assured moral or epistemological program. However, Rorty does not offer arguments against the sufficiency of ontology as this would place him in the role of the epistemological skeptic. Rather, he only provides a way of thinking that does not assume that reality is the proper subject of theory. This is the crux of his antiauthoritarian pragmatism and social circumvention. He *redescribes* without assuming there is anything to ground such descriptions or that they uniquely make contact with the world (Rorty 1989, 8).

In "Cultural Politics and the Existence of God," Rorty illustrates both his approach to the subject of ontology, specifically in terms of his understanding of social justification, and his understanding of its relevance to contemporary ethical-political life. "Cultural politics," which Rorty initially used pejoratively (e.g., Rorty 1997, 35),[3] refers to discourses within a society about what vocabularies, terms, and topics it is useful to employ. The problem, for him, within this process is the argument that some things, because they simply do exist or are fundamental to our experience, must be discussed.[4] The paradigmatic example is the insistence by religious believers that religion must be part of public discussion because God does exist. For Rorty, this argument assumes that "ontology precedes cultural politics" (Rorty 2007b, 3–5), that reality trumps cultural practice in determining what language a community uses and what objects they discuss through this vocabulary.

Rorty flatly opposes this claim to the priority of the ontological. Instead, he wants "to argue that cultural politics should replace ontology, and that whether it should or should not is itself a matter of cultural politics" (Rorty 2007b, 5). He is concerned not with disproving the existence of God but with arguing for the priority of social and cultural categories over ontological ones. Drawing on the work of Robert Brandom, he summarizes this as "the ontological priority of the social." Under this view, all arguments, analyses, revelations, etc., as cultural politics, are leveled out in authority and primacy. By referring to the presence of an authority (God, empirical reality, etc.), ontology attempts to take a privileged stance. However, as long as there is dispute, in any social context, about what a purported authority actually holds, the very idea of authority is out of place. "'Ontology' is not the name of an expert culture, and we should stop imagining that such a culture would be desirable" (Rorty 2007b, 24). Thus, discussions that appeal to ontologies are moves within the game of cultural politics. They are just ones that claim an authority by referring to another, nonhuman and noncultural, sphere. For Rorty, at the metatheoretical level, we would be better off with cultural-political limits to philosophical reflection.

Once again, Rorty's concern here is the *disposition to justification*, not its source. This argument both summarizes and extends his view of social justification and prefaces his understanding of language as thoroughly contingent. The terms and categories we employ do not map onto reality and are only one of many ways to conceive of the subject at hand. The concept of cultural politics captures the sociopolitical process of justification where we contest which languages to use, categories to employ, and objects to speak about. The language of ontology, in contrast, assumes there is a neutral language through which to discuss it.

Presently, it is important to illustrate the consequences of this conception. Without neutral criteria, cultural-political contestation is comparative. We can do no more than understand our current practices and engage in cultural politics where those practices are contrasted critically with alternative past and proposed future ones. All cultural discussions, as cultural politics, become about the *use* of one vocabulary over another. "Debate about the utility of such logical spaces and about the desirability or undesirability of uniting them with, or disjoining them from, one another is the substance of cultural politics" (Rorty 2007b, 22). Linked to the discussion of purpose in chapter 1, the category of utility is undertheorized in Rorty.[5] He only argues that the sphere of cultural politics, which takes place between and above various vocabularies, concerns the *utility* of any one vocabulary over against another, in the first instance, and the *coherence* of any particular language, in the second. However, like purpose, this category occurs within his wide social-practice-based conception. Use concerns the practices (linguistic and otherwise) and relations enabled by a vocabulary. Thus, there is great freedom here; cultural politics, the process of weighing these up, is "the site of generational revolt, and thus the growing point of culture—the place where traditions and norms are all up for grabs at once" (Rorty 2007b, 21). Cultural-political contestation is the site of intellectual progress. Situated in a claim of the primacy of social categories, this conception of development is fundamental to Rorty's conception of sociopolitical criticism.

Rorty frames his opposition to ontology within the priority of the social in determining our linguistic practices. On his understanding, at the metatheoretical level, languages are separate from the world and from one another and are only capable of discussing their use and consequences within the social sphere of cultural politics. In this, he repeats his strategy I outlined in chapter 1. By arguing for the priority of the social over particular ontological frameworks, he sociologically circumvents ontological discussion. In contrast, Connolly's ontological method illustrates a very different account of ontology and politics and raises an implicit criticism of Rorty.

CONNOLLY AND THE INEVITABILITY OF ONTOLOGY

Connolly's theorization of ontology as necessary for political reflection flows from different concerns. Over the past few decades, his work has attempted to excavate the implicit ontological presuppositions within contemporary political thought. In this, he is a central figure in both the ontological turn in political theory and postfoundational continental political thought within the Anglo-American context. He has uniquely articulated and justified his methodology for an ontological approach to political theory. Understandably, there has been a surge of interest in his work recently (Wenman 2013, chap. 3; Finlayson 2010; Campbell and Schoolman 2008; Symposium 2008). I will focus mainly on Connolly's work from the 1980s and the early 2000s as it was during these years that he most significantly articulated his ontopolitical method. While sharing Rorty's criticisms of foundationalism, he offers an opposed, ontological, pathway away from foundations, one that contains a critique of Rorty around the latter's rejection. Thus the differences between them give shape to the space between the pragmatist and weak-ontological turns in political theory.

Connolly's methodological criticisms of the social sciences bear striking similarities to Rorty's. He also emphasizes the social nature of inquiry and the absence of a neutral framework to which social scientists can appeal when clashes between rival methodologies occur (Connolly 2004a, 339). Further, he opposes the logic of "representationalism" that dominates these debates (Connolly 1995a, 9).[6] In spite of these similarities, Rorty and Connolly differ in the alternative paths they chart. In contrast to Rorty's antiontological social practices, Connolly's work emphasizes the necessity of ontological reflection and the irreducibility of ontological assumptions. This raises the possibility of a hidden set of assumptions in the former's work that could have consequences for the viability of his approach.

Connolly's method of "ontopolitical interpretation," or "ontalogy," is a qualified endorsement that acknowledges that while an ontological method cannot offer an incontestable understanding of reality, it can argue for the inevitability of ontological presuppositions and the need for active engagement and affirmative declaration. For him, every political interpretation invokes a set of fundamentals about the necessities and possibilities of human being, about the nature of the world and our relation to it. These assumptions structure the sphere of politics and the nature of political activity. Ontology establishes the boundaries of political possibility. Nonetheless, much of Anglo-American political theory and social science marginalizes ontological reflection as irrelevant to politics. One prominent strategy is the argument of ontological minimalism. Employed by a diverse group of theoretical and political positions, this claim argues that ontological reflection is simply unnecessary in the postmetaphysical context. In contrast to the premodern, modernity is defined by its ability to subsist on the ontologically "minimal" understanding of a pliable world susceptible to technological control. The problems and tensions of modern life do not flow from deep-seated ontological differences between groups (Connolly 1995a, 1–3). Thus, even if they exist, they do not affect the ethical-political relations and actions of individuals and groups.

In response, Connolly asks: By what standard are the ontological assumptions of the modern period minimal? What if those standards only appear minimal when opposed to the premodern teleological traditions modernity defines itself against? For him, it is precisely the ontopolitical matrix of late modernity that needs critical reassessment and positive alternatives. One of the prevalent strategies used to sideline ontological issues is to claim the primacy of epistemology. Connolly's analysis here is particularly interesting because it suggests that Rorty may still be complicit in this project. Epistemology claims to circumscribe ontology either by accessing criteria for knowledge that make ontology redundant or by providing neutral tests that resolve ontological issues. Rorty similarly socially circumscribes ontology through a sociological analysis of the linguistic social practices of a context and their various critical and normative purposes. Connolly calls this a social foundationalism and claims that it reinserts the demand that truth, even if only as social justification, be unified and one. It repeats a social ontology of neutralism. "The primacy of epistemology short-circuits ontological issues by assuming once the right procedure for attaining truth as correspondence or coherence or consensus is reached, any remaining issues will either be resolved through that method or shown to be irrelevant" (Connolly 1995a, 6). This critique is introduced here and examined throughout chapters 3 and 4.

It is important to emphasize that Connolly is not overtly arguing for the primacy of ontology after epistemology. Rorty would be correct that this merely replaces one foundation with another. Rather, Connolly is arguing that the "dilemma of epistemology" does not refute the use of ontology in political reflection and that the inevitability of ontological assumptions necessitates interrogating them. He thus charts another course away from that dilemma, offering a disposition that attends to both the necessity and *limits* of ontology. As a *weak* ontologist, Connolly argues that decisive arbitration between contending ontological positions is impossible; they are fundamentally contestable. There is no way to prove that the notion of a pliable world or that of a world with an intrinsic purpose to being are incorrect. Equally, his own position, regarding the irreducibility of ontological assumptions and his positive ontology of discordance, cannot be ruled out of the field of contestation. Whether this is unproblematic will be addressed shortly. What is important now is that the ultimate contestabilty of ontology, as a method, and specific ontologies is an axiomatic part of his philosophy (Connolly 1995a, 16).

Connolly's key insight is to map the contemporary shape of ontopolitical assumptions in contemporary Anglo-American discourse. The matrix occurs along a horizontal axis between *mastery* and *attunement*. The former refers to the drive to subject nature to human control and the corresponding assumption of nature's susceptibility to this project. The latter assumes a higher purpose or telos in being and the ability of humans to enter into a harmonious relationship with it. While these positions are, in theory, inimical, Connolly argues they share an ontological disposition of compensation: the implicit demand for compensation in modernity for the loss of enchanted understandings of the world. They insist on a world that is predisposed to us in some way, either as a pliable medium susceptible to our mastery or a higher order through which we can gain communion (Connolly 1995a, 17–20).

Connolly's method intends to destabilize these positions and their assumption of a world predisposed to humanity and intelligibility. For this, he employs strategies of ontological detachment and attachment; deconstructive and genealogical strategies of critical detachment are matched by strategies of attachment to alternative ontological figurations. The latter, which Connolly refers to as "positive onto-political interpretation," involves projecting explicit presumptions into one's interpretations of actuality while acknowledging that one's presumptions exceed both the intention and ability to demonstrate their truth. This acknowledgment of contestability challenges closure in the field by both critically assessing other approaches and refusing to set up another absolute space. For Connolly, this dual movement is a "double-entry orientation" to politics. Critical detachments and affirmative attachments are treated as incontestable initially but are then withdrawn in an acknowledgment of contestability. For him, inquiry must proceed explicitly in the median space between these gestures (Connolly 2004, 344; see also Howarth 2010). Thus, the affirmations are not merely strategic gestures but comprise ontological assumptions built into and constitutive of both the critiques and the alternatives they present. Connolly emphasizes this when he refers to these viewpoints as "vague essentialisms" and "happy positivisms." The key point is that these projections are neither merely provisional nor prediscursive realities beyond question.[7] Rather, they are both affirmative (like prediscursive ontologies) and contestable (like a provisional ontology would be). As in the epitaph, this paradoxical pairing of opposites characterizes interpretation in general. The double-entry orientation to interpretation attempts to do justice to the inadequacy and contestability of ontology, the inevitability of ontological presuppositions, and the ambiguous nature of human inquiry.

TWO PATHWAYS FROM FOUNDATIONS

Rorty's and Connolly's approaches to ontology represent two positive pathways away from the problem of foundations and the resulting ironic situation of inquiry. As discussed in chapter 1, Rorty responded with a prioritization of social categories, a strategy that elided epistemological issues. He developed this approach in his mature work through his cultural-political conception of social change and its argument for the ontological priority of the social. The latter claims that all ontological analyses, whether of analytic investigations of the existence of objects or Heideggerian analyses of the conditions of Being, are subject to the categories of a given social community. For Rorty, there is no way to elide this condition and ensure that our claims (ontological or otherwise) actually condition humanity. The critique of foundationalism and the failure of the epistemological model necessitate the abandonment of the idea of a level of reality other than everyday contingent human reality (Rorty 1989, 45). For him, ontology relies on a notion of *unmasking*, of getting beyond the merely ontic to some deeper level somehow prior to ours. It is based upon an assumption of the appearance-reality distinction that Rorty, as a Nietzschean, rejects. "For without the traditional concepts of metaphysics one cannot make sense of the appearance-reality distinction, and without that distinction one cannot make sense of the notion of 'what is really going on.' No more metaphysics, no more unmasking" (Rorty 1996b, 14). In fact, much of Rorty's critique of contemporary continental political thought is that its use of ontology repeats the Platonic logic of a deeper reality that can be unmasked by some privileged means and, in so doing, repeats a claim to special access/authority.

The language of unmasking is especially significant. For Connolly, ontologies may be contestable, but they are also inevitable. "When an unfamiliar competitor challenges these terms of discourse, the ensuing debates condense some of this fog into a new series of beliefs and counter beliefs. Of course, only one layer of fog is lifted by such an intervention, and new layers roll in" (Connolly 1995, 37; see also Digeser 1995, 47). *New fogs always roll in*. Any active interpretation of the world for Connolly always includes a set of assumptions about Being, humanity, and their relations. Consequently, political thought requires an active ontopolitical method of interpretation that avoids this logic of unmasking while accounting for the irreducibility of ontological presuppositions. His double-entry orientation to interpretation attempts this, to remain critical in its original incontestable strategies of detachment while subsequently folding in a reflexive ethos of contestability.

This basic difference in the role of ontology after foundations characterizes the relationship between Rorty and Connolly. Further, each exposes a potential criticism of the other's approach: how the other potentially ignores a fundamental condition of politics. By singlemindedly placing ontology within a homogenized field of languages without priority, where ontology is merely another way of speaking, Rorty ignores how the inevitability of hidden ontological assumptions requires engagement. Thus, the possibility emerges that a set of compensatory ontological assumptions will recur in his brand of pragmatic ontological minimalism. In formulating his method, Connolly gives priority to ontological limitations on politics and avoids how ontological claims are always situated within social contexts and languages. Further, he consistently oscillates between two levels of argument, two different statuses for ontological analysis. On the one hand, he seems to claim that contestable ontological presuppositions inevitably structure all human thought. On the other hand, he periodically expands this to claim that the ontological conditions he identifies are actually *out there* in the world, structuring not only human thought but events. The former is subject to the same issues Rorty is often accused of (i.e., relativism). The latter would ultimately be another foundationalism. The common danger is that his methodology's relation to ontological categories does not allow for the critical reflexivity Connolly desires and is central to the weak-ontological project.

This debate has important ramifications for methodology within contemporary political theory. Rorty and Connolly expose the lacunae of contemporary political thought's problem of justification, how we continue to be caught between the attempt to say something valid to all (i.e., incontestable), as a necessary moment of political criticism, and the problem that this entails one more claim to neutrality and authority. The following section teases out this conflict, these two pathways, by examining the understandings of language and contingency that inform their respective positions on ontology and approach to political thinking after foundations.

THE PROBLEM OF AUTHORITY: LANGUAGE, CONTINGENCY, AND CONTINENTAL PHILOSOPHY

This section continues the investigation of this paradox within contemporary political thought examining Rorty's theories of language and contingency and his relationship to continental philosophy. For Rorty, the turn away from foundationalism requires a turn toward language. This discussion will develop the themes of antiauthoritarianism, social justification, and the linguistic turn introduced in chapter 1. However, while the project there was to examine his early engagements, this discussion clarifies subsequent developments. The antiauthoritarianism that structured Rorty's early critiques continues to function as the dominant motivating force of his work, leading him to his linguistic turn and a pragmatic reconception of language that continues the shift from external forms of authority to humanity. What emerges is the centrality of language as a nonfoundational framework for sociopolitical change.

Rorty employs continental philosophy to reinforce that shift. His relationship with this philosophical tradition is complex, and part of this study is to clarify it. This section focuses on his selective and critical appropriation of Heidegger's theory of historical contingency. For Rorty, Heidegger overcomes the Western philosophical tradition but ultimately remains bound by its authoritarian impulses. By way of contrast and critique, this section also examines Connolly's use of Heidegger in order to fill out the former's ontological method. What emerges is that their different views on ontology stem from opposed positions on a key aspect of Heidegger's project: the claim of the primacy of Being.

THE LINGUISTIC TURN: AUTHORITY AND CONTINGENCY

In his mature work, Rorty extended his behavioral critique of the authoritarianism of epistemology to include any discourse claiming privileged access. As discussed in chapter 1, antiauthoritarianism unifies Rorty's work as the central response to the main impasse in modern philosophy for Rorty: the problem of justification. We can no longer refer to foundations in our philosophical accounts of humanity and the world; that is, we must be broadly antifoundational. Yet we still need to be able to make normative claims in relation to our practices that transcend a single vocabulary; that is, we must avoid relativism. For Koopman, this project of "normativity without foundations" is "Rorty's most important philosophical ambition" (Koopman 2011b, 68). While most of Rorty's critics have understood him to argue for antifoundationalism while ignoring the problem of relativism, Koopman illustrates how his pragmatic theory of language and contingency is an invaluable methodological contribution to the problem of justification. For him, Rorty weds *antifoundationalism* and *antirelativism* in his linguistic turn.

The fundamental importance of the linguistic turn for Rorty was the methodological contribution it made on the path to antifoundationalism. While he was critical of much linguistic philosophy, shifting the focus to language undermined foundationalism by moving the emphasis away from experience (external reality) and toward actual linguistic behavior (Rorty 2007l). This allows naturalistic forms of analysis that understand it merely as a human practice. *CIS*'s achievement is to spell out how we might conceive of language in such terms. Key to this is a reading of the work of Donald Davidson, particularly his explicit rejection of language as a representational medium between subject and world. This notion, dominant in contemporary analytic thought, replaced earlier frameworks (e.g., mind, experience) and repeats the same confusion of cause and justification. In contrast, Davidson rejects the idea that language is something that must be adequate to either the world or the self. He keeps the focus on language while dropping it as an epistemological standard: he theorizes the nonfoundational priority of language (Rorty 1989, 10; 1991p, 150).

To claim that language is both nonfoundational and fundamental, Rorty offers an account of vocabularies as tools.[8] This shifts our conception away from external verification to the relationship between various forms of social practice. Rather than asking about the adequacy of language to the world, we focus on its efficiency as a tool. Further, languages on this account are not about discovery but invention, where new tools are created to surpass old ones. The point of these tools is that they allow us to cope with our environment and with one another. For Davidson, this entails philosophers taking on the position of the *field linguist*. This anthropological image of linguistic practice emphasizes language as a largely ad hoc, piecemeal process of interpretation. On an individual level, it is a process of constructing "passing theories" about the noises/inscriptions of another human just as an anthropologist will attempt to link up a "native's" utterances with their surroundings (Rorty 1991p, 132). Understanding is a process of learning to predict what will come next. These theories are passing in the sense that they are constantly revised in order to account for things that are not explained by the current theory (Rorty 1989, 14). It is in this sense that vocabularies allow us to cope through shared understandings of one another and our environment.

This understanding of language shifts our approach to other vocabularies. The social-practice view emphasizes the autonomy and social nature of languages. In terms of justification, vocabularies are closed-off spheres that allow people to cope and that can only be approached through a piecemeal behavioral method. They do not uniquely link up with the world or some other neutral framework that allows for commensurability. However, this also raises a potential problem: maintaining too strict a division between languages suggests the impossibility of critical-normative exchange between them. While this potential weakness and its resolution will be discussed at length in chapters 5 and 6, it is important now to clarify that Rorty, in his linguistic turn, precludes this possibility. He follows Davidson in rejecting the scheme-content distinction, between our conceptual schemes and what flows into them, arguing that no languages are, in principle, incommensurable. This is the basis of his imperative to the field linguist's disposition to intervocabulary engagement. This clarification is important. It offers important resources for avoiding the reification of language and for pluralizing/democratizing linguistic engagement. For Rorty, giving language priority also requires contingency.

RORTY AND THE CONTINENTAL TRADITION: CONTINGENCY WITHOUT DEPTH

While the language of contingency is by no means the property of continental philosophy, this concept became central to Rorty's work through engaging that tradition. Specifically, through a reading of Nietzschean and Heideggerian theories of language Rorty injected contingency into his account of language as tools. This combination is one of the most original and overlooked contributions of his thought. Both his pragmatist and continental critics tend to examine this aspect in relation to their own focus. Consequently, there has been little examination of this mixture. Beginning with language (this continues into his naturalism and historicism), Rorty's understanding of social practices is a distinctive combination of his readings of Heidegger, Nietzsche, and postanalytic philosophy of language (Davidson and Wittgenstein). While the latter contributions have been examined, his relationship to continental philosophy has never been systematically clarified.

Rorty's work is fundamentally concerned with the nature of concept change. Following this re-visioning of language and the role of philosophy, he offered a view of intellectual history that emphasized its priority and contingency. Central to this is a Nietzschean understanding of metaphor as the prime agent in vocabulary shifts. For Rorty, the purpose of placing metaphor at the center of the history of human languages is to emphasize its nonteleological and nonpurposive nature, to portray it as a contingent process of tool change. New vocabularies are created and either gradually socially accepted or rejected, according to contemporary needs and values. This account develops Rorty's discussion of scientific revolutions. However, in *CIS* it broadens to the "metaphoric redescriptions" central to all linguistic change. Importantly, the centrality of metaphors to this process reveals the contingent nature of social change (Rorty 1989, 16–17).

Rorty follows Nietzsche in describing truth as a "mobile army of metaphors." He weds this to Davidson's opposition to the distinction between the metaphorical and literal as two distinct types of meaning or interpretation. Instead, this distinction is merely the difference between familiar and unfamiliar (normal and abnormal) noises. Metaphors are sentences that have no place, or meaning, within a given language. They are "unparaphraseable," pure possibilities, unfamiliar events analogous to new phenomena within the natural sciences. All we can do is grapple with them and revise our theories in response. If a metaphor is taken up within a language, if it becomes habitual and regularized, it is killed and only then given a meaning within a vocabulary. For Rorty, concept change occurs through this process of the literalization and death of metaphors. In this sense it is contingent; metaphors have no meaning and thus no necessary place within language. The way a language changes depends on which metaphors are taken up, how they are used, and the community where they are integrated into regular social practice (Rorty 1989, 17–19; 1991m, 12–13; 1991u, 163–65).

Rorty's point in this model is to emphasize the contingency, priority, and autonomy of language. Languages, as tools, allow us to cope through structuring our world. History is a process of one language replacing another through the adoption of some new metaphors or descriptive schemas. With each change, our purposes and ends also change. Furthermore, there are no neutral criteria against which to compare alternative languages. Rather, languages are normatively separated from the world and cannot draw on it for epistemological criteria or norms. We can only compare one language with another in pragmatic terms of their purposes and ends. For Rorty, this realization of contingency necessitates that we remove nonhuman bases for authority in our language. Only our purposes (the practices and relations facilitated by tools) can provide such direction (Rorty 1989, 22). For these reasons, for Rorty, conceiving of languages as tools keeps the authority within human sources while retaining the capacity for normative claims. In this manner, contingency moderates his tool account. How this moderation occurs can be clarified by examining Rorty's relationship to the continental tradition.

Rorty's relationship to continental thought[9] was established in the 1980s and 1990s through readings of Nietzsche and Heidegger (Rorty 1982a, 1991k, 1991b). However, pragmatism set the terms of this engagement. As he outlines in *EHO*, Rorty wanted to put "post-Nietzschean thought" in the context of pragmatism. It is unsurprising, then, that Rorty's reading of Heidegger, his most sustained analysis in this period (spanning three books and ten years of publications), when it has been commented upon by continentalists has only been lamented (Guignon 1986; Caputo 1983). This is because Rorty appropriates only a particular aspect of Heidegger, his sense of historicity and contingency. There are really two dimensions to this. First, Heidegger established the historicity of Dasein as a situated entity. It is notable that Rorty speaks much more positively of the early Heidegger than the late. For him, this is the pragmatic Heidegger who rejected philosophies of eternity and universality by arguing for the "primordiality of the *Zuhanden*, on the fact that everything was always already related" (Rorty 1991v, 60). For Rorty, and for pragmatists generally, this Heidegger gives ontological priority to social categories and also sees authority as socially derived (Brandom 2005, 216; see also Okrent 1988). Importantly, this perspective allows Heidegger to reconstrue history as a series of contingent developments.

While Heidegger did contradict this earlier pragmatism for Rorty, his second contribution was to provide the most thorough narrative of Western thought, illustrating its fundamental contingency. Rorty focuses on a particular text, "Sketches for a History of Being as Metaphysics" (Heidegger 1975), to bear this out. There Heidegger offers a series of terms, beginning in antiquity and moving up to the modern technocratic present, which represent the various stages of our fundamental determinations of Being. For Rorty, this illustrated the type of contingent language shifts he understands as inherent to linguistic change and cultural development. In fact, he goes as far in this interpretation as to claim that Heidegger's "Being" really has no useful sense beyond what he calls a vocabulary (Rorty 1991d, 37).

What Heidegger's narrative reveals is quite close to Rorty's own history in *PMN*. The development of Western thought is the movement through various attempts at philosophical certainty (Rorty 1991o, 73). This is the historical pathway from Plato to Nietzsche. The necessity is that "if you begin with Plato's motives and assumptions you will end up with some form of pragmatism" (Rorty 1991d, 27). For Plato, inquiry's end is certainty, the attempt to get in touch with something external that compels and assures belief. Importantly, this quest for certainty has undergone many forms, culminating in Nietzschean pragmatism. For Rorty, in illustrating this, Heidegger reveals the contingency of our various vocabularies (Rorty 1991m, 16). Each stage in this narrative is a failed attempt at certainty. What Heidegger illustrates is that

> this quest for certainty, clarity and direction from outside can also be viewed as an attempt to escape from time, to view *Sein* as something that has little to do with *Zeit*. Heidegger would like to recapture a sense of what time was like before it fell under the spell of eternity, what we were like before we became obsessed by the need for an overarching context which would subsume and explain us ... he would like to recapture a sense of contingency, of the fragility and riskiness of any human project.
>
> (Rorty 1991d, 34)

Heidegger's narrative illustrates the failure of the quest for certainty and the contingent nature of humanity and its history. By illustrating this, he more fully "overcomes the tradition" than any other thinker (Rorty 1982f, 46).

The problem with Heidegger is his normative evaluation of that history; he argues that pragmatism (and modernity) is still complicit in the Platonic project. Pragmatism is simply the most recent iteration in the onto-theological tradition. It is the final form, once skepticism about the entire Platonic project enters. It still assumes that certainty requires unique contact with the world and that, in its absence, all we have is our desires. In this manner, pragmatism for Heidegger is the most overt form of the technocratic interpretation of thinking because it places instrumental rationality entirely at the service of human desires not subject to that very rationality. It is still within the assumption of truth as power, which is fundamental to the modern technocratic mode of thought.[10] The fact that pragmatism (and Nietzsche) is the dialectical end of Platonic certainty means it represents a fallen and irredeemable tradition; this necessitates a complete rejection of the modern world.

For Rorty, this position reveals a fundamental metaphysics within Heidegger's project to give philosophy a radical role in relation to the present. Heidegger seeks to speak outside the present and thereby free us from its constrictions. In his "poetic" conception of philosophy, "the aim of philosophical thought is to free us from the language we presently use by reminding us that this language is not that of 'human reason' but is the creation of the thinkers of our historical past" (Rorty 1991m, 16). Heidegger seeks to undermine the present through the exposure of its contingency. However, there is a basic ambiguity in the status of the framework he offers. He seeks both to place the philosophies of the past in context, to reveal their historicity, but also to retain a justification for how his thought, his model of questioning Being, manages to break through that barrier and achieve a unique perspective. For Rorty, this reinserts an "unexplained explainer": a transcendental criterion beyond relationality. This is a conditionless condition, a normative claim for the authority of one entity over another, and it is susceptible to the same objections that have afflicted all previous options (e.g., God, Platonic forms, Kantian noumena). The understanding of Being that goes beyond vocabularies constitutes Heidegger's attempt to escape from time and contingency (Rorty 1991e, 69–70, 77).

Retaining this distinctive capacity for philosophy leads Heidegger to criticize the contemporary period as inadequate, as fallen from the truth of Being. For him, modernity is both contingent and *belated*.

> To say that it is contingent it is enough to show how self-deceptive it is to think things had to be as they are, how provincial it is to think that the final vocabulary of the present day is "obvious" and "inescapable." But to say that this vocabulary is belated, to contrast it with something more primordial, one has to give "primordial" some kind of normative sense, so that it means something more than just "earlier."
>
> (Rorty 1991d, 43)

In this, Heidegger succumbs to the same criticism the latter makes of Nietzsche. Metaphysics reemerges within Heidegger's philosophy through his nostalgia for a pure time before the Platonic quest for certainty and his resulting desire to escape the present moment. Consequently, he understands authentic philosophy only as the rupture of the present vocabulary, a movement beyond beings to the primacy of Being.

Several important points emerge in Rorty's reading of Heidegger. First, it is highly selective. Rorty focuses solely on Heidegger's identification of historical contingency. His value is in overcoming that traditional project of philosophy (Rorty 1982f, 52). In focusing only on this, Rorty's critics are right to clarify that there is no fusion of horizons here. Rorty reads Heidegger from within his own pragmatic priorities (much as this criticism amounts to).[11] However, this selective use is explained by Rorty's larger project. Like his reading of Nietzsche, he combines continental contingency with his pragmatic vision of social practices in order to address the problem of justification, to provide for a philosophy that is both antifoundational and antirelativistic. For Rorty, each moderates the other's problematic tendency. As we will discuss in chapter 3, naturalism (even the pragmatic) has a tendency toward a reductive scientism. Equally, continental thought tends to reify contingency. In Heidegger this manifests in the primordial nature of language as the disclosure of Being.

Second, more importantly, this reading reveals a clear link between Rorty and Heidegger. They share a "nonabsolutistic philosophy of finitude," a sense of the situatedness or "thrownness" of human existence. Further, they share a deconstructive project for the history of metaphysics, criticizing the history of Western philosophy as a series of attempts to insulate us from that finitude and preserve absolute knowledge, certainty, or universality (Caputo 1983, 682–83). However, they are divided by several fundamental differences. First, Rorty and Heidegger *conceive* of that finitude differently, especially in relation to language, and correspondingly seek to address it via different *approaches*. Rorty's addresses finitude by reconceiving language solely as a social practice, a tool we use for other purposes. In this way, it is divested of ontological and metaphysical significance through a model of the linguistic turn that avoids foundationalism. Rorty breaks the bond between language and Being and turns it in upon itself. Importantly, language also gains priority in this move as the primary site of normative claims and social change.

While language is similarly essential to our finitude for Heidegger, it is for very different reasons. Language is the house of Being, not in the sense that we are limited to language but because the event of Being always occurs in language, through which we encounter, experience, and disclose the world. Thus, for Heidegger, humanity can't help but speak Being, and so we must shed the history of our metaphysical languages, which ignored this, and attempt to speak authentically by returning to the thought of Being and how it conditions us. On this basic difference in the conception and response to finitude, as one commentator has aptly observed, "each is for the other the latest victim in the history of metaphysics" (Caputo 1983, 680). For Heidegger, Rorty would be the apotheosis of the technical interpretation of language. By separating language from Being and reducing it to a tool, he gives thought over to beings. Contrariwise, for Rorty, by retaining a distinction of depth, by seeing our language and life as conditioned by Being and thereby distinguishing between authentic and inauthentic discourses, Heidegger reinserts an unexplained explainer and conditionless condition, one more claim to authority that steps back in the infinite regress that is the history of metaphysics.

This contrast amounts to a difference in definitions of metaphysics and finitude. For Heidegger, metaphysics is the forgetting of Being and the sole focus on beings. Returning to finitude requires understanding how we are limited and framed by Being and our construal of it. For Rorty, in contrast, metaphysics is the attempt to invest authority in a nonhuman source, and finitude is relocating that authority in the social practices of justification that exist between humans. This key difference results in the tense relationship of appropriation and rejection that characterizes Rorty's relationship to post-Heideggerian continental thought. Rorty and Heidegger are linked by a rejection of the metaphysical history of philosophy and a common emphasis on the finitude and situated nature of humanity, while having fundamentally different understandings of that finitude and its consequences. Connolly's ontological critique of Rorty illuminates how this difference develops into a criticism of Rorty from a more recent version of Heidegger's ontological approach.

CONNOLLY'S CONTINENTALISM AND THE CONTINGENCY OF THE WORLD

As a prominent member of the contemporary ontological turn in political theory, Connolly's work is situated within an account of this "thrownness." However, this was not always the case. The central role of ontology in his double-entry orientation to ontopolitical analysis replaced his earlier postpositivism, which was in certain respects much closer to Rorty. This shift seems to have principally occurred between two of Connolly's works, *Appearance and Reality* (1981) and *Politics and Ambiguity* (1987).[12] My claim is not that there is a fundamental division here, for many common themes and ideas carry over (e.g., contestability, the role of interpretation in politics), only that there is a key shift in the sources of Connolly's analysis and thus in his approach in this period. While that earlier work argued for an interpretivist framework, one not wholly unlike Rorty's hermeneutics, the latter takes an explicitly ontological approach. This turn is generally ignored in the burgeoning literature on Connolly, which only focuses on work he produced after his ontological turn.

While he is not usually considered to be one of Connolly's main sources, that turn in Connolly's work was prompted by a reading of Heidegger. This basic fact links Rorty and Connolly, while their divergent uses of Heidegger drive them apart, giving some shape to the space between recent pragmatism and weak ontology in general.[13] Unlike Rorty, weak ontology flows from a basic Heideggerian framework. For White, Heidegger is crucial to the story of the ontological turn in the same two senses as for Rorty. In his early work, he demonstrates the necessity of questioning Being through the examination of the situated nature of human being (*Dasein*); in his later work, he illustrates the impoverishment of the history of metaphysics, including modernity, as the attempt to "grasp" Being (White 2000, 4–5).

Connolly takes on both of these imperatives in his framing of ontological analysis. However, while he enacts the former situated project through a reception of twentieth-century French philosophy (particularly Michel Foucault), his understanding of modern thought and its conditions is decidedly Heideggerian. In fact, it is in his discussions of ontology in general and modernity's relation to it that the most frequent references to Heidegger occur. Here, Connolly takes from Heidegger an understanding of the ontological conditions of human thought and a fundamental understanding of modernity's veiling of this structure.

For Connolly, the real significance of the epistemological tradition is not its failed projects but its obscuring of a more fundamental dynamic. Heidegger reveals that the truth/falsity pairing common to epistemology and modernity, rather than just misunderstanding truth as correspondence instead of justification, *conceals* the presence of a fundamental untruth.

> Modern "truth" is a mode of revealing that enables judgments of correctness and incorrectness within its frame. But every historical regime of revealing also conceals. It conceals possibilities of being that cannot be brought into a particular way of life without confounding its basic principles of organization. "Untruth" is deeper than truth and falsity, then: untruth is that which cannot achieve sufficient standing within the terms of discourse of a time without stretching contemporary standards of plausibility and coherence to their limits of tolerance.
>
> (Connolly 1995, 5; see also Heidegger 1998)

For Connolly, Heidegger's ontological mode of questioning and understanding of truth draws that concept out of the epistemological framework of modernity in order to undermine its truth/falsity pairing. This pairing conceals the "untruth" that exceeds it. The consequent imperative is to explore the historical conditions that allowed truth to be reduced to "reliable criteria for knowledge" and to engage thinking that is not commensurate with that current determination of thought. Truth is not epistemology but the attempt to understand how truth was reduced to epistemology.

Connolly is certainly critical of aspects of Heidegger's framework. Particularly, he rejects Heidegger's eventual abstraction of the "eventing" of Being away from the embodied human subject and thus turns to Foucault, Nietzsche, and recent literature from the neurosciences in response. Nonetheless, he takes on the importance of the structure of Being, that is, Heidegger's understanding that Being is always limited in a particular determination and thus that any eventing of Being is both an unconcealing and a concealing (White 2000, 110). This is especially evident in how Connolly reforms, without contradicting, his understanding of language.

In his much-praised *Terms of Political Discourse*, Connolly's understanding of concepts as "essentially contestable" occurs within a postpositivistic and naturalistic framework. There, he rejects the idea of language as a neutral medium and instead construes concepts as complex, open, and appraisive (Connolly 1994, 1-2, 22). This framework is not incompatible with Rorty's conception of language. While there are different emphases (especially around the internal complexity of language and the resulting contestation), both stress how concepts are situated within networks of other concepts and thus are relative to the criteria of that language. Like Rorty, this makes concepts fundamentally cultural for Connolly (Schoolman 2008, 25). However, in *Politics and Ambiguity*, where the influence of continental philosophy and Heidegger is apparent, the ontological dimension of language and its consequences hold center stage.

In that text, Connolly interrogates contemporary theories of language through a discussion of the relation between articulation and the world we attempt to articulate. However, instead of expanding his earlier analysis, he focuses on Heidegger's view that words are essential to the being of things, that "where the word breaks off no thing may be" (Connolly 1987, 144). For Connolly, this phrase demonstrates the paradox (i.e., conditions) of articulation (in general). "For things to be, they must be brought into a web of articulations which gives them boundaries, specificity, complexity; but any particular web of discourse fixes things in particular ways and closes out other possible modes of being" (Connolly 1987, 145). The similarities with the discussion of modern truth are obvious. Connolly understands language as fundamentally poetic. It calls forth and brings things into being yet is structured by a limitation. By speaking, we determine a thing, isolating it within one level of articulation; this excludes, and ultimately conceals, its other possible modes of being. Thus, where Rorty elides the relationship between language and world and internalizes justification to social categories, Connolly, following Heidegger, identifies a fundamental structure of limitation within language. He asserts an essence for it.

Connolly attempts to articulate this structure of *determination as limitation* within a conception of contingency. Rorty resists defining contingency. His concern throughout his work is to "avoid hinting that this suggestion [contingency] gets something right, that my sort of philosophy corresponds to the way things really are" (Rorty 1989, 8). In contrast, for Connolly, if all determinations are a limitation, then contingency is necessary and, in this, has a *general reality*, one that turns out to be multifaceted:

> By contrast to the necessary and the universal, it means that which is changeable and particular; by contrast to the certain and the constant, it means that which is uncertain and variable; by contrast to the self-subsistent and the causal, it means that which is dependent and effect; by contrast to the expected and the regular, it means that which is unexpected and irregular; and by contrast to the safe and reassuring, it means that which is dangerous, unruly, and obdurate in its danger.
>
> (Connolly 1991, 28)

The final description here highlights the difference. While Rorty would agree that contingency precludes neutral frameworks for inquiry and any teleological sense for human knowledge and communities (i.e., changeable, uncertain, dependent, and unexpected), the contingent for Connolly is also necessarily beyond control (obdurate). In his ontology contingency is not simply an acknowledgment of the historicity, fallibleness, and socially situated nature of humanity. Rather, contingency is something *in* the world. "Suppose internal and external nature contains, because it is neither designed by a god nor neatly susceptible to organization by human design, elements of stubborn opacity to human knowledge, recalcitrance to human projects, resistance to any model of normal individuality and harmonious community" (Connolly 1991, 31). By giving contingency a determinate nature and figuring it as something "obdurate in its danger," Connolly gives the world intention and agency. It not only lacks susceptibility to human intentions but actively resists them.

When the world actively resists human intentions, when contingency is a general condition, ontological analysis becomes necessary. This is not for the foundationalist reason of discerning the unity of reality but because of the postfoundational imperative to understand its necessary disunity (contingency) and how that conditions human thought and action. Further, it necessitates the continual investigation of our concealments of Being. As discussed above, Connolly follows Heidegger in arguing that modernity's central flaw is obscuring the presence and necessity of the ontological veil. The imperative of both their ontological projects is to "let the veil appear as what veils" (Connolly 1991, 31; Heidegger 1977b, 16). There is no exposure of Being or harmonious relationship in the ontological approach for Connolly. Rather, *new fogs roll in*. The consequence of the irreducibility of ontology, because of the partial (contingent) nature of our languages and understandings, is that contingency, contra Rorty, becomes ontologically necessary as a part of the world. It is an irreducible part of reality that makes all of our understandings partial and the presence of unjustifiable ontological assumptions inevitable. Consequently, the goal should not be the absence of a veil or its (sociological) circumvention, as in Rorty, but the revelation of the presence and necessity of that veil. Presently, we must examine the critique of Rorty that results out of this, for although there are problems with the relation to ontology Connolly establishes, problems that continue in his thought and that Rorty's framework identifies, there is also a potential critique of Rorty.

CONNOLLY AND THE TWO RORTYS: METHODOLOGICAL REFLEXIVITY

Connolly's most extended critical engagement with Rorty focused on the consequences of his critique of foundations and his alternative pathway. Endorsing Rorty's critique of epistemology in *PMN*, Connolly expresses frustration with his subsequent alternative. "Rorty closes the door he has just opened as the new converts are walking through it" (Connolly 1987, 118). Rorty's pragmatization of language wards off dangerous possibilities and isolates us within our current cultural discourse. Closely mirroring Rorty's liberal critics, Connolly accuses him of providing no resources for sociopolitical criticism. There is no capacity to question one's own presuppositions here, no critical reflexivity, but only a "tinted mirror held up to American technocracy" (Connolly 1987, 123). This is especially frustrating for Connolly, as it seems to have been for several continentalists, because Rorty's work matches the Nietzschean and Heideggerian critiques of Western philosophy.

Connolly's central and most important charge is that Rorty reinstitutes grounds in the form of a *social foundationalism*. While he fails to justify this claim, his arguments more expressions of frustration than analysis, it is a keen observation. As discussed above, Rorty does argue for the ontological priority of the social. In this, he isolates us within languages and reduces sociopolitical change to linguistic development. He thus regrounds his philosophy in an understanding of normative development that ignores nonlinguistic factors (including the ontological). He also assumes that the only important level of the social is the most overt, ignoring that there could be persistent assumptions within. While implicit, Connolly's main complaint is that Rorty incorrectly links sociopolitical criticism to epistemology. Consequently, his rejection of the latter circumscribes human thought to the social, to cultural politics. In contrast, Connolly and his sources (here Heidegger and Foucault) "extend it [critique] by encouraging us to experience strangeness in its prevailing form" (Connolly 1987, 125). While Connolly never exactly clarifies this difference, he suggests that they extend the critique of metaphysics they share with Rorty to our cultural norms and institutions in a way he refuses. For Connolly, this refusal institutes a social foundationalism. It is the difference between pragmatic complacency and continental criticism. "Heidegger questions and illuminates; Foucault disturbs and incites; Rorty comforts and tranquilizes" (Connolly 1987, 125).

Connolly's criticism both makes an important observation and fails to grasp the true significance of Rorty's moves with respect to ontology, language, and contingency.[14] As discussed above, for Connolly, ontological assumptions are inevitable. He follows Heidegger in arguing that every revelation of Being is simultaneously a concealment, that all interpretations of the world are necessarily partial, and that they reveal certain aspects while concealing others and are thus imposed. Further, by rejecting ontological analysis, Rorty *seems* to ignore the possibility of such assumptions within his own work. His social-practice-based understanding of language as a tool for interacting with one another and the environment might contain such assumptions. Further, his model of social justification, which posits use as the only measure between vocabularies and coherence the only measure within them, suggests he assumes the susceptibility and pliability of the world to human purposes (Heidegger's enframing and Connolly's mastery). Thus, Connolly's criticism that Rorty's failure to go beyond an epistemic criticism of contemporary thought results in a sociopolitical complacency does identify the potential of a real set of problematic assumptions.

For Connolly, this illustrates the need to posit the necessity of contingency. It is not only that our languages can never represent reality but that the latter actively resists our attempts to confine it to one interpretation. These two conditions, the inevitable presence of ontopolitical assumptions within all political thought and the necessity of contingency, necessitate engaging ontology. We must both examine the ontological assumptions behind the various positions on the matrix of contemporary thought and explicitly articulate the ontology that motivates our own interpretations. Both of these allow for the incorporation of a critical reflexivity that ultimately acknowledges one's own interventions as contestable. This is the second move in his double-entry orientation, which ensures that Connolly's method avoids the problems of strong foundationalism while still being critical.

We also saw above that both Rorty's early linguistic turn and late concept of cultural politics attempt to satisfy these two exact criteria. Rorty also seeks to avoid foundationalism (antifoundationalism) and retain critical power (antirelativism). Each of these moves contributes to the possibility of a pragmatic brand of critical reflexivity that illustrates Rorty's important methodological contributions. First, he undertakes the linguistic turn in order to shift normative authority to language, a sphere that can retain the capacity to make justificatory claims without descending into authoritarianism. This central project in his work can be summed up as "authority without authoritarianism." Rorty's unique contribution was to shift the focus to language, undermining foundationalism *methodologically rather than metaphysically*. Rorty's claim is not that language holds a privileged viewpoint, as Heidegger claims, but that starting with language helps us explicate our forms of normativity without appealing to foundations. Importantly, this transition also avoids relativism by naturalizing language. When language is understood as a social practice, as a tool with consequences for our interactions with the world and one another, its normative significance is no longer a metaphysical mystery. Rather, linguistic behavior becomes a set of practices where we justify our beliefs to one another. Further, justification is leveled out as a relation that exists between language-using humans rather than as a nonlinguistic relation that exists between human thought and some nonhuman reality. In this manner, shifting our attention to the languages humans use in their social practices provides a methodological field that understands normative claims as necessary (Koopman 2011b, 70–72). Our languages, for Rorty, are always subject to a series of authoritative structures we have to employ, negotiate, and, hopefully, reconstruct. This dedivinizes language in a manner directly opposed to Heidegger's and Connolly's investment of it with nonhuman significance while emphasizing its sociopolitical importance.

This point clarifies an important motive in Rorty's combination of pragmatic naturalism and continental contingency. As discussed in chapter 1, Rorty is cognizant of the tendency within pragmatism and naturalism to scientism and methodism. Because both focus on the human relation to the world, our ability to interact reflectively with one another and our environment, pragmatism and naturalism are given to reifying their approaches into neutral methods. Thus, when he comes to offer his own reconstruction of language as social practice, he infuses that account with Nietzschean contingency (metaphor): a reading of the continental tradition, particularly Heidegger, that emphasizes its theorization of historical contingency. However, while pragmatism is given to methodism, Heidegger and continental thought tend to reify language and contingency. For Rorty, the question of ontology quickly slides into the question of essence and the assumption of the hidden nature of that immutable essence. This is "the assumption that philosophy might explain the unhidden on the basis of the hidden, and might explain availability and relationality on the basis of something intrinsically unavailable and nonrelational" (Rorty 1991v, 60). For Rorty, language no more has an essence than humanity does; both only have histories. The problem with essence is that it functions as a conditionless condition or unexplained explainer, a unique entity that requires a privileged access that ultimately cannot be justified. Rorty thus infuses Heideggerian contingency with naturalism. He makes it a social property of our languages instead of a metaphysical property of the world.

The balancing act Rorty establishes between pragmatism and continental thought allows each to moderate the other's problematic tendency. Pragmatic naturalism checks the continental reification of language; the latter's contingency checks the former's scientism. This is a Madisonian solution of checks and balances that illustrates the meliorative, reconstructive disposition Rorty derives from Dewey. It is within this project that he calls for an alliance between these two frameworks. For Rorty, they can be linked in a common pragmatism without method and a continentalism without depth (Rorty 1991i, 77; see also Rorty 2007d). However, it is important to emphasize that there is a prioritizing of pragmatic naturalism, evident in Rorty's juxtaposition of the later Wittgenstein and Heidegger.

> From the later Wittgenstein's naturalistic and pragmatic point of view, we can be grateful to Heidegger for having given us a new language game. But we should not see that language-game as Heidegger did—as a way of distancing and summing up the West. It was, instead, simply one more in a long series of self-conceptions. Heideggerese is only Heidegger's gift to us, not Being's gift to Heidegger.
>
> (Rorty 1991v, 65)

Rorty's second important move in his reconstruction is to enshrine this approach within a new model of sociopolitical change. His late concept of cultural politics is his clearest expression of an understanding implicit within much of his previous work. This is the claim that after foundations, the only way theory can be both antifoundational and antirelativistic is to situate it primarily within current sociocultural discourses. Philosophy as cultural politics must be understood as both a descriptive and a normative claim. It is the argument that justification is a sociolinguistic process and that recognizing this allows us to reconstruct present problems more effectively. Recent trends in political thought to situated forms of political thinking bear out the success of this idea. Chapter 6 will connect Rorty's methodological move to this literature; chapter 5 will illustrate how it overturns his overt public-private divide and minimalist liberalism.

Connolly's (and the ontological turn's) objection to ontological minimalisms like Rorty's is that they implicitly assume the neutrality of their own categories. That in whatever form they come (e.g., Rawlsian public reason, Habermasian communicative rationality), their attempts to avoid in-depth ontologies obscures real assumptions and results in a claim to neutrality that excludes other perspectives. This compromises their critical reflexivity. However, while Rorty's model of cultural politics may have subterranean assumptions, as we have seen, it successfully retains this reflexivity through its fundamental leveling of the discursive field. Rorty does offer us a vocabulary with which to speak about the many linguistic frameworks that exist, a "vocabulary of vocabularies," as Brandom has called it. This may entail a type of neutrality. However, operationally this model is thoroughly *pluralistic* and *democratic*. In its imperative to approach the evaluation of languages on the model of assessing tools as more or less useful for certain purposes, it asserts the present and future contingency of those purposes and tools. Thus it acknowledges the multiplicity of goals and solutions without erecting a universal standard by which to judge either (Brandom 2000b, 168).

Rather than erecting a single framework, question, approach, or lens that is somehow privileged, this "democratize[s] philosophy itself by expanding who counts as a competent audience and conversational partner" (Voparil 2011b, 133; see also Voparil 2011a; Rorty 2000). This insight reforms our previous understanding. It is often assumed that Rorty excludes ontological perspectives, and occasionally his language slides into this. However, on this model, ontological languages, such as Heideggerese, are *not* de facto excluded. They are simply not given priority within the give and take of cultural politics; that is, they are subject to the same processes of social justification as all other languages. This includes Rorty's vocabulary of vocabularies (cultural politics), which he acknowledges is subject to these same constraints. The implied question behind this debate can then be clarified as over how best to speak about the plurality of languages. The problem, for Rorty, with the metavocabulary of ontology is that it implies that "relating to Being" or disclosing Being is a purpose all vocabularies share—a neutral standard they can all be compared according to. Rorty's approach, in contrast, makes both his own perspective and political theory in general participants in rather than arbiters of democratic society. It allows us to remain critically reflexive in relation to all the languages within the discursive field. How does this compare with Connolly's own method for reflexivity, his onto-ethical-political concept of contestability?

Contestability is the second move in Connolly's double-entry orientation to ontopolitical interpretation. It is an ethical moment of humility acknowledging the comparative contestability of different perspectives, and it is folded back into every ontological analysis in order to prevent the exclusion of other perspectives. In this, it shares much with Rorty's pluralizing and democratizing of discourse. In fact, it could be understood as Connolly's response to Heidegger's primordial urge and the tendency to reify contingency and Being within ontological approaches. However, there is a fundamental difference. Connolly's mechanism of contestability is not internal to his ontological method or his understanding of Being. It is an externally imposed outsider enforced on his ontology to moderate that tendency. As an external humbling mechanism it could be applied to any approach, and for Connolly, it in fact should be.

This reveals an ambiguity in his thought. Connolly's framework is simultaneously too strong and too weak. There is a tension there that pushes it in either one of two directions; *toward either the priority of ontology or the priority of contestability.* Both are problematic. If the former is given priority, as we have seen above, the necessity and reification of contingency violates his critical reflexivity. The contingency of being becomes another external standard. However, if contestability is given priority, then Connolly follows Rorty in reconfiguring languages as vocabularies without providing for an understanding of the normative resources within language that ensures the same reflexivity. *Either*

Connolly violates antifoundationalism or antirelativism. In contrast, Rorty and pragmatism go beyond a mere claim to contestability by weaving it into a conception of language and social practice (Voparil 2011a, 135). Ultimately, this is the difference between a naturalistic conception of contingency and an ontological one. The former necessitates an equal sphere of overlapping exchange; the latter erects one more form of hierarchy based on the necessity of contingency. Subsequent chapters will illustrate the effects of this problem in the rest of Connolly's theory.

CONCLUSION

Rorty's understanding of language and engagement with continental philosophy informs his relationship to ontology and the pathway he charts away from foundations. As we have seen, he took the linguistic turn to satisfy two criteria for philosophy after foundations: antifoundationalism and antirelativism. For him, both of these are required for authority without authoritarianism: to be able to make normative claims without assuming foundationalist premises. This fundamental concern with authority led him to the methodological imperative to focus only on language, to draw resources for philosophical thought and social change only from the actual linguistic behavior of human groups. This is a call to situated thought and a refiguration of language in pragmatic, social terms.

This wider project structured Rorty's engagement with continental philosophy. In that tradition, specifically in his early engagements with Nietzsche and Heidegger,[15] Rorty found allies against the traditional image of philosophy and similar emphases on human finitude and historicity. However, their responses to these broad conditions are drastically different. Where for Heidegger the thrownness of human being requires a turn to the question of Being in general and to the ontological conditions of and assumptions behind politics, for Rorty it necessitated a turn to actual language and practice. For Rorty, the ontological turn reinserts an unexplained explainer and a consequent claim to the authority of one standard and one perspective over all others. Unfortunately, as it seems, post-Heideggerian philosophy has been unable actually to address this criticism. Stephen White demonstrates this well. He notes that Rorty's framework provides a ready criticism for weak ontology and that the latter exceeds the philosophic limits it sets for itself in employing ontology as it does. His only response is that this criticism has gotten stale (White 2000, 16–17). This illustrates a tendency within ontological responses to Rorty that fall short of words when engaging this central philosophical issue that he poses.

This is not to imply that ontological forms of analysis have no critical insights on Rorty. As illustrated here, Connolly persuasively argues for the inevitability of ontological assumptions. Further, his own analysis of Rorty, incomplete as it is, does raise an important claim, which we will develop in chapters 3 and 4. For him, Rorty's pragmatization of authority and language results in a social foundationalism. In rejecting ontological analysis in general, Rorty does ignore the possibility of implicit assumptions within his framework and, if Connolly is right, this may reintroduce a structure of authority within his prioritization of social categories. The next two chapters examine the significance of these assumptions and whether such a foundationalism emerges in Rorty's thought through an analysis of his naturalism and historicism.

Here, we have also identified important methodological contributions within Rorty's models of language and contingency. Unlike Connolly, Rorty integrates critical reflexivity seamlessly within his conception of cultural politics. Conceiving of languages as tools for diverse sets of purposes entails that the vocabulary of cultural politics bears no special authority over other languages. It thus allows for an *internal equality* that makes it fundamentally pluralistic and democratic. Concept change and sociopolitical criticism then take the form of new vocabularies for new purposes and situated interventions within established languages. There are, of course, many lingering questions, especially around how this model provides resources for critical interventions and how we can think new languages and purposes in the context of the ontological priority of the social. While much of the critical literature assumes Rorty has no answer, this analysis will expose his alternative resources for these exact tasks. The present discussion has set the stage, establishing the threads of analysis to be picked up over the subsequent chapters.

3

RECONSTRUCTING NATURALISM

Pragmatic or Ontological?

The big difference between an undesirable sense of humility and a desirable sense of finitude is that the former presupposes that there is, already in existence, something better and greater than the human. . . . A Greek sense of wonder requires us to think that there is something sufficiently like us to be enviable but so superior to us as to be barely intelligible. A pragmatic sense of limits requires us only to think that there are some projects for which our tools are presently inadequate, and to hope that the future may be better than the past in this respect.

—RICHARD RORTY, "A WORLD WITHOUT SUBSTANCES OR ESSENCES"

This chapter and the next continue the critical reconstruction of the themes of naturalism and historicism in Rorty's work. In chapters 1 and 2, I argued that, following the problem of justification, Rorty shifts the focus to language, to discussing what communities say about their political practices and institutions, to identify a set of resources for normative critique and reconstruction that allow us to be both *antifoundational* and *antirelativist*. This avoids repositing external standards for our explanatory and normative claims while still allowing us to identify resources within language that let us to make those claims.

In addition to language, naturalism and historicism comprise Rorty's positive articulation of philosophical practice following his critique of foundationalism. While he is never overt, they function as a pair[1] of limiting and enabling injunctions, proscribing certain types of approaches to theorizing politics while offering alternative resources for sociopolitical criticism. With naturalism, Rorty theorizes how theory can be realist and, importantly, how that realism offers important resources for being antifoundational and antirelativist. His historicism, as with his use of continental historical contingency (described in chapter 2), establishes an important limit on human thought while also providing a means to transform our practices. What will emerge throughout this chapter and the next is the complex relationship between these two resources, one of mutual development and limitation. Naturalism and historicism each contribute important elements to the task of critical analysis and normative reconstruction while moderating problematic tendencies in their counterpart.

While initiating this reconstructive reading, the possibility of a social foundationalism within Rorty's thought was raised in chapter 2 through the work of William E. Connolly. These chapters also extend this initial analysis by examining both Connolly's overt alternative to mastery (chapter 3) and his critique of the ontology of mastery within modernity (chapter 4). The latter ends by arguing that this criticism, which Connolly deploys against much of modern political thought (including pragmatism), is an ontological version of the criticism of acquiescence, which I discussed in the introduction. This analysis illustrates that while there are valid concerns behind this criticism, it relies on a superficial understanding of Rorty's model of critique and normativity under naturalistic and historicist conditions, and that mutual moderation between these two themes explicitly addresses these concerns.

Instead, in clarifying Rorty's pragmatic approach to naturalism and historicism, my analysis turns back upon the ontological method. It will illustrate that while Rorty's naturalism and historicism together constitute a strategic and methodological injunction to holism, Connolly's articulation of these themes reifies ontology as a method and pluralism as an ontological dynamic. The result is a furthering of democratic pluralistic reflexivity in Rorty and a compromising of these resources in Connolly. In this manner, Rorty's work contributes to a growing literature criticizing the ontological turn in general, through its clarification of an alternative set of resources for critically reflexive normative practices of political theorizing.

NATURALISM: A SOCIAL-PRACTICE-BASED VOCABULARY

This chapter explicates Rorty's understanding of naturalism. It illustrates both how this theme is a strategic methodological response to the problem of foundations and how it extends the project and resources in Rorty's turn to language and continental philosophy. This chapter continues the analysis of his relation to that tradition, particularly to (one of) its most prominent contemporary forms, the weak-ontological method of William Connolly, by extending the latter's critique of his work and drawing out the implications through a comparison to a more fully developed version of Connolly's method. Connolly raises the possibility of two readings of Rorty's naturalism. On the one hand, extending the critique of social foundationalism, he suggests that Rorty's naturalism assumes a form of mastery. On the other hand, Rorty's naturalism may evade this criticism through a deep methodological reflexivity. In turn, this exposes a series of reifications and idealizations within Connolly's ontological naturalism that undermines his explanatory and normative aims. The consequences of these analyses will be discussed in chapter 4 in terms of Rorty's historicist method of sociopolitical criticism and Connolly's critique of pragmatic political thought.

RORTY'S PRAGMATIC NATURALISM: ANTIAUTHORITARIANISM AND SOCIAL PRACTICES

Naturalism remains opaque within Rorty's thought; it is not so much an account of the natural world as it is a way of speaking about the human social life that accounts for it. It occurs within his account of the strategic priority of language as social practice and is part of his antimetaphysical and antiessentialist vocabulary for sociopolitical thinking that escapes the two dangers of foundationalism and relativism. It is in this sense that it must be understood methodologically. It is both an injunction against external forms of justification and an identification of and imperative to use the normative resources already within human languages and practices.

The development of Rorty's naturalism and its mature form cannot be detached from his early work in the philosophy of mind. His early "eliminative materialism" in the mind-body debate and his subsequent epistemological behaviorism emphasized the relativity of epistemological criteria, that is, that competing frameworks were describing the same event but within different sets of criteria for explanation. He thus reoriented discussions to the social sphere of language use and cast justification not as an epistemic or ontological relation of language and world but as a social relation between language-using subjects within a community.

As a result, Rorty asserted the need to distinguish between causes (physical) and justifications (social). The world *does* impinge upon us; it *does* stand in a causal relationship to us. Thus, the ontological priority of the social is not a social form of idealism. The priority of language does *not* entail that the world is an effect of our language. Rorty distinguishes between two claims: that the world is out there and that the truth is out there. The first is a causal point beyond dispute. The second posits an external justificatory source in the world. It assumes the presence of a nonhuman language that provides immutable and universal criteria for justification (Rorty 1989, 4–5).

Rorty's naturalism is not an account of the material but of the resources within language and social practice for critical and normative political claims. What is important is that the broad vocabulary of the natural sciences, the vocabulary of causes, has its own set of *uses* and *purposes*. The flaw of representationalism as a vocabulary was to assume that correspondence with reality (a criterion from within the vocabulary of causes) is a purpose that all vocabularies share and thus a universal point of assessment. We should replace the distinction between sentences that access reality in some way and those that do not in favor of distinctions between the various uses of vocabularies for equally various purposes (Rorty 1991j, 113–16).[2] In this way, this use of materialism is compatible with Rorty's strategic prioritization of language. He can be a physicalist (asserting the use of the vocabulary of the sciences) without falling into idealism or reductionism.

Previously, we saw that Rorty turned to language to address the problem of justification, where we can no longer refer to foundations in our philosophical accounts of humanity and the world—that is, we must be broadly antifoundational—while still requiring normative claims in relation to our practices that transcend a single vocabulary—that is, we must avoid relativism. Rorty undertakes the linguistic turn, with an account of languages as tools, to provide an understanding of language that avoids implicit criteria for their justification. This is part of the larger project of antiauthoritarianism, to remove nonhuman standards from our forms of social and political justification. I argued that viewing languages as tools achieves this; understanding them as social practices democratized and pluralized languages while avoiding reifying them. Principally, this was a naturalization of language that turned it away from external standards and toward actual behavior.

The question arises of what Rorty's naturalism actually entails, what uses and purposes it serves, and what conditions and resources for critical and normative inquiry it provides. Principally, it is a way of understanding and speaking about languages and language-using communities that maintains the plurality of their justificatory frameworks and avoids implicitly establishing a single set of criteria against which they can be judged. To do this, it is both a frame, that is, a set of concepts and ways of speaking that enable political thinking to employ the critical and normative resources for sociopolitical criticism already in languages, and a set of injunctions excluding external explanatory and normative standards. As I will discuss in chapter 4, historicism, on the other hand, focuses on enabling intermethodological exchange, to allow different vocabularies to make explanatory and normative claims to one another, from within these nonhierarchical relations. Together these constitute a *holism* that not only enables but explains normative political practices.

It should be clear that Rorty's naturalism is nontraditional. Scientific naturalism is still the orthodoxy among many Anglo-American political philosophers and theorists. Here, the natural is figured strictly in the scientific image of the world. This can take the hard form of an ontological doctrine that the world consists of nothing but the entities that successful scientific explanation reveals, or it can employ the softer "methodological" argument that scientific inquiry is the only genuine source of knowledge of such entities and that all other forms are illegitimate or reducible to it. Rorty is part of a recently identified "liberal naturalist" alternative.[3] This alternative is linked to scientific naturalism by a rejection of the supernatural, where normative claims are justified wholly independently of human practices. Liberal naturalism goes further in problematizing this division between the natural and the supernatural. It seeks to do justice to the range and diversity, both within the social sciences and outside, of forms of understanding. Specifically, it seeks nonscientific *and* nonsupernatural understandings of normativity (Macarthur and De Caro 2010, 3–4, 9). This concern with the plurality and movement of conceptual and linguistic difference is a basic motivation for Rorty. What is important is that while he rejects the dominant form of naturalism (as Connolly does), his pragmatic reconstruction thereof is also guided by the central naturalist question of how to construe the presence of normativity in our world. Do our normative commitments flow from or are affected by the "natural" world? Or are they purely the imposition of human creativity and social life? Rorty's naturalism balances these two options to slip neither into the former's foundationalism nor the latter's relativism.

While Connolly employs an ontological understanding of pluralism to reconstruct naturalism, Rorty deploys its own critique against itself. Specifically, he offers a form of naturalism that removes the authoritarian structure of epistemological justification in the scientific variant. It is in this sense that his naturalism is very much a *naturalization*, a process of ascribing a certain status to our conceptual categories that avoids authoritarianism. At its broadest point, it is a naturalization and behavioralization of social practice that allows Rorty to understand cultural and biological evolution as continuous (Rorty 1998g, 125).

In a later article, Rorty clarifies his naturalism, contrasting his own "subject" or "pragmatic" naturalism with the "object" or "reductive" naturalism that dominates the natural sciences and holds the ontological and methodological claims just discussed. These assumptions result in their concern to identify perennial philosophical problems of word-world relations and address these problems through the explanation of nonparticles by particles, or language by the world. In contrast, Rorty's pragmatic naturalism opposes the task of picturing (ontologizing) these relations. Rather, it begins with the understanding of humans and communities as "natural creatures in a natural environment." Asserting our continuity, rather than distinction, with the real in this way, our conceptual systems are better described as systems of linguistic behavior. As organisms thrown into an environment, we are merely attempting to cope with one another and that environment through language, which on this reading is a social practice, a way of speaking and thinking that enables (and proscribes) certain practices and relations. Thus, in opposition to discoveries of fundamental word-world relations, we have narratives of development about how our practices and vocabularies have changed to cope better amid our shifting purposes. Behavioral explanation is all we have outside these narratives to distinguish between organisms. Pragmatism thus escapes the whole idealism-realism argument by eschewing the question of representation/correspondence "in favor of descriptions of the interaction of language-using organisms with other such organisms and with their environment" (Rorty 2007g, 158).Unless particles (as physical) are somehow given an ontological status prior to organisms (as language using), these narratives of cultural evolution are as naturalistic as explanation can be.

In this behavioral model of naturalism, Rorty utilizes the language of evolutionary theory, what he calls "Darwinian naturalism." For him, the evolutionary model of contingent and nonteleological responses to changing circumstances and developments is a nonessentialist way to think about language use and social change. "Davidson lets us think of the history of language, and thus of culture, as Darwin taught us to think of the history of a coral reef. Old metaphors are constantly dying off into literalness, and then serving as a platform and foil for new metaphors" (Rorty 1989, 16). This naturalistic account of language use and worldview change illustrates how Rorty's view of contingent social practice is nonteleological and nonpurposive. Changes in our behavior and practices occur neither according to predetermined pathways nor under some inherent logic. However, this language of nonpurposive contingency does not entail that humans have no agency in linguistic and social development. The point is that there is no necessary ground for that agency but only a contingent set of historical resources for critical reflexivity within modernity (see chapter 4).

This radically rewrites the naturalist tradition. Rorty is still employing the language of the natural sciences. However, he alters their status and, as a result of resituating their justification to the question of their consequences for the groups employing them, dramatically changes how we consider them. This approach should recall the strategy discussed in chapter 1, where Rorty did not argue against the representationalist problematic. He did not argue that it would never be able to provide the foundations it seeks but only that it had failed so far and that its problems could be avoided through recourse to a different, *sociological* vocabulary. Here, his strategy confines our discussion of the norms of linguistic justification to actual languages and practices we can engage rather than to standards that stand above, within, or beneath those concrete activities. Thus, he argues that his naturalism avoids the inevitable problem of the infinite regression (and resulting problem of access) of foundational standards.

Rorty's naturalism offers an understanding of relations that is explicitly framed in opposition to a transcendental mode of ontological explanation. Transcendental explanation, or the explanation of actuality by eternal verities or conditions of (im)possibility, is impossible because it is one more attempt to escape from (temporal) contingency. Rorty reads the history of philosophy as the history of successive, privileged a priori conditions. Whether it is mind/consciousness, experience, logic, or language, all privileged principles can, after Darwin, be explained naturalistically as a particular social practice serving a particular set of purposes, a view that Rorty in one instance refers to as "making Spirit continuous with Nature." Further, each transcendental condition, or "unexplained explainer," incurs the self-referential problem of explaining its own possibility. This is the problem of how entities used as explanatory metacriteria are themselves known. This problem arises because transcendent conditions always function as the source of explanation for the rest of reality. Thus, everything and every entity must always stand in some sort of relation to these conditions before they are accessible to experience, description, etc. For Rorty, transcendental (external) explanation assumes that no entity is available for experience or description without being in a relationship that exceeds the relationship between everyday available entities. External entities, as conditions of (im)possibility, provide this necessary transcendence. However, this leads to the aforementioned self-referential problem of access. How are external entities themselves known (Rorty 1991v, 54)?

Rorty's naturalism is antitranscendent. It is the understanding that anything might be otherwise (might be put into a new set of relations) and that there are no conditionless conditions, no philosophical abstractions identifying some condition of (im)possibility that explains this world without being explainable by it. These are by definition relations outside of our web of relations that, by default of their externality, gain a privileged status. "I shall define as naturalism the view that anything might have been otherwise, that there can be no conditionless conditions ... that there is no such thing as a noncausal condition of possibility" (Rorty 1991v, 55).[4] This summarizes one of the key methodological injunctions of Rorty's nonreductive naturalism: the imperative to *avoid reference to any extranatural properties or functions*, of what exceeds the realm of lived human experience broadly construed, as sources of explanatory or normative criteria.

This makes all explanation of the actual, causal. It is about the present state of relations between entities. Whether language or physical reality, we adopt a *holistic* view that rejects any distinction between available and unavailable (privileged and unprivileged, ineffable and effable, masked and unmasked, etc.) entities in favor of "a seamless, indefinitely extensible web of relations" (Rorty 1991v, 55).[5] Thus Rorty's naturalism, as antitranscendent, chooses to exist solely on the level of the actual relations of the physical and linguistic worlds. On this definition, naturalism is neither scientistic nor reductive; it is a contingent figuration of our embodied, finite, social limitations that resists reifying this into a necessity. It is a simultaneous articulation of contingency and pluralism and a rejection of metaphysics and foundationalism.

In sociopolitical thought, Rorty's naturalism leads to his pragmatic vocabulary of social practices. Its advantage is how it avoids these problems while still enabling critical and normative reflection. It avoids positing any external standards, removing the illusion of depth, and moves beyond the central problematic of the idealism-realism debate, the contrast between the world and a way of representing it. Rorty is aware that this position will garner accusations of linguistic idealism, of suggesting that there were no objects to discuss before people began discussing them. For him, this confuses two different questions: "How do we pick out objects?" and "Do objects antedate being picked out by us?" The existence of objects (the world) before language about objects, which he in no way denies, gets us no closer to essence. This antiessentialism is the crux of his naturalism (Rorty 1999a, 47–58). His pragmatic naturalism, Darwinism, and critique of transcendence are all designed to *remove the question of essence* and the appearance-reality divide. However, they do not radically disconnect our languages from the world. For Rorty, vocabularies, as fundamental tools within our social and natural lives, are both causally affected by and have great consequences in the world. They are inseparable from our relation to it, as they enable and preclude (depending on which we employ) our actions.

All of this has important consequences for normativity. On this understanding, norms are inevitable and entirely social. Without external standards, and when "all awareness is a linguistic affair," the use and coherence of our norms becomes the main basis for asking about the justification of a vocabulary on the whole and for intervocabulary dialogue.[6] "If our awareness of things is always a linguistic affair, if Sellars is right and we cannot check our language against our nonlinguistic awareness . . . there is no authority outside of convenience for human purposes that can be appealed to in order to legitimize the use of a vocabulary. We have no duties to anything nonhuman" (Rorty 1998g, 127). For Rorty, without nonhuman authority, we must examine our vocabularies and practices to make their details coherent and explicit. Norms are always already present. They are a consequence of the fact that vocabularies enable and preclude certain purposes through practice. As a result, he defines norms as "just a certain kind of fact—a fact about what people do—seen from the inside" (Rorty 2007f, 196). They are thus already present in the choice of purposes and their relation to other practices and purposes.

Theoretical reflection makes these explicit, to enable critical and normative claims in relation to them. Naturalism emphasizes the former; historicism, as we will see, emphasizes the latter. While this is presently opaque, the point is that this naturalistic perspective on normativity and the extent of possible human reflection on it that Rorty draws is a fundamentally antiauthoritarian and antiessentialist move that avoids the problem of justification by shifting our focus to the behavioral level of the actual linguistic and social practices of normativity used by political subjects:

> There is no way for human beings to get beyond their own practices except by dreaming up better practices, and no way to judge these new practices better except by reference to their various advantages for various human purposes. To say that philosophy's task is to make human practices explicit rather than to legitimize them by reference

to something beyond them is to say that there is no authority beyond utility for these purposes to which we can appeal.

(Rorty 1998g, 128)

It is important to emphasize that this naturalism does not simply reinforce present norms. As Brandom noted, it is a constitutive feature of norms for Rorty that using them also changes them. To employ a norm comes with a type of freedom. Not only does that norm already enable certain sets of behavior, but it also can be deployed in new ways. How we go about both making norms explicit and deploying them in new ways, and with what type of method, is the subject of the rest of this book. Presently, it is important to understand that this naturalism sets the limits for what types of resources can be identified and employed within Rorty's model of sociopolitical criticism, that is, his reconstruction of philosophy as cultural politics. It does this through the aforementioned negative methodological injunction against transcendence and the resulting shift to attend to the practices of normativity available to us in the shared languages and practices of sociopolitical life. Currently, this study engages an alternative reconstruction of naturalism gaining prominence within contemporary political thought in order to clarify the strengths and potential criticisms of Rorty's.

NEW MATERIALISM AND IMMANENT NATURALISM: COSMOLOGIES OF DIFFERENCE

Across the matrix of contemporary political thought, there is a cluster of perspectives also involved in reconstructing naturalism. However, while Rorty's naturalism focuses on the behavioral level of the use and purposes of actual languages and social practices, "new materialism" offers an ontological version of naturalism. To assess Rorty's model, here I ask: What are the methodological advantages to a new-materialist approach to political theorizing and the task of sociopolitical criticism? Specifically, what are its resources for thinking pluralism? Do these overcome the problem of justification? After contextualizing this emerging trend, the discussion turns specifically to Connolly's new-materialist naturalism and its ontologization of pluralism to do this.

Within the ontological forms of political theory that have dominated the critical continental sectors of that discipline recently, a new materialism has emerged that extends those ontological approaches.[7] As discussed in the introduction and chapter 2, both weak ontology and Connolly's early ontopolitical approach are defined by a focus on the conditions of human being, and subsequently Being in general, and their effects for political inquiry, both explanatory and normative. These conditions result in a fundamental paradox of inquiry where ontological assumptions about the being of the world and humans are both unavoidable and contingent. This necessitates an ontological method that relied on an understanding of linguistic determination as a fundamental limitation. This claim in turn relied upon an assumption that contingency was necessary, that it is out there in the world in some sense (rather than just being a condition of our relation to it, as it is in Rorty). How do new materialists, and Connolly within his more recent work, develop these claims and methods?

The surge of recent new materialisms applies the principal claims of the ontological turn to the material world. The latter is understood to include both physical reality as well as social and economic structures. As such, several projects have been outlined in the literature. What concerns us is the ontological and methodological project that undergirds its applications to biopolitical analysis and political economy (and other areas). In the edited volume credited with identifying this trend, this project is glossed as reconsidering the material world in a similar manner to how the linguistic and cultural turn reconsidered human subjectivity. Thus, new materialists seek "to subject objectivity and matter to a similar radical re-appraisal" (Coole and Frost 2010, 2). From this ontological project they formulate a new methodology for political theory that attends to the complexity and importance of the material. I will address each of these projects.

New materialism attempts an ontology that performs three crucial functions: attending to recent advances in the sciences that require updating our theories of materialism and their significance for politics, responding to the new ethicopolitical issues raised by the creation of new technologies and these scientific models, and reconceiving the model of sociopolitical criticism dominant since the rise of social constructivism and the linguistic turn.[8] This project relies upon a critique of social constructivism as inadequate to the task of thinking the material and its relevance for politics. This criticism is that social constructivists ultimately share the modern Cartesian understanding of matter as a passive and calculable side of the world fundamentally distinct from and subject to human agency.[9] While social constructivists have done much to undermine the understandings of knowledge and subjectivity there, such as in Rorty's and Connolly's discussions of epistemology (see chapter 1) and language (see chapter 2), for new materialism they fail to apply these criticisms to the understanding of matter itself. As a result, they retain the previously mentioned image and the series of flawed distinctions that support it: nature versus culture, human versus nonhuman, modern versus nonmodern (Coole and Frost 2010, 5–6; see also Latour 1993).

In light of this critique, new-materialist ontologies share several features. First, in contrast to the traditional images of matter as inert and passive, they emphasize the dynamic nature of materialization (which is always a process) as complex, pluralistic, and relatively open. Consequently, they turn to traditions like vitalism and radical empiricism (e.g., Spinoza, Deleuze, Henri Bergson, William James, etc.) and to recent work in the sciences to produce new ontologies of becoming. For example:

> "matter becomes" rather than ... "matter is." It is in these choreographies of becoming that we find cosmic forces assembling and disintegrating to forge more or less enduring patterns that may provisionally exhibit internally coherent, efficacious organization: objects forming and emerging within relational fields, bodies composing their natural environment in ways that are corporeally meaningful for them, and subjectivities being constituted as open series of capacities or potencies that emerge hazardously and ambiguously within a multitude of organic and social processes.
>
> (Coole and Frost 2010, 10; see also Coole 2013, 453–54)

Emphasizing the immanent nature of these conditions, they argue that "materiality" always exceeds current material processes. It exceeds "mere" matter in including "an excess, force, vitality, relationality, or difference that renders matter active, self-creative, productive, unpredictable" (Coole and Frost 2010, 9). As a result of these ontological imperatives, in their various forms and articulations they offer ontological figurations of reality that prioritize this common dynamic of becoming throughout the material world. These are "flat ontologies," which do "not privilege some kinds of entity or agency over others and... in which new assemblages and unstable hybrids are recognized to be constantly emerging and dissipating across a normatively and ontologically horizontal plane" (Coole 2013, 455). Importantly, like Rorty, the purpose is an antiauthoritarian leveling of normative authority.

In light of the new materialists' critique of the exclusive focus on subjectivity within the linguistic and cultural turn, and their identification of a Cartesian subordination of matter to language there, one particular focus for this leveling is agency. Embracing a broad posthumanism, they reconstruct agency on a distributive model where it is not solely the property of humanity. Consequently, they emphasize the "agentic capacities" of nonhuman matter, which, in their ontologies, bear emergent, generative powers "with trajectories, propensities, or tendencies of their own" (Bennett 2010, viii, chap. 3).The purpose is to recast the traditional aspects of humanity (rationality, subjectivity, self-reflection) that have been the basis of a firm human-nonhuman division. For them, this is a corrective to the anthropocentrism of social constructivism and political theory in general.

Mirroring Connolly's move I described in chapter 2, new materialists resort to ontology to recode concepts of agency and enact this general leveling of the material and human worlds. It is this feature that brings them within the broader ontological turn within political theory. However, they see it as having particular methodological consequences, requiring a turn to "methodological realism," which involves two distinct moves. First, this method points to the situated nature of political thinking and action. Such claims are not only situated within particular linguistic and social circumstances but also material ones. Given their flat ontologies, this amounts to the claim that "the creativity and intransigence of materiality [can] verify or negate, guide and inspire, theoretical and empirical investigations of evolving structures" (Coole 2013, 456). Materiality here has intrinsic normative consequences. Thus, the first outcome of methodological realism is a shift in the normative status of humans relative to the world. The latter now comes with its own normative significance.

Second, new materialists turn to a wider plane of ontological actants in the analysis of any political situation. For Jane Bennett, a major voice, a turn to materiality requires a turn away from negative demystification within critical sociopolitical theory and toward "positive utopian thinking." The former still resides within a prioritization of human agency, where the task is to uncover how social structures either enable or disable that capacity. In contrast, Bennett focuses on offering positive affirmations of alternative figurations of events that emphasize the nonhuman aspects of any political situation and how they impinge upon and limit human agency. This serves the important purpose of working against the tendency within the social sciences toward narcissistic anthropocentrism (Bennett 2010, xvi).

> Thus, New Materialists in general tend to embrace a positive project of ontological affirmation. The prevailing ethos of new materialist ontology is consequently more positive and constructive than critical or negative: it sees its task as creating new concepts and images of nature that affirm matter's immanent vitality.
>
> (Coole and Frost 2010, 8)

Taken together, these two methodological moves, the intrinsic normativity of the world and the turn to affirmative thinking, radically change the task of political theory and the status of human thought. William Connolly's recent work reveals its methodological and political consequences.

While Connolly's recent political thought is by no means representative of new materialism, as with the ontological turn he is a central figure in its development. Since the 1990s, Connolly has gradually drifted from a Heideggerian framework to one exhibiting many of the features outlined in new materialism. Thus, his development of these themes preceded the self-conscious emergence of this group. Further, as in his relationship to weak ontology, his detailed methodological and ontological framework of ontological pluralism contains one of the most in-depth justifications of this approach to pluralism and naturalism available. Consequently, it offers a privileged point of comparison.

Connolly's ontological framework of immanent naturalism is his solution to the mastery-attunement problematic discussed in chapter 2. As examined there, Connolly schematized the matrix of contemporary Anglo-American political thought along an ontological axis between mastery, where the world appears as an object for human control, and attunement, where the purpose is to place human communities in line with a preexisting order to being. Both, for Connolly, are compensatory ontologies that assume the world in some manner is "for us." In contrast, he posited an ontology that rejected this unity, symmetry, and convenience for human purposes. It offered a fundamental structure of determination-as-limitation and stressed that any language or framework always excludes other modes and understandings of being. As a result, contingency is a necessary ontological reality that conditions human thought, action, and, even, the nonhuman world. The latter, further, entailed an element of resistance to humanity and its projects. Consequently, ontological analysis is necessary to expose the existing determinations as limitations.

I argued in chapter 2 that this fundamentally Heideggerian structure of Being pervaded the ontological turn in Connolly's work and conditioned the development of his explicit ontological method for political thought. What is important now is the development and transition of this project. It is in the context of this Heideggerian framework, and its configurations of *contingency as recalcitrance* and *determination as limitation*, that Connolly's naturalistic materialism emerges and his ontological method develops. The previous framework was centered on the question of identity and difference. It sought to destabilize the image of the autonomous and "disengaged self" that dominated Anglo-American thought (and their ontologies of concord) at the time (Connolly 1987, 10). Instead, Connolly emphasized "the contingency of life and the fragility of things" (Connolly 1991, 25).[10] To counter the implicit demand of political thought that the world be for us, he cast these identity/difference relations in terms of a "protean vitality of being," a constant becoming of 'the abundance or richness of being" (Connolly 2005a, 244–45) that always overflows established identities and the limits of social forms.

Since the late 1990s, Connolly has developed this positive ontopolitical account, which has served as the basis of his critiques of existential resentment (around a variety of social problems) and his theory of agonistic democracy and its ethical virtues of critical responsiveness and agonistic respect. In terms of its ontological sources and figurations, these have moved through several stages. From an articulation of the "protean vitality of being," he turned to a "deep rhizomatic pluralistic universe" and subsequently to an "onto-cosmology of becoming and fragility." This series of figurations have held one common terminology, what Connolly calls his materialist ontology of *immanent naturalism*. This framework has developed throughout a series of works over the past fifteen years: initially appearing in an article in *Radical Philosophy* (Connolly 1999a), it was subsequently articulated in *Why I Am Not a Secularist* (Connolly 1999b), *NeuroPolitics* (Connolly 2002), *Pluralism* (Connolly 2005b), and *A World of Becoming* (Connolly 2011). While it dropped out of his most recent work, *The Fragility of Things* (Connolly 2013), its key themes have been furthered there.

This materialist ontology "depicts the world as a layered immanent field of 'infrasensible forces'" (Wenman 2013, 126). From readings of Spinoza, Nietzsche, and Deleuze, Connolly takes on an image of the world as a "common plane of immanence" in which all bodies, institutions, minds, and individuals are structured. Deleuze's inorganic vitalism is especially important, figuring life as a constantly emerging multiplicity of forces, periodically coalescing into assemblages before once again dissolving, without an inherent end or purpose. To return to Heideggerian language, this is a figuration of Being not as always partial or concealed but as becoming. It is an elementary flux: categories traditionally understood as distinct (e.g., nature and culture, mind and body, etc.) are mixed immanent processes always in movement. Connolly employs perhaps as the clearest image William James's model of the pluralistic universe. This intentionally metaphysical pluralism rejects the idea of a logic or "allform" and posits a universe in which there is "litter," that is, remainders and instabilities deviating from and undermining stable forms. The idea is that "the overlapping forces propelling the world are themselves messy. Pluralism is the philosophy of a messy universe" (Connolly 2005b, 70).

Connolly has further developed this ontology in a variety of themes, including temporality, embodiment, complexity, becoming, and fragility. The point has been to emphasize the creative, unfinished, self-organizing, and emergent nature of the world and human life. Further, to support this ontology he has moved beyond the traditional boundaries of political theory and the social sciences to developments in the natural sciences. Anticipating new materialism, he drew on new theoretical models in the sciences, such as those of Ilya Prigogine, Stephen J. Gould, and Stephen Wolfram, all of whom challenge classical determinist models in their fields. All have notably (and controversially) modeled how complexity, instability, and disequilibrium characterize natural systems and offered new explanatory models and tools for understanding such systems under these conditions.

This framework is overtly ontological. It offers a detailed model of the complexity and interdependencies of reality and explains, ontologically rather than epistemologically, why conceptual systems always fall short of understanding the complexity of the world. The immanence of immanent naturalism immediately recalls the idea of a single immanent plane of existence. Connolly includes this to illustrate his opposition to transcendence as a mode of philosophical and moral explanation.[11] By naturalism, Connolly means the view that nature and human culture persist without the aid of any divine or supernatural force (i.e., attunement). However, like Rorty, his naturalism also opposes the lawlike model of nature endorsed by the natural sciences (i.e., mastery) (Connolly 2005b, 72; 2002, 86).

Connolly uses this pluralistic ontology to rethink some of the core concepts of the social-scientific method and to offer a new immanent naturalist approach to political theory. His most detailed examinations of this occur in two chapters of works from the last ten years (Connolly 2004a; 2008, chap. 3).[12] For Connolly, every political interpretation invokes a set of fundamentals about the necessities and possibilities of human being, about the nature of the world and our relation to it. These assumptions structure the sphere of politics and the nature of political activity. Thus he holds to the inevitability of ontological assumptions and the necessity of interrogating them. "Ontopolitical interpretation" was designed specifically to interrogate the compensatory ontologies that posit a world predisposed to humanity. Two two-part mechanisms were fundamental here. On the one hand, Connolly's method employs strategies of critical detachment *and* strategies of attachment to alternative ontological figurations. On the other hand, his method requires a "double-entry orientation" to political theorizing, where these critical detachments and affirmative attachments are treated as incontestable in their first instance but are then withdrawn in contestability. The double-entry orientation to interpretation attempts to do justice to the inadequacy and contestability of ontology, the inevitability of ontological presuppositions, and the ambiguous nature of human inquiry resulting from these conditions. It attempts to provide for a critically reflexive method from within the problem of justification.

His later method still contains these mechanisms. For example, the same two-part structure of strategies of detachment and attachment and a double-entry orientation of incontestable and contestable operate here (Connolly 2004a, 336, 344; 2008, 73, 85). However, the emphasis, language, and roles of certain elements have shifted. Connolly expands his claim for the significance of ontology and strategies of positive attachment. This depends upon an understanding of the relationship between ontologies, methodologies (in political theory and the social sciences generally), and the problems that motivate inquiry. For him, every ontology, what he now calls an "existential faith,"[13] is not only assumed by our beliefs and inquiries, and in turn has those same assumptions about human being that structure politics, but is also layered into our affective dispositions, habits, and institutional priorities. They are embodied, lived, and structured. Further, these existential faiths have deep connections to the methods of inquiry and political problems employed in any approach. Importantly, these connections cannot be schematized, as there is no "general formula" for how they are connected. Thus, he rejects the idea of a method of adjudicating between such competing frameworks because this assumes a superproblematic capable of absolutely resolving intermethodological disputes (Connolly 2004a, 338–39).

In the absence of such neutral arbitration, how are we to govern intermethodological relations? How are we to speak to one another across ontological, methodological, and political differences? This is the crux of the issue, and it extends beyond the discipline of political theory to the situation of engagement across cultural-political difference in contemporary democracy. Connolly's answer resembles his model of agonistic democracy: intermethodological engagement should be governed by an *ethos of engagement*. Such an ethos repeats the above resources, with one important omission.

> The first thing is to articulate comparatively the problematic you support with as much energy and skill as you can, pressing others to take it seriously as a possibility to respect.... The second thing is to come to terms publicly with the persistent element of contestability in the eyes of others of the faith infusing your problematic.
>
> (Connolly 2008, 90)

Positive attachment and the critically reflexive mechanism of contestability. Strategies of critical detachment fall out of this methodology.

For these reasons, Connolly's methodological statements always include positive articulations of immanent naturalism. There are two important claims in this account for our purposes. First, Connolly rethinks causality as *emergent* in opposition to the lawlike model of *efficient causality* that dominates most methods. In emergent causality, causal relations are not susceptible to full explanation or knowability. Rather they have real elements of uncertainty and creativity (e.g., when complex systems of relations enter periods of "disequilibrium" or interact). Importantly, this "*naturalize[s] a place for mystery,* incorporating a modicum of intrinsic uncertainty into patterns of emergent causality" (Connolly 2008, 84). Second, Connolly links this naturalized mystery to a broadened concept of agency that extends beyond humans. Like new materialism, this "distributive" sense of agency appreciates the multiple sites and degrees of agency in the world. Such elements bear "agentic capacities": the ability to respond creatively to situations that are not entirely determined. Equally, human agency is more limited than traditionally supposed. The contingencies of our history, evolution, embodiment, etc. mean that humanity is limited by its determined nature. The point now is that this view necessitates a broadening and leveling of agency. Actors become "actants," which includes anything that responds creatively with effects on the systems and actants around it (Connolly 2013, 145; 2011, 21–32). Examining the consequences of this (e.g., for the traditional nature-culture divide) leveling and applying it to sociopolitical issues occupies much of his two most recent books.

This account illuminates Connolly's ontology and his method for political theory. While some of the dynamics I identified in chapter 2 remain, they have shifted in emphasis. Regarding ontology, in Connolly's recent work there has been a decided shift from his broadly Heideggerian framework, and its configurations of the necessity of *contingency as recalcitrance* and *determination as limitation*, to a more determined figuration of the world as inherently pluralistic/complex/becoming/fragile/etc. This is not insignificant. On this model, uncertainty becomes more explicitly inherent and manifest in the world, which now not only implicitly resists mastery but also has creative agency, a naturalized mystery, of its own kind. This gives it a normative status that impacts on his method, which has equally developed.

Previously, Connolly's method focused on challenging the dominant ontologies of Anglo-American modernity that he argued circumscribe ethical-political life through a set of unexamined ontological assumptions setting the parameters of the political. Using strategies of critical detachment and positive attachment, he undermined these assumptions and provided an alternative figuration as a new source of normativity. In contrast, here Connolly's method is similar to new materialism, imbuing the world with normative value via methods of positive affirmative attachment to counter those ontologies. It is in this sense that there is, in this phase, a "fidelity to radical contingency itself" (Howarth 2010, 39). As noted above, explanatory critical methods seem to be deemphasized here. This is perhaps why Connolly's most recent works have focused almost exclusively on clarifying his "ontocosmology" of becoming and fragility in the world and the conditions it sets for human action and politics (Connolly 2013, 9). When they have critically examined perspectives that fall short of both accounting for and normatively valuing it, they have done so only and explicitly from these normative commitments. For Connolly, such accounts exhibit "existential resentment" against the pluralistic and unstable nature of Being.[14] In this manner, both his method and ontology of immanent naturalism are designed to achieve the single aim of investing normative and explanatory significance in the world in order to encourage attachment to it.

This is important because, as we saw above, these developments in his methodology are undertaken within the question of how to engage in intermethodological pluralistic exchange. In the absence of any general superperspective for engaging the intricate complexes of existential faiths (matrices of methods, ontologies, and problems), Connolly argues that the best way to address deep explanatory and normative differences is through *articulations* of their normative sources. We then, just as before, deabsolutize these accounts in a secondary gesture of contestability meant to provide for critical reflexivity in these methods.

COMPETING POSSIBILITIES: MASTERY AND NATURALISTIC MINIMALISM

My account of Rorty's and Connolly's naturalisms extends the criticisms and strengths identified in these frameworks previously. Once again, we encounter two sets of competing possibilities. On the one hand, there are the various readings of Rorty's framework as mastery or as situated sociopolitical criticism. On the other hand, there is the critical comparison of the latter with Connolly's weak-ontological and new-materialist method. However, the ontological critique of mastery in Rorty is overcome by my second reading of his work. Instead, the strengths of this framework continue to illuminate tensions and concerns within Connolly's ontological method; here, this is specifically to do with his naturalism and its consequences on his recent method for political theorizing.

In chapter 2, this analysis considered Connolly's criticism of a hidden ontology of mastery in Rorty. Chapter 4 will examine Connolly's extended analysis of mastery and connection of it to pragmatism. Presently, the task is to understand how his critique applies to Rorty's naturalism. Connolly defines mastery generally as the drive to subject nature to human control and the corresponding assumption of nature's susceptibility. In *The Ethos of Pluralization*, he explicitly included Rorty within the cluster of contemporary Anglo-American thought that displayed this presupposition (Connolly 1995a, 17). Previously, in *Politics and Ambiguity*, he accused Rorty of a social foundationalism (Connolly 1987). While he didn't sufficiently develop this analysis, it predicts Rorty's naturalism and highlights his investment of humanity with explanatory and normative authority. As discussed above, Rorty does restrict explanation to behavioral and social categories focused on human beliefs and practices. His evolutionary language and understanding of humans as "natural creatures in a natural environment," while overtly nonmetaphysical, does argue that normativity is solely a human issue. Further, his focus on the use and purposes of human languages, and the relativity of those to human groups, seems to repeat a naïve anthropocentrism dangerous in this contemporary age of global environmental crises. All of this implies both that Rorty circumscribes human thought to the social, to cultural politics, ignoring persistent (ontological) assumptions within our beliefs and practices, and that humanity is the sole object of normative value.

Such concerns are reinforced by Rorty's own statements regarding the relation of humans and the world. One consequence of Rorty's antiessentialist naturalism is that language use, as a uniquely human practice, makes humans fundamentally exceptional in relation to nature. Language use involves the ability to describe. All elements relate to one another, but only humans relate through a relationship of description and can measure the success of their descriptions in allowing us to cope with and utilize the world. Darwin is so significant because he replaced the image of humans as having an intrinsic faculty of reason with an evolutionary account of our "increased cunning." The development of symbolizing abilities can explain the uniquely complicated interactions humans have with one another and their environment. "These interactions are marked by the use of strings of noises and marks to facilitate group activities, as tools for coordinating the activities of individuals" (Rorty 1999a, 64). Naturalism, on this account, is about viewing language not as a representative medium but as a process of relating tools to what they manipulate for a particular purpose. For Rorty, this has two distinct effects. First, it allows us to view all human behavior in naturalistic terms and thereby see it as entirely continuous with animal behavior. This effaces the nature-culture divide, a project Connolly and new materialism share. Second, it also changes our relation to nature in a manner that does not *necessarily* invest normative authority in it. Humans are no longer meant to represent or correspond to nature; instead, now "our task is to master it, or adapt ourselves to it" (Rorty 1999b, 269). Understanding our languages and practices as tools allows us to do this more effectively. It allows us to see them as ways to master both our practices and environment. They are alternative means of "grabbing hold" of the causal forces that surround us and altering them and ourselves to our purposes. It is for this reason that languages should not be viewed as "veils between us and objects, but as ways of putting the causal forces of the universe to work for us" (Rorty 1991s, 82). Thus, naturalism seems to lead to an ontological disposition of mastery.

I am not arguing that Rorty's naturalism and his view of language are without problems.[15] However, the ontological critique of Rorty fails for two reasons. First, as discussed in chapter 2, his model does not de facto exclude ontological languages. His antiauthoritarianism only precludes a claim that ontology offers a privileged perspective. Equally, his naturalism and its understanding of how languages, as social practices, arise from communities coping with one another and the world do not preclude an ontological language being given normative authority by a community. So while Rorty may have often demonstrated hostility to vocabularies such as ontology (or a strong notion of reason), his naturalistic framework does not prevent such languages from having normative authority (Ramberg 2004, 45).

Second, there is the question whether this naturalism contains covert assumptions of mastery. Does viewing humans as complex-tool-using social organisms who are the sole creators of normative claims entail the assumption that the world is only a resource available and amenable to our use? The problem with this accusation is that it misunderstands the scope of Rorty's project, assuming he aims to give an exhaustive ontology or metaphysics. In contrast, if his framework is only understood as an account of critical and normative resources without foundations, authority without authoritarianism, such a criticism quickly dissolves (Koopman 2014, 156; Rorty 2001b). Being able to extrapolate from a very specific understanding of some aspect of human social practice to an account of the world or the human condition in ontological/metaphysical terms does not illustrate the intrinsic connection between these two descriptions. It does not make that metaphysics internal to that understanding. Thus, even if some ontological assumptions seem intuitively linked to Rorty's method, and even if these are bolstered by some incendiary comments, it is not necessary that these assumptions are inherent to his model of sociopolitical criticism.

To support this defense, my analysis needs to explicate this modest methodological project in terms of Rorty's naturalism as just described. The key claim is that Rorty's naturalism supports the methodological claims for a linguistic approach to normativity, which I addressed in chapter 2, where he described languages behaviorally as a social practice in order to meet the two aims of antifoundationalism and antiskepticism. It does this via two elements. First, it contains an antitranscendent *negative methodological injunction* to avoid any reference to external critical or normative standards that exceed the realm of lived human experience. Within social and political thought and the question of normativity, this means descending to the level of social practices and the languages that enable and preclude them. Thus, the second aspect of this naturalism is a *methodological imperative to holism*: we can only criticize linguistic practices through other linguistic practices and the consequences of each. We thereby judge our assumptions about humanity in relation to some practice by how that accords with other areas of behavior (chosen and deployed for certain sets of reasons). The languages of subject naturalism and Darwinian naturalism are vocabularies, sets of terms and concepts, that Rorty offers to social and political theorists to frame and *enable* such a level of discourse.[16] They both enable political critique and normativity and avoid essentialism, metaphysics, and foundations. Further, they are examples of exactly the type of criticism Rorty is offering. He takes one language from another area of culture (natural sciences), reconstructed, to bolster his model of political theorizing.

It is in this sense that I described his naturalism as a *process of naturalization*, something enacted upon our categories to keep them at the level of linguistic social practices. It is a process of ascribing a certain status to our conceptual categories that avoids authoritarianism. Naturalism is a methodological, not metaphysical, suggestion that when we ask questions of normativity we focus on the languages actually employed by groups. Further, that when we seek to understand what languages are, we see them as socially situated frameworks of belief and meaning that function as tools for communities and individuals to achieve certain ends. This approaches language as something we do, as one type of social practice among many. However, it is a social practice that gives us access to normative reflection. Languages are already inherently normative in that they enable certain practices and preclude others. The advantage of this specifically linguistic form of naturalism is that it does not run afoul of the problem of justification; it allows for the diversity of languages without an in-built external mechanism of judging between them. It is thus ideally suited to the methodological pluralism of contemporary social and political theory and the social and cultural pluralism of contemporary democracies.

In contrast, Connolly employs naturalism for a different set of purposes and with different consequences. Connolly and new materialism share two key developments in their political theorizing. First, they share a methodological shift away from negative critique to the articulation of positive affirmative ontologies as sources of normative motivation. This entails a strong emphasis on the development of detailed materialist ontologies emphasizing the complexity and pluralistic nature of the natural world, the human relationship to it, and sociopolitical life. Second, connected to this, they use such ontologies as normative bases for political theorizing; that is, they hold to the inherent normativity of natural dynamics within the world. This represents an important development in methodology. Previously, Connolly advocated the use of both critical strategies of detachment and positive ontopolitical attachment. Such incontestable analyses were then deabsolutized in a secondary external mechanism that acknowledged the contestability of all ontologies. However, the methodological moves within Connolly's naturalism shift this balance. He moves from the ontological thesis about the fundamental contingency of human thought to a cosmological thesis about "real uncertainty" and mystery in the world. This is the difference between a broad notion of contingency as recalcitrance (and determination as limitation) and a determined image of a pluralistic, fragile universe. While this is a difference of degree, it has important consequences.

All these effects circle around the tension identified in chapter 2 in Connolly's mechanism of contestability. There, I argued, as an externally imposed mechanism, this tension pushed his method in two directions, toward either the priority of ontology or the priority of contestability. If the former is given priority, the necessity and reification of contingency violated his critical reflexivity. The contingency of being becomes another standard for humans to match. If contestability was given priority, then Connolly was in danger of lacking the normative resources to avoid relativism. He violated either antifoundationalism or antirelativism.

This dynamic is repeated within Connolly's recent method, though with important alterations. The methodological move toward normative attachment through ontological articulation seriously undermines the operativity of critical reflexivity within these analyses that contestability is meant to provide. This is a strong, determined view of the world united around an inherent logic (or lack thereof). This point bears out a recent and important criticism of Connolly's work, that his whole model of ontological thinking assumes, without justification, that social and political dynamics (especially complex ones) can be modeled on natural and ontological ones (Wenman 2013, 128–31; McNay 2014, 205–6). With new materialism, he assumes that "materiality," some general dynamic new materialists assume can be abstracted to the entire material world (which itself seems problematic), is explanatory of sociopolitical events. Thus, his ontology ends up "too weighty," overdetermining and colonizing his sociopolitical analyses and normative prescriptions. This is a challenge Connolly never adequately meets. In shifting his methodology, the danger of reifying ontological contingency I raised in the last chapter is realized in this period of his work. This danger is located in the question of the *status* of Connolly's analyses. Rather than rejecting the whole transcendental mechanism of external criteria, as Rorty does, Connolly "naturalizes the transcendental" (Howarth 2010, 27).[17] External normative and explanatory authority remains in this model; it is just radically immanent to the world in a series of dynamics (e.g., self-organizing processes, systems in disequilibrium, etc.) that Connolly identifies and then applies back onto sociopolitical questions. The question of whether this problem afflicts theories of radical immanence in general (i.e., whether there is much less space between transcendence and immanence than is often asserted in continental political theory) is beyond the purview of this analysis. The point here is that these methodological developments further undermine the efficacy of his external standard of contestability.

Contrariwise, the lack of critical negative detachment only increases the relativizing effects of the contestability mechanism when it is applied in the second gesture of Connolly's double-entry orientation. This is represented well in the shift in language between his two methodological phases. Connolly moves from "onto-political frameworks" to "existential faiths." Within the former, unexamined ontological assumptions undermine the analytic value of many perspectives in contemporary political thought, circumscribing our analyses of politics. The point of his method was that ontological perspectives were necessary supplements. In contrast, the language of existential faith radically undermines the status of all of our methods of political theorizing. Such approaches lose any distinction from religious dogma or positivistic method. "Every faith and doctrine so far invented runs into zones of paradox, mystery, and enigma that could be drawn upon to reject it as incoherent *or* invoked to deepen faith in it" (Connolly 2008, 75). Consequently, within Connolly's method, across and in between faiths we lose the capacity to engage in any kind of activity of reason giving. However, this leveling of the authority of frameworks is different from Rorty's insofar as the purpose and use of these languages is not a sufficient basis for intermethodological discussion.

Rather, there is a making-faith here of all perspectives that leaves us isolated within our ontologies. It is for this reason that Connolly claims that changes of framework are "more akin to a *conversion* than to a change of opinion" (Connolly 2008, 77). This models intermethodological exchanges (and perhaps intercultural ones) as chaotic arenas of positive ontological articulation without resources for productive development.[18] In this manner, his recent methodological developments exacerbate the mechanism of contestability and its problems.

These two tendencies, the priority of ontology and the priority of contestability, while so far presented as distinct, are fundamentally connected. They are the consequences of Connolly's weak-ontological response to the paradox of contemporary sociopolitical inquiry. By resorting to the level of ontology to argue for the fundamental contestability of the various approaches to contemporary political theory, he has increasingly outlined the conditions of that contestability. In a sense, he has responded to the question of essence by reifying and ontologizing the lack of essence into a series of positive immanent conditions of plurality and instability. This keeps his framework within the problematic of foundations. His movement from the contingency of language to the pluralistic universe can then be understood as a natural development of his original methodological choices.

CONCLUSION

This insight allows us to see the real difference between Rorty and Connolly and between recent pragmatist and weak-ontological/new-materialist approaches. Rorty responds to the same problematic of foundations and methodological pluralism with a similar attempt to level the discursive field while retaining critical and normative resources. However, he does this *methodologically rather than metaphysically*, in a series of injunctions meant to focus political theorizing on actual human languages. It is in this sense that while Connolly's is a substantive naturalism, Rorty naturalizes philosophical theorizing itself, applying it to the methodology of social and political thinking (Ramberg 2004, 2). The result is that they invest normativity in very different places. Connolly places it in the world, repeating the model of external standards. Rorty places it in the service of humans and under our control. This is the difference between Greek wonder and pragmatic limits that Rorty outlines in the epigraph. As I will discuss in chapter 4, this is the beginning of an attempt, never fully developed in his work, to provide a pragmatist theory of human agency and resources for reflexive sociopolitical development.

I return to these differences, strengths, and weaknesses in the next chapter, which, following its accounts of history and modernity in Rorty and Connolly, concludes the account of the thematic frame of Rorty's positive model. This chapter has illustrated his naturalism and assessed it in comparison within Connolly and new materialism's recent moves to employ an ontological naturalism as the basis of political theorizing. The latter has only exacerbated the problems of Connolly's ontological method, while the former continues to provide viable resources for an antifoundational and antirelativist form of sociopolitical criticism that, though not without problems, enables critical and normative claims from within the contemporary condition of democratic pluralism.

4

HISTORY AND MODERNITY

Self-Assertion and Critical Reflexivity

> *What pragmatic naturalists with one hand take away from philosophy—the idea of ontology (whether as metaphysics or natural science) as a substantive enquiry into the legitimacy of vocabularies—they return with the other; we are left with a conception of philosophy as aiding our practical and ethical deliberations. . . . On this view, the job of a philosopher is to make vivid how our practices might change if we were to describe things—particularly human beings—in altered vocabularies, or if we extend particular vocabularies into new domains.*
> —BJORN RAMBERG, "NATURALIZING IDEALIZATIONS: PRAGMATISM AND THE INTERPRETIVIST STRATEGY"

Historical reflection is the central theoretical resource of Rorty's positive method for sociopolitical progress. It is also where he explicitly turns to political issues: history and narrative, for him, enable antiessentialist theoretical reflection for positive social change. This chapter illustrates how these themes, understood from within the contingency of language and the methodological injunctions of naturalism, lead to both a particular framing of the task of sociopolitical criticism and a particular reading/justification of modernity. Further, it also completes the analysis, built over the preceding chapters, of the question of an implicit human-centered mastery with Rorty's work. Finally, it begins the tasks of the remaining chapters: giving a more determinate shape to his implicit model of sociopolitical criticism, critically assessing it, and clarifying its future potential for contemporary political thought.

HISTORICISM, SOCIOPOLITICAL CRITICISM, AND JUSTIFICATION

As we saw in chapter 1, Rorty turned early from epistemological debates within the philosophy of mind to a cultural-critical conception of philosophy. The model of a hermeneutic-edifying philosophy he entertains in the final sections of *PMN* quickly develops in *CP* into a conception of "philosophy-as-criticism-of-culture," which was progressively developed throughout his career (Rorty 1982b, 74). In fact, it is this subterranean guiding project of transforming philosophy from a systematic, foundational discipline to a democratic voice within the larger conversation of Western culture that unifies the diverse periods and topics of Rorty's thought. Further, several of the guiding themes of this dynamic were already present in *CP*, including his opposition to according any one area of human culture an authority that allows it to determine the validity of all others. He rejected the image of " 'the Philosopher' who could explain why and how certain areas of culture enjoyed a special relation to reality" (Rorty 1982c, xxxix).

This led to Rorty's linguistic turn and his understandings of language and justification as social practice. The originality and importance of these developments is the methodological significance of focusing on language as the primary object of critical and normative analysis. Focusing on languages, with which we discuss the various practices and aspects of human life, gives us nonfoundational access into criticizing and normatively reconstructing those practices, by learning how to speak new languages and employ new concepts. The previous discussion of naturalism clarified that Rorty's philosophy as the criticism of culture entailed the linguistic social practices that allow us to perform and reflect on our interactions with one another and our environments.

A turn to history further enables this form of sociopolitical criticism and prioritization of culture within our political theorizing;[1] it also removes the types of external standard Rorty proscribes with his naturalism. For him, when we discuss human political practices, we must avoid discussions of biological necessity, ontological conditioning, etc. Rather, to understand our cultural practices, we must see them as distinct from the other conditions that make them possible. What remains is a historical holism that understands those practices in terms of their relations with other practices and our ways of speaking of them and with the past forms of those practices and our ways of speaking about them. To avoid running afoul of the problem of justification, theoretical disciplines access our practices through the creation of narratives, rather than by searching for perennial features of human life or the wider world (Rorty 2007d).

This changes the nature of inquiry. Rather than accumulating knowledge about the world, *redescription* is central. It is this aspect of Rorty's theory that requires history. When inquiry is redescription, philosophical debate becomes about the use, purpose, and consequences of any practice or vocabulary. For Rorty, this is debated through the descriptive comparison of a practice or vocabulary with a past and a proposed future one. Thus, theory becomes historical; it is turned toward the existing historical narratives of our languages and practices, and, importantly, it intervenes in those languages. This model of inquiry reorients our focus from the "methodologico-ontological" to the "ethical-political," ending the idea that certain objects and topics demand to be studied in a certain way, and redirects inquiry to the purposes it hopes to achieve and the alternatives available (Rorty 1991f, 110). Inquiry must approach humanity not with the aim of discovering the immutable but of understanding the past uses of various conceptualizations in order to understand how they led to the present conceptual landscape. This enables political theorizing to be a continual process of "reinterpreting and recontextualizing the past" (Rorty 2007d, 182).

On Rorty's model, history allows political theory to interrogate critically and reform our ways of speaking and acting. It is the *second-order task of describing our descriptions*, of accessing our common narratives and concepts, and reconstructing them to change those understandings and the practices they enable (Rorty 1982c, xl). This is obviously not a task that political theory is exclusively capable of but is a wider democratic activity within a plural culture. Nonetheless, it is one political theorists are likely to perform well because it relies on the capacity to develop wider synthetic visions of our cultural-political present and relate those to the concepts and narratives, implicit and explicit, of public culture.

RORTY'S HEGEL: SOCIAL CRITICISM AND SUMMARY

For this reason, Rorty often had recourse to a conception of philosophy, drawn from Hegel, of "its own time apprehended in thoughts" (Hegel 1991, 21). Rorty's relation to Hegel is complicated and has been insufficiently addressed. While it is not the primary concern here, his specific relation to Hegel is illustrative of the dynamics of Rorty's relationship to continental political philosophy and his argument about the use of history in sociopolitical criticism.

As Rorty and his critics have observed, he employs only a particular aspect of Hegel's thought: his *historicism* (Rorty 2000b; Redding 2002; Rotenstreich 1985; Matarrese 2006). For him, Hegel's "temporalization" of rationality in his history of varying rationalities dialectically progressing through European civilization was invaluable. This historicism made the criteria for rationality dependent on its language and epoch. However, for Rorty we must remove this historicism from the discourse of the Absolute in Hegel, a process he refers to as "de-absolutizing" or "de-ontologizing" Hegel.[2] What remains is the minimal part of Hegel's philosophy, where philosophy is understood as a project of cultural synthesis, "its time apprehended in thought." For Rorty, Hegel first posits the pragmatist notion that justification is internal to an epoch and shifts along with other sociocultural developments. Thus, he is instrumental for Rorty's own characterization of languages and truth as temporal, contingent developments. For this reason, he posits Hegel's "romanticism" (i.e., his sense of the temporal relativity of vocabularies) as his chief contribution to toppling nineteenth-century scientism. He exposed "how the passion which sweeps through each generation serves the cunning of reason, providing the impulse which drives that generation to self-immolation and transformation" (Rorty 2000b, 302). The stability each generation achieves with the creation of a new vocabulary is inevitably lost in the impermanence of all such vocabularies. This points us toward an important point about how linguistic social change occurs;

this is a question of how our purposes change and how existing tools/languages become inadequate to those purposes.

One of the difficulties with Rorty's historicism is the singular emphasis he places on its capacity for normative commitment. He often describes the investigation of history as a means not to criticize the present but to celebrate whatever aspects of it one chooses. For example, "holding our time in thought" is "finding a description of all the things characteristic of your time of which you most approve, with which you unflinchingly identify, a description which will serve as a description of the end toward which the historical developments which led up to your time were means" (Rorty 1989, 55). Rorty reiterated this emphasis in a later typology of the functions of history, which identifies four beneficial types.[3] The first two are historical and rational reconstructions. The former attempts to understand a thinker from within their historical context. This provides "self-awareness," the awareness of the difference (and contingency) of forms of intellectual life. In contrast, rational reconstructions are interpretations that integrate thinkers into the present. This provides "self-justification." Here, past thinkers are incorporated into the present debate to provide continuity and a rational line of progression. While anachronistic, this frames thought as a "long conversational interchange." It assures us of rational progress and, for Rorty, has deep cultural-political possibilities. "We need to think that, in philosophy as in science, the mighty mistaken dead look down from heaven at our recent successes and are happy to find that their mistakes have been corrected" (Rorty 2000f, 249–50).

The third and fourth types of history are similarly connected. Intellectual history, for Rorty, provides the raw material. Theorizing always occurs within a wider intellectual and cultural context. Intellectual history provides the material for canon reformation, a process that must be continual. But what decides the canon? For Rorty, it is specifically the fourth type, *Geistesgeschichte*. These "spirit-histories" draw on both historical and rational reconstructions (and the raw material of intellectual history). From the former, they derive the awareness of the relativity of philosophical vocabularies and problems. From the latter, they draw the project of justification. Yet they differ in scale. Where rational reconstructions focus on specific problems/thinkers, *Geistesgeschichte* engages *problematics*, asking the metaquestions of what philosophy is and should be. For Rorty, these metahistories fulfill several purposes. First, they illustrate the contingency of our own time. Second, they simultaneously provide us with an understanding of philosophical development that assures us that progress has been made, that we are "better off" than those before us. These upward narratives provide the hope to continue with the project of a community. Finally, these narratives point us to the future, to the ways in which it will be better than the present (Rorty 2000f, 270–73). The emphasis here is on how these various types of progressive narratives can intervene in the present by deploying one particular aspect of it, in order to justify it over against others. In this manner, we hold our time in thought by understanding how all the small developments that preceded the present were particularizations and contributions to a particular good within the present moment.

Several points are worth noting. Rorty strongly emphasizes an understanding of philosophy as a forum for intervening in our existing languages, especially those languages that reflect on our development. A historical perspective is crucial to this: it provides a unique opportunity to intervene within those languages and narratives by placing them within larger or alternative contexts. In this manner, we can both illustrate the contingency of our linguistic practices (i.e., their non-necessity and particular emergence) and engage in cultural-political intervention through novel narratives of justification that emphasize the aspects of those practices we seek to celebrate and carry forward (and implicitly those we want to leave behind).

HISTORICISM AND NORMATIVE CHANGE

This reveals an important weakness, only adumbrated up until now, in Rorty's account of sociopolitical critical reconstruction. When discussing history, he emphasizes the task of linguistic intervention for the purposes of normative commitment but ignores the equally important task of critique within political theorizing.[4] This imbalance is a problem Rorty shares with Connolly, especially in the latter's recent work, and is one my analysis returns to. Presently, it is important to note that it stems from a hesitancy (see the introduction) around the status of theoretical reflection. Rorty worried that a distinctive task for our capacity of theory, over other areas of contemporary democratic culture, entails a relationship of authority he wants to avoid as foundational. Thus, as Matthew Festenstein has noted, he subordinates critical and theoretical reflection to *the language of summary and narrative*, of redescribing rather than critiquing (Festenstein 2003, 17). In what follows, I challenge the idea that a distinction between the role of theoretical and nontheoretical disciplines must entail such a hierarchy and such a relation of critique to description.

Presently, it is important to meet the associated criticism, dominant in the 1990s, that this hesitancy reveals a fundamental conservatism—that in rejecting critique, as it is often mistakenly characterized, Rorty's theory is politically *acquiescent*.[5] The ubiquity of this view is odd given its circumvention of a key aspect of Rorty's thought and use of historicism. His entire account of the necessity of a historical perspective in sociopolitical criticism both highlights and enables conceptual invention within our situated linguistic practices. The holism that this perspective necessitates, where some linguistic practices are deployed against others, facilitates the single most important aspect of his pragmatic account of social change. When vocabularies are understood as tools to make possible certain practices and delimit others, the question of how we change tools is central. For Rorty, the historical perspective enables individuals and communities to "frame and formulate new ends" (Brandom 2000b, 169).

Rorty's vocabulary of vocabularies, his language for intervocabulary relations, focuses on how alterations in vocabularies change the purposes of our practices. While such changes are only understood *retrospectively*, which Rorty emphasizes to ensure his tool metaphor is not misunderstood as positing perfect control (i.e., mastery) over social change (Rorty 1989, 12), this method highlights "an absolutely crucial practical capacity that vocabularies give us: the capacity to frame genuinely novel purposes, and so in a real sense to remake ourselves" (Brandom 2000b, 171). There are two important points about this capacity. First, it is derived neither from some core feature of human nature nor some transcendental faculty. In the "vocabulary" vocabulary, applying and transforming a linguistic norm are two sides of the same coin. To use a vocabulary is to change it (this distinguishes vocabularies from other tools).[6] Second, this means that linguistic norms are both constraining and profoundly liberating. They both provide established practices to act within (which is limiting *and* enabling) and the possibility of transforming those practices (Brandom 2000b, 177).

This *constitutive space of freedom* within language use is the motivating reason behind Rorty's linguistic turn. It also points, albeit at this stage only tentatively, to the possibility of a *reconstruction of rationality*. While he was notably resistant to that concept, our freedom with respect to norms within language use raises the question of by what criteria we go about the task of transforming our purposes. Rorty often asserted that this can only occur by "our lights" and thereby encountered the charge of relativism.[7] However, while he may have thought no ahistorical standards could ground this activity, he also consistently maintains that this can happen in better and worse ways. Further, and this is the more contentious part, there are resources and strategies that can enable better forms of sociopolitical change.

In a late essay on Hegel, developing his antifoundational reading, Rorty moved incrementally toward a reconstruction of rationality as a strategic, situated resource for reflective social development. Focusing on Hegel's theory of the "sociality of reasons," he notes, "On this conception, reason is not a link between human beings and the nature of things, but rather a social relation between human beings" (Rorty 2003, 40). Rorty insists that this provides no basis on which to privilege one discourse over another in a wholesale (i.e., metaphysical) way. The only way languages can be better is in terms of serving specific human purposes or, in this case, by making us better able to effect new purposes. Thus, when we operate at the metatheoretical level of the vocabulary of vocabularies, the ability to consider various discourses and their comparative advantages and disadvantages, without metaphysical standards, is a type of freedom that enables better and more rational social practices. Though Rorty does not frame it in these terms, he argues that this develops resources for "self-reliance" and "cultural freedom" (Rorty 2003, 45). The suggestion here is that this entails a reconstruction of *rationality as critical reflexivity* that provides a nonessentialist criteria for social criticism.

We can appreciate the methodological importance and originality of Rorty's historicism. As the main theme of his positive conception of philosophy as sociopolitical criticism, it is the key element of his model of theorizing that moves past the problem of justification without seeking to overcome or reify it. Following his naturalistic methodological injunction, his historical perspective provides resources for sociopolitical intervention. While his dominant tendency is to emphasize only the narrative aspects and the project of normative commitment, his later reading of Hegel indicates the possibility of a critical conception of rationality as reflexivity that may address his oft-noted underemphasis on critique.

However, Rorty's account of historicism is not incompatible with a wider set of methodological resources, which may exceed his explicit model, as long as they avoid external standards that run afoul of his naturalism. The next section illustrates how this theory of critical reflexivity is manifested in his rereading of modernity.

SELF-ASSERTION VERSUS MASTERY: TWO MODELS OF MODERNITY

Given the centrality of history, it is unsurprising that a narrative of modernity initiates Rorty's conception of critical reflexivity.[8] On a more overt level, his account of modernity illustrates the type of historical justification he envisions as possible within his model of sociopolitical thought. It is also where Rorty most overtly responded to the charge of an ontology of mastery in his work. Unsurprisingly, Rorty's accounts of the development of Western thought center on the question of authority/foundations/metaphysics/justification. The common thread in these accounts is a view of this development as a process of dedivinization and secularization.[9] For Rorty, from the religiosity of the medieval period, through the love of reason in the Enlightenment, and finally to the romantic love of the inner truth of man in the nineteenth century, we have looked to idealizations and external absolutes to justify human ends. The imperative now is to reject all divinations, to have history and narrative "replace God, Reason and Nature as the source of human hope" (Rorty 1999b, 265). Modernity, for Rorty, is where this continued secularization becomes possible, where the project of *authority without authoritarianism* (normativity without foundations) can be furthered through a certain set of linguistic practices/resources.

RORTY'S MODERNITY: SELF-ASSERTION AS CRITICAL REFLEXIVITY

Rorty's most detailed justification of these claims is in a review of Hans Blumenberg's *The Legitimacy of the Modern Age*, which connects narrative, history, and modernity to his ethic of mastery and critique of continental philosophy.[10] For Rorty, the significance of Blumenberg's work is an understanding of modernity that defends the Enlightenment without recourse to the foundational nature of reason; essentially, it offers a *Geistesgeschichte* that engages in a narrative of justification and development through conceptual invention. Further, he contrasts this account with continental critiques of modernity (his main targets are "Nietzscheans, Heideggerians, and Marxists"). Elsewhere Rorty criticized the broad continental tendency to treat modernity as a "philosophical problem."[11] For him, there are no privileged criteria that can transcend the epoch in the manner this assumes, nor is there a deeper essence behind it (Rorty 1999c, 213–16).

In this review, he builds on this criticism in terms of its recourse to "unmasking" in its critique of the "belatedness" of the modern age. As discussed in chapter 2, Rorty critiques Heidegger (and much of continental political philosophy) for employing a logic of unmasking in philosophical critique. For him, this logic assumes an appearance-reality distinction in its attempt to penetrate through some distorting veil to a hidden reality. It is the source of a return to metaphysics within Heidegger, which I argued ended up as an undue methodological prioritization of ontology within Connolly's work. "Belatedness" is the critical view Rorty identifies within continental thought, which rejects modernity as fundamentally impoverished in comparison to some idealized past. In this it assumes a distinction between some "pristine old and nasty new" that smuggles the appearance-reality distinction back in. In contrast, Blumenberg offers a novel justificatory narrative of the Enlightenment that shifts our understanding of its authority and purposes without a totalizing metaphysics (Rorty 1983, 3). Essentially, he combines a recognition of historical contingency with a creative defense of modernity that takes its strengths while junking its weaknesses.

This is just the contest of narratives Rorty identifies as the essence of cultural politics and the object of his model of sociopolitical criticism. Is modernity where humanity has become freer in its projects of disenchantment and democracy? Or is it merely a secularized form of ancient and Christian eschatologies, as various continentals have charged? The latter is the main point of opposition for both Blumenberg and Rorty, who see in it the source of a common rejection of modernity. What this critique ignores is the distinction, which Blumenberg introduced, between two projects within enlightened modernity: *self-foundation* and *self-assertion*. Self-foundation is the project of discovering an ahistorical framework for human knowledge and existence. It is precisely the project of authority Rorty rejects. Self-assertion is the "mode of life" that places human aims, desires, and happiness at the center of its reflections. There, neither absolute knowledge nor primordial truth is the standard of justification, only possible human futures. Importantly, while this includes the projects of "technological mastery" and "the acquisition of Baconian knowledge-as-power," they are not unreflective, because self-assertion includes a self-conscious practice of critical interrogation that replaces external metaphysical standards with "historical self-consciousness":

> The way to stop the pendulum swinging between "irrationalism" and "defenses of reason" is to let historical self-consciousness take the place of metaphysics. Such historical self-consciousness would not require ahistorical metaphysical or epistemological back-up, but merely a vocabulary which, as he [Blumenberg] says, has "a durability that is very great in relation to both our capacity to perceive historical events and the rate of change involved in them."
>
> (Rorty 1983, 3)

Modernity's significance is its potential to raise and eclipse the problem of justification/authority/metaphysics that has engendered this pendulum swing. Its "historical self-consciousness" enables a mode of reflection on human social practices and ideas that allows us to intervene and develop them. This stems from the fact that the disposition to self-assertion and its "proliferating curiosity, its urge for technical mastery, its refusal to be interested in something larger than itself which contains it and makes it possible, and its consequent orientation toward an unknown future" encourage us to place humans, and our various practices, at the center of our critical and normative reflections (Rorty 1983, 3). In this sense, for Rorty, in modernity humanity is "asserted," which is why he speaks of it as "courage" here and as "self-reliance" in the essay on Hegel.[12]

By distinguishing these two sides of modernity, Rorty believes he can save the best features of the Enlightenment. For him, in contrast to continental narratives, it is only the project of self-foundation that is "bankrupt." Further, he argues that the logic of unmasking upon which their critiques depend, "the demand to unmask completely, to make all things new, to start from nowhere, to substitute new true consciousness for old false consciousness," is the foundationalist legacy (Rorty 1983, 3). Whether the narrative is an upward Hegelian one of the teleology of absolute spirit or a Heideggerian downward fall away from primordial knowledge of Being, both rely on the logic of grounding (either as presence or absence). In contrast, history does not occur according to either the logic of absolute rationality or absolute contingency but the "sufficient rationality" of a "series of rational rejections of alternatives. These were not rational in some ahistorical sense, but only in the sufficient sense of being a pragmatic choice among tools" (Rorty 1983, 3). Once again, Rorty edges closer toward a kind of reconstruction of rationality as the growing ability and set of resources, seen especially in modernity, to reflect on and critique our linguistic practices of normativity.

CONNOLLY, MASTERY, AND MODERN MALIGNANCIES

Connolly offered an extensive critique of modernity that challenges Rorty's reading and use of history while clarifying the difference between their approaches. It is important to note that this account occurs from within the Heideggerian ontological structure that characterized his earlier period (see chapter 2). Nonetheless, as illustrated in chapter 3, the problems of that period (the tendencies to a priority of ontology and priority of contestability) and the structure of determination as limitation only change emphasis in his recent work. Further, this critique is particularly relevant because in it Connolly connects mastery explicitly to pragmatism. This allows us to extend the ontological critique of Rorty developed across the previous two chapters. Connolly's analysis of modernity argues that the self-assertion of human reason contains hidden ontological assumptions and demands, that beneath Rorty's use of history is the unifying demand for a truth that can be grasped and dominated.

Developing his discussion of the ontological matrix of contemporary thought in *Political Theory and Modernity*, Connolly targets the mastery assumption of a world predisposed to humans. In modernity, control of the world is the ultimate concern. The natural, individual, and social worlds are approached as at the disposal of humanity. "Nature becomes a set of laws susceptible to human knowledge, a deposit of resources for potential use or a set of vistas for aesthetic appreciation." (Connolly 1993b, 2). The world loses its enchanted nature, where divine will and realities were inscribed upon it and order was obvious through some great hierarchy of Being. Instead, it becomes resources to mine and material to augment.[13] All modern approaches are governed by the desire to form and reform, to perfect control over change and thereby assure progress. In such a world, modernity becomes a continual process of critique, absorption, and reform, a way to guarantee continual temporal progress (Connolly 1993b, 20).

Yet for Connolly, contra Rorty and Blumenberg, modern values are fundamentally undermined by hidden ontological assumptions. His central charge is that *these values assume a model of truth that fixes identity and excludes difference*. This is true even of their explicit rejections of the traditional correspondence and representational understandings. Coherence, consensus, and pragmatist theories of truth continue to presume that "truth be one, that a doctrine or theory not be treated as true unless it is the only one that meets the established standard of truth" (Connolly 1993b, 10). This is an admittedly confusing claim, and Connolly does not substantiate it with evidence from particular pragmatists. However, when he clarifies it, it relates to the central issue of pluralism. In assuming that truth is one, pragmatists assume that two or more readings of the world could not be "equally able to render it intelligible to humanity." For Connolly, every framework will encounter "slippage and undecidability in its structure" (Connolly 1993b, 10). Ignoring this results in modernity's continued faith and its failure to address the appearance-reality distinction.

Connolly develops this charge in a reading of Nietzsche's "How the Real World at Last Became a Myth" (Nietzsche 2003, 50–51)[14] and in a critique of the pragmatic use of Hegel. In the former, Nietzsche provides a succinct, six-stage history of truth within Western thought that narrates the death of the appearance-reality distinction. It is stage five that is important here. "The 'real world'—an idea no longer of any use, not even a duty any longer—an idea grown useless, superfluous, consequently a refuted idea: let us abolish it!" (Nietzsche 2003, 50). For Connolly, this is the moment of pragmatism and utilitarianism when human use and organization exhaust the true. Citing Rorty as an example of this "naturalized Hegelianism," he notes that this view is still too "cheerful." It seeks the ontological minimalism of truth as pragmatic action and ignores the possibility of alternative (and resistant) ontologies (Connolly 1993b, 145).

Connolly critiques Marx in a manner that explicates this assessment of pragmatism and its use of Hegel. For Connolly, Marx pairs an explicit critique of Hegel's ontology of Spirit with an implicit counterontology of plasticity in nature. If the world is not progressively realized in Spirit through the dialectical march of history, it is becoming progressively more susceptible to human mastery. This converts the world from standing against humanity to a deposit of resources utilizable for human ends. Hegel and Marx (and Rorty) still share a fundamental "pattern of insistence" that the world be for us in its fundamental structure. Rorty's version is simply a Hegel without Spirit. It "is Hegelianism by other means. It is the conversion of Hegelianism into a set of presumptions more credible and amenable to modern sensibilities" (Connolly 1993b, 132). This language closely resembles Rorty's own. The question now becomes what the further step beyond pragmatist stage five is. What approach eclipses the modern problematic?

The final stage of truth is the abolition of the apparent world. For Connolly, this is not an idealism but a statement on the nature of knowledge without the appearance-reality distinction. "We must stop comparing belief to the pure model it seeks to copy and start appraising beliefs according to standards of living. We might even begin to discern that knowledge—an authoritative organization of experience—is both a support and danger to life" (Connolly 1993b, 144). With pragmatism, Nietzsche assumes that knowledge bears utility; it is a mode of power, a way of imposing form on the world to make it comprehensible and utilizable.[15] Here, knowledge is not simply power but a form or "tool" of power. Like Rorty, Connolly compares knowledge (language) to a tool in that it shapes. It does not merely reveal the world but acts on it and organizes it, "willing it," in Nietzsche's language. The will to knowledge is the will to change the world, to bring it in line with human purposes. Yet Nietzsche goes further. Knowledge is both a support (like a tool) and *a danger*. He does not assume, with the pragmatist, that the world is susceptible to our purposes.

> Thus a residue of the providential view of the world clings to the categories through which the pragmatist seeks to organize it. The pragmatist

naturalizes Hegel and forgets that a naturalized world may not be as responsive to human capacities as one filled with Spirit. The ghost of Hegel's Spirit still roams the world of pragmatism.

(Connolly 1993b, 145)

For Connolly, the world resists our interpretations. Instead of merely rejecting truth and the real world (the "let us abolish it!" of stage five's pragmatism), Connolly offers an alternative ontology of resistance (Connolly 1993b, 132). As we saw in chapter 2, all views of the world are partial because they all both reveal and conceal elements therein (determination as limitation). Connolly moves from this to a thesis about the necessity of contingency and from there to an overt ontology of resistance/recalcitrance. In chapter 3, we saw how this developed in his recent work into a type of ontological naturalism that emphasizes the plurality, complexity, and becoming of the natural and sociopolitical worlds. Resistance becomes nonhuman powers of self-organization and a distributive sense of agency. The point here is that this generalized ontology of resistance and its later versions are better ontological dispositions than mastery for Connolly, because they do not assume the plasticity of the world on the sociopolitical level. This better suits it to the diversity of contemporary pluralistic democracies.

Connolly claims that this overt ontology of resistance more effectively responds to the problem of foundations in its explicit commitments and its nonexclusionary model of belief, which does not rely on a hidden insistence of truth. For him, modernity still participates in the faith that truth is one. Rorty's pragmatism, in this criticism, assumes that it is done with truth in its antifoundational and postmetaphysical self-assertion of humanity. The latter is particularly relevant because the inevitable failure of postmetaphysical thought is a central criticism posed by weak-ontological approaches to a variety of models in contemporary political theory, including Rorty's.[16] Yet, in placing humanity at the center, it contains a demand that reality be one in its plasticity and susceptibility to human purpose and assumes the neutrality of its pragmatic method. It is still an ontology of coherence and concord and thus is "a demand for external guarantees inside a culture that has erased the ontological preconditions for them" (Connolly 1993b, 11). This is the paradox of modernity and its faith. It claims to overcome the past in exceeding dependence on a deity for authority. However, it implicitly relies on a faith in the authority of truth and as a result assumes the legitimacy of one model, excluding others and ignoring the existence and partiality of its ontological assumptions of mastery.

Connolly's contrasting reading of modernity and critique of the pragmatic view of truth is ideally placed to test Rorty's historicism and justificatory account of modernity as critical reflexivity. First of all, it challenges Rorty on two key claims that I have identified as his strengths: first, the capacity of his theory to accommodate the plurality of vocabularies in modern, pluralistic societies and, second, its relation to the very problematic appearance-reality divide, a central issue in discussions of the problem of justification/metaphysics/foundations and that Rorty, in turn, accused continental theory of assuming in his critique of unmasking. Connolly argues that the project of a naturalized Hegel without Spirit contains hidden ontological assumptions of the plasticity of the world and the susceptibility of it to human purposes that assume that truth is one. This extends Heidegger's initial critique of pragmatism as the highest stage of technological thinking and Connolly's development of that into the charge of a social foundationalism in Rorty. Here, the focus on reconstructing modernity and deploying new narratives from within our existing languages would, from Connolly's ontological perspective, bear out these criticisms. If he is correct, Rorty's model of sociopolitical criticism and implicit resource of critical reflexivity fail to achieve normativity without foundations. The next section gathers together the various threads of this chapter and the previous two in assessing these possibilities.

NATURALISTIC HISTORICISM: PHILOSOPHICAL RESOURCES FOR SOCIOPOLITICAL CRITICISM

The strength of this ontological criticism turns on the claim that ethics of mastery like Rorty's contain hidden ontological assumptions of the plasticity/susceptibility of the world and that truth is one, that this is the only legitimate disposition to the world (as nonmetaphysical, rational, etc.). These assumptions, for Connolly, exclude otherness/difference, which makes these frameworks less capable of addressing contemporary pluralistic sociopolitical life. The social foundationalism of pragmatic naturalism is so dangerous because it lacks the resources to delineate critically its own assumptions and gain a reflexive distance to make new normative claims. For Connolly, these naturalized models are typical of modernity: its rejection of the divine, ontological minimalism, and refocusing of the sociopolitical to the authority of humanity. For all these reasons he offers his counterontology of resistance and immanent naturalism.

This analysis poses a serious challenge to Rorty and contemporary pragmatist political theory. It suggests that his attempts to develop modernity in a manner that does not run afoul of the problem of justification (antifoundationalism) but retains the capacity to enable normative claims (antirationalism), by distinguishing self-foundation and self-assertion, and to offer a naturalistic framework and historicist method for sociopolitical critique are incapable of the reflexivity it attempts. However, this charge ultimately fails, as it misunderstands both Rorty's project, in terms of its status and the resources it identifies, and the critical and normative capacities of ontology in sociopolitical thinking.

As discussed in chapter 3, the problem with the ontological critique of mastery is that it misunderstands the scope of Rorty's project, assuming that he attempts an exhaustive ontology or metaphysics. In contrast, his framework is only an account of the critical and normative resources within languages and a method for intervening in these for sociopolitical development. Extrapolating from a very specific understanding of some aspect of human social practice to an account of the world or the human condition in ontological/metaphysical terms does not illustrate the intrinsic connection between these two descriptions. It does not make that metaphysics internal to that understanding. Thus, even if a complex series of ontological assumptions seems intuitively linked to Rorty's method, it is not necessary that these assumptions are inherent to the account of his model of sociopolitical criticism developed here. As previously noted, Rorty's tool-based accounts of language and discussion of the centrality of metaphor to linguistic development are exactly intended to oppose the idea that sociopolitical development (let alone the natural world) is subject to total mastery. Rather, such development is contingent and complex, and mastery for Rorty is only a disposition he recommends to meet that situation, not an ontology that has any sense.

This point holds equally true for modernity. Rorty's narrative of self-assertion and his support for it as a disposition highlights the resources within modernity for an independent relation to our critical and normative standards that does not measure them against external criteria but against the purposes we hope they serve or against proposed alternative purposes and what our wider practices, institutions, and life would look with those ends. Thus, for Rorty, there is nothing inherently wrong with the project of "technological mastery" or "the acquisition of Baconian knowledge-as-power," because modernity can be reconstructed to have a disposition of self-assertion without the project of self-foundation that excludes others and assumes the plasticity of the world (Rorty 1983, 3). It has no particular or necessary essence. Rather, this version of modernity is mastery, but it is only a mastery of our own social and political lives. Further, as I will discuss in chapters 5 and 6, this is ideally suited to pluralistic democratic societies where competing normative standards meet in the public.

In contrast, it is Connolly's ontological analysis of modernity and mastery that fails its intended purpose. Once again, the two tendencies of the priority of ontology or the priority of contestability emerge here. When the reading is on the strong end, Connolly slips back into the foundationalist paradigm, claiming to have discovered the essence of modern thought (i.e., as compensatory ontologies). However, broad historical periods, as human constructions, are not characterized by a unity of thinking, practice, and politics in this manner. Recognizing contingency means understanding that there are aspects of the present constellation we can retain and those we can reject. To reiterate, we don't have absolute control over this. But this is not for an ontological reason but for the naturalistic and sociological reason that shifting meaning and practice in a collective context is a difficult, cumulative process. Rorty makes this point well when he criticizes the continental homogenization of the Enlightenment for confusing a criticism of a mode of justification with a criticism of the mode of life being justified (Rorty 1983, 3).

While a full analysis is not possible, this problematic tendency to essentialization may arise often within contemporary continental political theory (at least its Anglo-American form). Stephen White has argued that this tradition is premised on a radical questioning of authority. In the broadest sense, this includes not only epistemic and ontological standards but ingrained sociopolitical forces. However, unlike Rorty, this opposition to authority includes the identification and critique of a *fundamental malignant logic* within modern thought. For White, this leads continentals to systemic critical understandings of modernity and (in most cases) complete rejections of the progressive and universalistic narratives of Enlightenment progress. One dominant way of enacting this line of criticism, epitomized by Connolly and other agonistic democrats, is to emphasize the antagonistic and conflictual nature of contemporary sociopolitical life. From this, various ways of transforming practices away from the universalism of the modern frame have been offered. Importantly, it is through ontological characterizations of, in the first instance, human individual and collective being and, in the second instance, general plurality and becoming that these conflictual elements are argued for (White 2011, 482–95). It is for this reason that Connolly's work is so significant: his development from the earlier Heideggerian focus on human "being-in-the-world" to theorizing "Being-as-such" (in his immanent naturalism) is representative of the drift of the tradition.

There is much of value in these approaches, and Rorty is sympathetic to many of their aspects. Further, this critique of essentialism has not suggested that the assumptions of mastery and their effects on practice are not present in the modern world. They surely are. The point is that they are not *essential* to modernity. The question Rorty raises is whether ontology is the best way to analyze and argue for their critical and normative reconstruction. This concern is prescient given that continental political theory's criticisms are largely motivated by a version of the problem of justification and the necessity of acknowledging philosophical, cultural, and political pluralism. Is an ontological approach suited to criticism and normativity without foundations?

Tellingly, this concern has also arisen within continental political theory. Nathan Widder argues that *weak*-ontological approaches cannot maintain a contestable relationship to their own foundations. For him, no perspective can continually problematize its own basic claims, and so weak ontology ends up an idealization (Widder 2012, 9). This bears out the previous criticism that Connolly fails to achieve his aim of folding contestability back into his ontological figurations to provide for a critically reflexive position that is "enacted rather than just announced" (White 2000, 8). Contestability is not internally present in ontological approaches but is only an external standard applied back at various moments. As a result, weak ontology cannot be critically reflexive, and so its ontological method ends up essentialist, ignoring the differences and potentialities within modernity. This illuminates the problem with these approaches to political criticism. Malignancies are degenerative and, unless radically addressed, eventually terminal situations. On the face of it, this seems an inappropriate de facto logic for sociopolitical issues, especially within a method employing weak rather than strong forms of justification.

On the other hand, when the reading is weak, that is, when the external mechanism has been applied, Connolly's understanding of modernity offers too few reasons to endorse it, and a general relativizing of positions occurs. If modernity is simply one faith among many, as Connolly's language suggests, the reasons to prefer one faith over another fall away. Connolly's general move to a language of faith (see chapter 3), which in terms of overt methodological statements occurs after *Political Theory and Modernity* (though seems to anticipate this feature), ignores the possibility of distinguishing between a mode of justification that has the reflexive capacity to interrogate its own assumptions critically and one that does not. If the modern claim to rationality is reconstructed along these lines, as Rorty suggests, it becomes a much more plausible way to distinguish between faith and nonfaith and provides a strong reason not to reject modernity as a fundamentally malignant logic. Like any viewpoint, it just needs particular forms of critical development.[17]

While this analysis has tended to emphasize the weaknesses of Connolly and the ontological approach, there are strengths that make these deficiencies all the more tragic. He tells a convincing narrative about the presence of a series of assumptions within modernity that, if present, are in need of critical revision. The problem is that his framework of analysis, because of the status given to ontology, doesn't allow us to identify the problematic aspects of our practices and languages in need of development (and then reconstruct them) but calls only for an ontological solution: a new determination of being and a corresponding set of categories, manifested in his immanent naturalism. As a result, it ends up being capable of offering few reasons to endorse its reading or its normative conclusions.

Rorty directly addressed this problem of the status of ontology. His naturalism, discussed in chapter 3, criticizes visual metaphors of worldpicturing. While ontological frameworks generally follow Heidegger's rejection of this language (Heidegger 1977a), Connolly, especially in his shift not only to a determination of Being but a cosmology of immanent naturalism, repeats the logic of world-picture in the all-encompassing and determinative nature of ontological lenses. In opposition, in sociopolitical criticism, Rorty attends primarily to the ways of speaking we employ.

> We do not need a synoptic view of something called "the world." At most, we need a synoptic narrative of how we came to talk as we do. We should stop trying for a unified picture, and for a master vocabulary. We should confine ourselves to making sure that we are not burdened with obsolete ways of speaking, and then ensuring that those vocabularies that are still useful stay out of each other's way.
>
> (Rorty 2007g, 150)

Ontological frameworks like Connolly's remain within the logic of picturing when they seek to relate languages, as social practices, to something beyond themselves (in this case, Being). In this, they repeat what Davidson called the scheme-content distinction, where a framework is judged against what it seeks to represent. Beyond the problems with the logic of correspondence this entails (see chapter 1), this imposes an artificial unity on the world (Rorty 1991q, 152). In contrast, Rorty's holistic use of history is *methodological rather than metaphysical*. It does not posit unity but offers a strategic injunction to, when engaging in sociopolitical criticism, restrict ourselves to deploying some sets of descriptions and practices against others rather than appeal to external critical and normative standards (e.g., whether something accords with radical contingency).

This reraises the question of the relation between naturalism and historicism in Rorty. These two categories are mutually enabling and limiting injunctions; they both proscribe external critical and normative standards and prescribe the use of situated languages and practices (past and present) as tools for critical political thought. In a later essay, Rorty provides an important framing of this mixing, clarifying how deabsolutized versions of each avoid their respective problems. In this account, he discusses the vitalism (a view of the unity of experience in its vibrant, living aspect) and panpsychism (a view of the unity of experience in a mental aspect) in the thought of James and Dewey. The former theme is often associated with naturalism, the latter with historicism. Both were intended to overcome the problematic distinction between subject and object, mind and world, by seeing them as ontologically continuous. For Rorty, both are also the most problematic versions of their respective themes (as well of James's and Dewey's philosophies). The reason is that in positing a fundamental unity within the wider world, they suggest that the world shares in what is the distinctly human activity of framing collective sociopolitical projects. That is, a wider unity within a continuous reality suggests that there are purposes inherent to nature and the history of our interaction with it. This would mean that there are standards, beyond our practices and their consequences, in the world for judging our sociopolitical lives (Rorty 2000b). This tendency emerges within Connolly's thought in its placement of inherent normative value in the world (chapter 3).

This engenders two problems. First, it reraises a series of issues around the problems of access and justification because it depends upon an appearance-reality divide in positing a unity (and set of purposes) inherent to the world, despite not being otherwise apparent. Second, it exacerbates the problem pluralism poses to contemporary sociopolitical life by bringing in the variety of ontological and comprehensive frameworks various groups will always have when discussing how to construe the world. Importantly, this raises two important questions about how such assumptions could be excluded, as this is a central criticism Connolly poses to ontological minimalism, and what the task of political theorizing actually is in this context. We will return to this in chapters 5 and 6. Presently, the relationship between naturalism and historicism remains.

Opposing pictures of unity, Rorty deemphasizes Darwin's vitalism and Hegel's idealism.[18] This amounts to removing any hint of intrinsic purpose from both a naturalistic understanding of the world and of historical development. This allows naturalism and historicism to function as a set of mutually limiting and enabling injunctions. Naturalism "grounds" us in our present purposes, removing external standards and mandating a form of holism that situates us within the present nexus of languages, practices, and purposes. It, necessarily, does come with a vocabulary of social practices that is not without links to the natural sciences. This entails assumptions, as well as a history and set of concepts, that can be framed in ontological terms (e.g., as mastery). As a language with a history and a context, this is unavoidable; there is no view from nowhere. However, historicism pushes us beyond this framework by emphasizing the contingency of our present and enabling us to frame new ends. Naturalism and historicism together give the capacity to intervene reflexively within our present sociopolitical worlds. Paired in this way, they are resources that save Rorty's model from Connolly's criticism of social foundationalism (as well as the charges of acquiescence and conservatism).

Given our concern with sociopolitical criticism within the context of plurality, that is, different sets of linguistic practices, historicism's capacity to regulate intervocabulary relations is especially important. Naturalism contains injunctions that root our critical and normative reflections in linguistic social practices rather than external standards and allow us to deploy some practices against others. This enables reflexivity in the present. Historicism illuminates how we achieve this through narratives of our development, that new understandings of the developments of those practices enable not only removing old, problematic practices, by weaving them out of the narrative of our present and its future, but also formulating new purposes, by crafting new narratives that recontextualize the past and present in terms of a new line of progress. This enables reflexivity between past, present, and future. Further, the best way to be naturalist and historicist, to satisfy the limiting injunctions of each, is to take the linguistic turn and treat language as a collective practice. Languages are available and already contain critical-normative practices; criticism is just something we do.[19] For Rorty, undertaking this turn makes our thinking more flexible, complex, and self-aware. While he does not use the language of reflexivity, he emphasizes that these virtues allow for progress in sociopolitical life: "Societies evolve into other societies by finding that the moral language they have been using brings with it consequences they do not like.... To say that moral progress occurs is to say that later societies are more complex, more developed, more articulate, and above all more flexible than their predecessors" (Rorty 2000b, 303–4).

Fundamental to a reflexive mode of sociopolitical development that embodies these virtues is a deontologization of our wider understandings of our context (naturalism) and its progress (historicism). In this, Rorty offers a way of thinking space and time that doesn't reengender the problem of foundations. To this end, we must have a conception of the present world and history that does not make a problematic nature-culture distinction and thus *does* see humanity, the wider world, and history as continuous but *not* as fundamentally linked by some guiding ontological dynamic. Teleology and metaphysics might be inevitable, but they can also be more or less problematic. Thus, he reconstructs Hegel's claim that the real is the rational simply to mean that there is an element of the present that is better than the past and that this can be developed by our thinking (Rorty 2000b, 305).

Rorty's naturalism and historicism do not provide a sufficient method but only a promising pathway for sociopolitical criticism. Its strength is the possibility of a critical and normative form of reflection that avoids positing a fundamental and underlying unity that reengenders the problem of foundations. This framing is important. Rorty and Connolly's models, and pragmatism and weak ontology more broadly, are two different pathways from Nietzsche and his critique of metaphysics. As we saw above, Connolly interprets Nietzsche ontologically. The death of God, on this reading, is not only a cultural event but a manifestation of an essential aspect of the human condition. This is the urge to truth, the urge to organize and determine human social life into established, predictable categories. This urge inevitably encounters not just limits, for Connolly, but active resistances, recalcitrances, and subversions. Thus, "human life is paradoxical at its core" (Connolly 1993b, 139). Connolly figures the limits of the human ability to organize the world as an active ontological feature of embodied social life.

Rorty interprets this differently. The novelty of Nietzsche's death of God is the notion that God's existence depended on human thought and practices. This is the ontological priority of the social; the claim that the *authority* (not the truth) of our various claims (e.g., normative or ontological) is always given socially. Importantly, the point of Rorty's social understanding of normativity is not that we cannot invest authority in nonhuman things. We often do and in many cases have good reasons to (e.g., avoiding environmental destruction).[20] The point is that it is something *we do*. Nothing has that authority in and of itself. The fact of the social origin of normative status requires a way of assessing, judging, and critically developing these normative statuses we ascribe, so that our practices are under our reflective guidance rather than subject to the authority we have, through the development of our practices, already invested somewhere (Brandom 2013, 24–29). Thus, the priority of the social requires mastery, but this mastery is only the intellectual acknowledgment of fallibility and incompleteness, that we always have and will continue to revise these standards, and of the contingency of these standards, that we do not in any sense have to be at our present set of standards but that they are the product of a series of decisions taken, possibilities pursued, and alternatives discarded. This provides the *possibility* of reflexivity.

What it does not require is ontological backing. In *Political Theory and Modernity*, Connolly confronts this question of the contrast between pragmatist and ontological figurations of the limits of knowledge.

> Why, then, bother to postulate resistance rather than, say, speaking with the pragmatist of the incompleteness and fallibility of knowledge? The Nietzschean idea that an element of resistance is encountered in every formation—in the various formations of the human through history into a coherent self, in every form of social life, in every organization or use of nature—is a coordinate of his treatment of being as will to power.
> (Connolly 1993b, 145–46)

This is a circular claim that Nietzsche ontologizes contingency because it is his ontology, repeating Connolly's logic of faith. Because faith, to some degree, inflects every method and approach to political theory, it is necessary to engage in the act of overt faith articulation. In fact, normative theorizing in general can only be a pronouncement of our ontological faiths.

The argument here is that this project does not offer a fruitful pathway for political theorizing. While it was initially framed as a response to the problem of justification and the need for critically reflexive forms of thinking that question their own standards, Connolly's ontological approach fails to provide the resources to achieve this. So while we might want to invest authority in an ontological account of the world, that account cannot give us the reasons to do so, and it cannot give us a framework for assessing and ascribing that normative status, because it places authority not in humanity, where it originates, but in ontological conditions it identifies as universal. This is why Lois McNay argues that Connolly's method, and other ontological approaches, results in a "socially weightless" form of political thinking. In focusing on the essence of politics as contingency and reifying that essence into the nature of the political, Connolly's model is so removed from the actual languages and practices of social life that its analytic and normative relevance becomes unclear (McNay 2014). This means that its critical and normative claims, while theoretically interesting, are practically meaningless.

CONCLUSION

This chapter has focused on the role of historicism in Rorty's thought and the type of political reflection it enables. It built on the analyses of language in chapter 2, which addressed Rorty's rationale for the linguistic turn and critique of continental political theory, and my discussion in chapter 3 of his naturalistic frame and its injunctions on political thinking. Historicism is the positive pathway away from these themes. As the epigraph to this chapter notes, when political thought is situated only within our social practices, and when an understanding of the world and humanity's relation to it is necessary to frame the account of social practices, and when language is understood to provide the only unproblematic access to the critical and normative resources already present within language, then narratives of the development of those languages and practices become critical political resources. Further, as Rorty hints in his work on Hegel and his justification of modernity, all of these themes together, in both how they limit and enable sociopolitical criticism, provide for the possibility of a critically reflexive method for political theory that remains both antifoundational and normative. This discussion has raised the question of what political theorizing is for and how best to achieve its ends. The point here has been that it can't simply be first-order normative pronouncements of faith but must engage in second-order critical clarification. This is properly the subject of the next two chapters and their overt turn to Rorty's methodology for sociopolitical thought.

III

RORTY AND CONTEMPORARY POLITICAL THEORY

Pragmatic Sociopolitical Criticism

5

PRAGMATIC POLITICAL THINKING AND CONTEMPORARY CRITICAL SOCIAL THEORY

> *This substitution of objectivity-as-intersubjectivity for objectivity-as-accurate-representation is the key pragmatic move, the one that lets pragmatists feel they can have moral seriousness without "realist" seriousness. For moral seriousness is a matter of taking other human beings seriously, and not taking anything else with equal seriousness. . . . Pragmatists think it will be better, not just because it will free philosophers from perpetual oscillation between skepticism and dogmatism, but because it will take away a few more excuses for fanaticism and intolerance.*
>
> —RICHARD RORTY, *TRUTH AND PROGRESS*

While the preceding chapters established the frame of Rorty's positive theoretical framework, vocabulary, and method, this chapter outlines the critical and normative political thinking that follows from those. The overriding aim is to clarify the connections to and insights for contemporary political theory. To this end, this chapter addresses Rorty's engagements with critical social theory. His continuing debates with both its major clusters of perspectives, Habermasian critical theory and what Rorty terms "radical thought," around the role and capacity of theory in critical and normative political thinking further reveal the shape of his implicit method and the consequences of its maxims.

This achieves three principal aims. First, it extends the reconstructive reading of Rorty's thought around his conception of philosophy as embedded sociopolitical criticism. Second, while previous chapters allowed us to meet certain criticisms, this analysis confronts the political criticisms of his thought that have dominated discussion since the 1990s and that are, at least partially, addressed by alternative dynamics implicit in much of his work and clear in his later philosophy as cultural politics. Third, it furthers the account of Rorty's relation to continental thought by addressing two of his most persistent interlocutors: Jürgen Habermas and Michel Foucault. Rorty's ambivalent relation to both focuses on the status and appropriate disposition of sociopolitical criticism, not on substantive political positions. Further, for him, they paradigmatically represent the two problematic pathways in contemporary political thinking he mediates.

These are not distinct projects. Rorty's framework for political thinking and his readings of critical social theory are interwoven. Further, neither is explicit. I impose some form on these dynamics to bring them into my reconstructive project. The emphasis is not on the accuracy of Rorty's readings of particular figures. While I am not assuming their inaccuracy, the question is their usefulness for contemporary methods in political theory. I argue that his critiques of Habermas and Foucault, of critical theory and radical thought, are analytically revealing and corrective of problems in ontological political theory.

For any reader of Rorty, the primacy given to critical social theory, and the methodological focus in general, will raise questions of where liberalism falls within this account. While I do address Rorty's controversial articulation of liberalism, it is *not* the main lens for developing his political relevance. There are several reasons for this. First, this invocation is not the only aspect of Rorty's political thinking. The reconstructive effort to convert theory into a form of situated sociopolitical criticism stands alongside this trend. Second, this dynamic has significant claims to be Rorty's more mature form of political thinking. On this reading, his attempt to provide a political language that fits within the metaconditions of inquiry engendered a turn first to a rereading of liberalism and, subsequently, a move to the overt language of social criticism and cultural politics. This chapter argues that this reading allows us to tease out more useful insights for political theorizing.

Nonetheless, Rorty's identification with liberalism is relevant. In fact, his initial turn to this literature, like his turn to critical social theory and his mature form of sociopolitical criticism, was prompted by the problem of justification and the philosophical antiauthoritarianism and pragmatic method discussed throughout the preceding chapters. It was a consequence of his social account of justification and his subsequent rethinking of the nature of political critique and normativity from within the antifoundational and antirelativist imperatives where grounded perspectives are precluded and a diversity of vocabularies are always present.

Thus, Rorty's liberalism and critical social theory are not distinct. Common theoretical concerns led him first to debates in political liberalism, where he tried to offer a substantive postmetaphysical account of liberalism structured around a public/private divide. While never repudiating this, he shifted his focus to the question of the methodological constraints and ethos within which political thinking should proceed. In critical social theory, Rorty found a substantial engagement with the problem that would dominate his political thought and model of social criticism: the problem of "taking others seriously," as the epigraph notes, of proceeding inclusively both theoretically and politically.

HOW TO READ RORTY POLITICALLY

Concerned with the status, nature, and proper role of theory, there is a question of how to read Rorty politically. This question is particularly important because of the vitriolic nature of the secondary literature. However, it is equally necessary in light of the emerging alternative readings of Rorty and the reconstructive strategy pursued here. This section will briefly examine this critical history and its myopias, chart some alternative possibilities, and justify its own Rortian reading strategy by focusing on the conversations around sociopolitical criticism.

As discussed in the introduction, in the 1990s Rorty's work was attacked from all the dominant theoretical frameworks, often with similar charges of political acquiescence and for lacking the conceptual resources for anything but a conservative apology of the status quo. Much of this criticism focused on his invocation of liberalism, his problematic claims for its sufficiency, and its central public-private divide. That is, it focused on his initial and overt concern with liberal theory rather than on his emerging conception of sociopolitical criticism. The latter did receive critical attention, but it was not the primary analytic focus of the literature.

This negative reaction was both curious and unsurprising. On the one hand, Rorty's liberalism is deeply uncontroversial. In form and substance, he largely agrees with the conclusions and prescriptions of Mill, Rawls, and Habermas, some of the most widely accepted liberal theorists (Rorty 1989, 63–67; 2006c, 43). The often-noted broadness of his account of liberalism and its lack of disagreement with either the central guiding principles or key institutions of mainstream liberal democracy seem to raise the question of why any liberal would disagree (Curtis 2015, 45).[1] While this would raise criticisms from communitarians and post-Marxists (the two other dominant strands of political theory at the time), his views on the theoretical and political role of the community and postmodern themes around contingency suggest he would be equally affable to these groups.

On the other hand, in approach Rorty undertook a very different type of project than most liberals. Rather than seeking guiding principles (or unveiling the deep contingency and violence of them, as critics often did), he attempted a fundamental shift in the vocabulary of liberal democracies. Rorty theorizes liberalism to answer two implicit questions. First, how can liberalism as a political culture and democracy as a political method be justified without reference to philosophical foundations, that is, pragmatically and historically and from within contingency? Second, what would such a postmetaphysical liberal culture and democratic vocabulary look like? This concern simultaneously to justify and redescribe liberalism in terms of postmetaphysical, pragmatic thought frames Rorty's liberalism (Rorty 1989, xiii–xiv).

Standard liberal objections focused on two fronts. On the one hand, some were deeply concerned by the extent of irony in his model. While Rorty did try to address this issue (Rorty 1989, 85–86), there was clear concern that his liberal culture would be disunited (Horton 2001; Conway 2001; Owen 2001). On the other hand, others were concerned with the ethnocentric *manner* in which Rorty justified liberalism. Contingency and historicity entail that any present is the chance development of a particular history in a particular community. To great ire, this was the purpose behind his "postmodern bourgeois liberalism" (Rorty 1991n, 198). This resulted in a deep concern with his purported lack of argumentative resources to justify liberalism to both internal and external nonliberals. Richard J. Bernstein voices this well. While a close colleague and one similarly influenced by Dewey's social democracy and by continental philosophy, he argued Rorty's liberalism was merely "inspirational"; its lack of theoretical resources, rejected by Rorty in his excising of metaphysics from politics, denied him the capacity to offer practical and institutional alternatives, leaving it "little more than an *apologia* for the status quo" (Bernstein 1987, 541).

Rorty's claims for the superiority of liberalism thus often seemed naïve and dangerous to liberals, who found them lacking rigor. Equally, to critics of liberalism his knee-jerk support of liberal positions seemed insufficiently thought out, conformist, and contradictory of his philosophical critiques of Enlightenment rationalism and opening of philosophical reflection to new sorts of critical and normative claims. For example, in one of his moments of greatest excess, Rorty claims: "Indeed, my hunch is that Western social and political thought may have had the last *conceptual* revolution it needs" (Rorty 1989, 63). While such statements beg (and raise) many questions, disproportionate critical focus has prevented reading Rorty in a more holistic manner. As I will argue, this is true of much of the criticism from critical social theory.

Equally problematic is the central structuring device of the liberal period of Rorty's politics: his much-maligned *public-private divide*. This division is the source of the central limitations of Rorty's model that this study addresses. While the general discussions around this division have softened in the last few decades of liberal theory, as a result of persistent critiques from feminists, poststructuralists, and multiculturalists (among others), it is still functionally assumed by many liberals.[2] As such, it was not a primary object of criticism for liberals[3] and thus will recur in our discussion of critical social theory. What is important here is its role in Rorty's thought, its problems, and the avenues open for melioration.

On his own telling, the public-private divide is one of the central insights of Rorty's politics. As he notes in his autobiographical essay "Trotsky and the Wild Orchids," the central project of his work was to push against the philosophical demand to hold "reality and justice in a single vision." This is the demand to bring together philosophical beauty with sociopolitical progress, to find an immutable theoretical foundation to political life (Rorty 1999f). The public-private divide is a way to prevent such a demand, which for Rorty inevitably falls into the foundationalist problematic. As a result, he frames it not as a division among social spaces, as is common to versions focused on negative liberty, but between two "normative spheres" (Curtis 2015, 100). This should immediately recall Rorty's theory of justification and the social origin of normative authority. Public and private denote different sorts of vocabularies, two ways of speaking with different structures of authority. One is public facing, a process of justifying to others. The other is private facing, about speaking to ourselves, and "has nothing to do with . . . relations to other people" (Rorty 1989, 142). Rorty's project in CIS and its surrounding political writings is to provide space for both.

The nature of this division is clarified by the notion of *purpose*. As discussed previously, for Rorty vocabularies, as sets of linguistic practices, enable and disable all sorts of conduct and relations. Metatheoretically, they can be assessed relative to the purposes they purport and actually enable. Further, there are no purposes, beyond the blandest and most abstracted claims, that all vocabularies share. In terms of the public-private divide, he claims: "The vocabulary of self-creation is necessarily private, unshared, unsuited to argument. The vocabulary of justice is necessarily public and shared, a medium for argumentative exchange" (Rorty 1989, xiv).

Rorty typologizes vocabularies into those conducive to shared, public purposes, which he equates with building solidarity among a democratic community, and those suitable to private purposes, which he glosses as self-creation, something democratic societies provide for but separate off. Why this particular binary? Given the diversity of human languages, it can't be meant to catch all aspects of linguistic practice (e.g., theoretical physics would seemingly fall into neither). The answer is historical and contingent to the particular histories of Western societies. For Rorty, there continues to be a strong theoretical demand, implicit and explicit, that we philosophically justify our form of political life, that a form of politics is only as good as its foundations. In fact, this is the basis of much of his criticism of liberal and communitarian political theories in the 1980s; they assume that a political system and theory is only as good as its theoretical grounding. For Rorty, this assumed a natural order to justification that places theory in a primary relation to political life (Festenstein 1997, 118; Rorty 1991t, 175, 190). This is an assumption repeated, in a different form, within contemporary ontological political theory.

For Rorty, philosophical founding is not an intervocabulary standard; nor is there good reason for it to be. So he typologizes to avoid reductively judging one type by the other's standards. The real basis of the distinction is a divide between vocabularies that are outward pointing, and thus seek agreement, and those that do not. His point is that not all vocabularies serve public, collective purposes of seeking agreement.[4] As we saw, at the metatheoretical level, this is the purpose of achieving solidarity rather than truth or justice, which for him requires external validation from an established moral or epistemic order, where solidarity places agency in human values and our ability to re-create them. This is of course a contestable rewriting of the political, but it is one Rorty believes more appropriate to the contemporary need to engage diverse frameworks. His claim, in contrast, is that private purposes of self-creation explicitly reject agreement and solidarity through a fundamental prioritization of autonomy, a disposition inappropriate to the public. Rorty's project is once again inclusive and pluralistic. His division makes space for more vocabularies and traditions by preventing us from assuming a single set of justificatory standards.

The public-private divide thus speaks to one of the most important aspects of this period of Rorty's thought: his attempt to think the relations between diverse justificatory frameworks within public democratic culture. This question flows from his theories of the social justification of normative authority and the diversity of purposes in linguistic practice. The weaknesses occur in some of the indeterminacies of this account and its primarily negative orientation. Here I will discuss these weaknesses and their possibilities for rectification. The larger argument is that Rorty overcomes them in his positive project of a democratic ethos for sociopolitical criticism.

It is important that Rorty's division is intended as a defense of pluralism. The problem at this phase is the frame and his consequent understanding of how to support it. Rorty situates his liberalism in *CIS* in an account of Isaiah Berlin's "Two Concepts of Liberty," where the latter argues that to understand freedom, we must acknowledge the necessary incompatibility of our diverse human ends (Berlin 1969). However, misreading Berlin like most, he takes this as a defense of negative liberty: the imperative to ensure the demarcation of a sphere for private self-creation, not ensuring its use (Rorty 1989, 63, 85; 1991t, 194). Chris Voparil has convincingly argued that Rorty misses an important point. Berlin's argument is not only a defense of negative freedom but a public defense of pluralism, with negative freedom as a means to achieve it. The result is that while Rorty takes up his repudiation of the single true solution to political life, he neglects the full implication of the pluralism of ends on which it is based. Voparil draws the line on the reason for protecting pluralism. In Berlin and Mill, there is a public reason to defend plurality as constitutive of democratic politics. In contrast, in a more negative vein, Rorty's division is based on a logic of mutual protection. The private must be protected from the shared standards of public life, which would prevent self-creation, and the public must be prevented from the corrosive and antisocial possibilities of the private (Voparil 2006, 119–23).

Nancy Fraser termed this the "partition position." For her, it is the product of an essential tension within Rorty's liberalism, revealed in his public-private divide, between pragmatic liberalism and romanticism. This observation is especially insightful given that he came to articulate these two thematic sources in his work in this manner in his final writings (Rorty 2007i). Further, it places pluralism only in the private in this period of Rorty's political thinking. The public is, as a result, homogenized to one liberal solidarity, and there remains no room "for genuinely radical discourses rooted in *oppositional* solidarities" (Fraser 1990, 316). Rorty's divisional logic leads him to place plurality only in the private realm of self-creation. Wrapped up with romantic themes as ideas of self-creation are, he frames the self-creative endeavor in a narrowly poetic cast. Why else would Harold Bloom's strong poet end up his cultural ideal and literary criticism come to stand in for sociopolitical thinking![5]

Beyond the political problems this engenders, it is in tension with Rorty's social picture of justification and resulting methodology. First, it ignores the ethic of inquiry that democratizes and pluralizes our normative orders (see chapter 1) and his critical relation to Heideggerian and continental ontology (see chapter 2). Second, it confuses two types of argument for why we might distinguish public from private. On the one hand, Rorty claims that "there is no way to bring self-creation together with justice *at the level of theory*" (Rorty 1989, xiv, my emphasis). This is the claim, which we have seen before, that theory has no algorithmic consequences, that philosophical positions have no *necessary* political consequences. However, Rorty extends this claim, suggesting that "we drop the demand for a theory which unifies the public and private, and are content to treat the demands of self-creation and of human solidarity as equally valid, yet forever incommensurable" (Rorty 1989, xv). On the one hand, the language of "content to treat" suggests a pragmatic claim to speak a certain way. On the other, this violates several core Rortian claims. Purposes can be in tension, but vocabularies cannot be incommensurable and thus untranslatable. This is an unsustainable ontological claim that would ignore the fact that socialization permeates every level of awareness.[6] It would treat public and private as distinctions of kind rather than merely of degree.

This clarifies one of the central problems of Rorty's thought: his tendency to go from a perceptive critique of the persistent forms foundationalism takes, such as what emerges in radical ontological political theory, to a circumscription of theory unnecessary in light of his own methodological claims.[7] Many of the discourses he criticizes are only problematic in terms of their self-understood status and the normative authorities they appeal to in making their validity claims. However, instead of attempting to install his pragmatic understanding of linguistic diversity and social justification at the public level, he chose to partition off any theory that violated his antifoundational and antirelativistic standards. In this manner, the public-private divide, in fact, offers an important insight into both the context of his reading of critical social theory and of the areas for improvement within his theory. In turn, this reading and later developments in his theory that nuance rather than elide these concerns with the theory-politics relation in a manner more consistent with his understanding of normative authority, create a space to overcome these limitations.

Before addressing this reading, there is one further question in this dissociation of Rorty and liberalism. This is his oft-noted support of John Rawls, mainly articulated in "The Priority of Democracy to Philosophy" (Rorty 1991t). Importantly, this allegiance is related to his public-private divide in its focus on the status of the theory-politics connection and the manner in which a pragmatist framework can provide for internormative exchange.

A nuanced wedge between Rorty and Rawls is necessary because their positions have been taken to be so similar as to make Rorty susceptible to all of Rawls's criticisms.[8] However, while Rorty generally celebrated Rawls's transition from *A Theory of Justice* (1971) to *Political Liberalism* (1993) as paradigmatic of the historicist justification of liberalism, they have very different understandings of these themes. While they both reject the traditional project of providing philosophical foundations for liberalism, Rawls's minimalism argues that a commitment to liberalism can be ethically undemanding, spanning the present diversity of comprehensive doctrines within Western liberal democracies. Rorty does want to eliminate metaphysical language from the tradition of liberalism, which is why he praises Rawls's approach as "thoroughly historicist and antiuniversalist," avoiding philosophical issues in the manner that Jefferson avoided religious ones (Rorty 1991t, 184). Further, he acclaims Rawls's method of engaging in normative construction through situated engagements of the discourse of constitutionalism. This reveals Rawls's pragmatism, which does not transcendentally deduce principles for, or philosophical foundations of, democratic institutions but is only "trying to systematize the principles and intuitions of American liberals" (Rorty 1991t, 189). This fits Rorty's image of normative construction and the task of political theory, where constructing principles is a backward-looking process of idealizing and formalizing relations and norms among our existing set and the practices they govern and inform. We do not provide foundations; we provide idealizations that render our various practices more coherent and consistent and thus informative for future practice (Rorty 1996a, 333). This is the political upshot of his notion of the theorist as "holding their time in thought."

In spite of this, Rorty is not committed to Rawls's problematic criterion of public reason and the accusation that it illegitimately excludes the diversity he and Rorty purport to respect through its criterion of reasonableness. Rorty is not arguing for an institutional norm that prevents all comprehensive doctrines from introducing their substantive claims into public discourse. Rather, he offers ethically thick virtues for pragmatic democratic life, ones that would not entail actually excluding views but would just culturally engender a certain way of reacting to the making of such claims.[9] While there are passages where Rorty seems to take on the minimalist mantle, he emphasizes that his "ethnocentric" liberalism is a substantive "form of life" turned outward toward deepening inclusive relations with others (Rorty 1991l, 203–4; 1989, 198). In fact, in one defense of minimalism, Rorty claims: "The procedural republic tries to instill in its citizens the virtues of compromise and tolerance, and to educate them out of other virtues (those of the warrior or the nun, for example)—the kind of virtues which might get in the way of compromise and tolerance" (Rorty 1998a, 118). Thus, his liberalism is not a neutral set of principles grounded in human commonality but a contingent and fragile form of ethical life particularly adept to the needs of diverse societies and the difficulties of democratic engagement. As such, Rorty had no intention of providing an ethically minimalist articulation of liberalism and so is neither committed to the core of political liberalism nor susceptible to its criticisms (Curtis 2015, 112–24).

This difference pushes Rorty away from political liberalism and toward the macropolitical project that initially elicited his interest there and that emerges in its strongest form in his later work on philosophy as cultural politics. This is the "utopian, inclusivist, human community," and cultural politics is the theoretical mode of engagement best suited to achieving it (Rorty 2000g, 1). This links Rorty's politics with the previous account of his social mode of justification and ethical approach to inquiry. His engagements with critical social theory around the shape of sociopolitical thinking are crucial to this project of inclusivist critical and normative exchange.

The virtues often framed in ideological (i.e., liberal) terms are construed here as theoretical and methodological, aimed at a form of political thinking adept to inclusion within pluralistic conditions.[10] This is supported by a later essay on Rawls where Rorty offers a sociological, metatheoretical account of justice that works against Rawls's antihistoricist intentions in favor of his constructivism. For Rorty, justice is better framed as the process of using existing thick identities, which are always built on exclusivist Sellarsian "we-intentions," as building blocks for thinner and larger inclusivist identities (i.e., cosmopolitan loyalties). To do so, he largely accepts Rawls's criterion of reasonableness in relation to the law of peoples (Rawls 1999, part 2) in spite of acknowledging it as a prioritization of

Western standards. For him, contingent, situated, and ethnocentric as it is, the strength of this standard *is not its universal validity but its universal reach*. As a standard open to continuing contestation and development, insofar as it is aimed at and allows for the inclusion of all willing voices, it offers a possibility for the nonauthoritarian pursuit of cosmopolitan commonality (Rorty 2007e, 47–50).[11] While such a project is broadly procedural, it does not predetermine the nature of consensus but simply the disposition to others in engagement, something developed further through the discussions of critical social theory.

This clarifies Rorty's invocation of Rawls. The framing of justice, under Rorty's reconstruction, is the end of an appeal to authority in its shift from metaphysical to political thinking. When justice, rather than an antecedent moral order, is the focus, we are free from nonhuman (nonsocial) authority. This is his "freedom as the recognition of contingency";[12] this is not freedom as the recognition of a philosophical condition but freedom as the recognition and practice of normative exchange and creation. This occurs when we engage in the linguistic exchange of reasons, without reference to external authorities (God, the real world, human nature) that would elevate one normative vision over another. Rorty invokes Rawls's exclusion of comprehensive doctrines to exclude conceptions of human nature or reality as bases for normative arguments (Rorty 1991t, 185). While he often assumes freedom in its negative sense, his more consistent usage refers to the freedom this exclusion engenders; freedom as social and historical autonomy (i.e., a linguistic community of exchange free from self-imposed and external forms of authority). This is freedom as the recognition that we are finite, linguistic, historical communities with no ultimate basis for our social practices and vocabularies. It is a constitutive freedom that recognizes that only we create and justify those languages and habits through recourse to discussions of the relations and practices those vocabularies enable and preclude.

While one could ask why Rorty invoked Rawls on these metatheoretical aims, they are the primary motivation of his political thinking. Rawls's proceduralism is fundamental for Rorty because it rejected the foundational project of building prescription on universal human nature in political theory. However, he moves away from Rawls in offering a thin set of virtues to condition our relation to the engagement of others and the building of internormative commonality, "a sort of intellectual analogue of civic virtue—tolerance, irony, and a willingness to let spheres of culture flourish without worrying too much about their 'common ground,' their unification, the 'intrinsic ideals' they suggest, or what picture of man they 'presuppose'" (Rorty 1991c, 171). Rorty offers virtues derived from his social model of normative authority, conforming to the negative injunctions and positive imperatives of his ethos of pluralistic engagement. For him, these constitute a productive disposition for engaging in public internormative engagement inclusively. This is the aim of his later philosophy as cultural politics. Contemporary metadebates about the role of political theory circle around these issues.

RORTY AND CONTEMPORARY SOCIOPOLITICAL CRITICISM: WITHOUT PROFUNDITY OR GRANDEUR

If his reconstruction of liberalism in the 1980s was his first attempt to offer an inclusive ethos for politics, Rorty's engagement with critical social theory was the increasingly dominant framing for this project. Through it, he questioned the status and appropriate way to pursue a project of human commonality within the context of pluralism. Importantly for this argument, it is also the context of his theorization of the shape of non-authoritarian theory as sociopolitical criticism, illustrating the fundamental link between the problems of justification, as it relates to both theoretical diversity in political thinking and social diversity in the world, and the political problem of pluralism. The constraints on inquiry and internormative engagement have a deep significance for the question of how to arrange democratic engagement in a diverse world. Thus, the primacy of the problems of justification and pluralism to Rorty's political thought are revealed in this attention to reconstructing the project of commonality among difference. How can this occur without assuming the superiority of one standard and thus without running afoul of these fallacies, and what form of theory can best engage in this critical-normative project?

In his engagement with critical social theory, Rorty inserted himself into a divisive literature in a manner unacceptable to every position.[13] On the aforementioned questions, he attempted to split the difference between Habermasian critical theory and what Rorty termed "radical thought." He does this by largely agreeing with the substantive political norms of critical theory, while placing them within a theoretical framework more akin to radical thought. This entails a different understanding of the status of inclusive norms, an understanding he hopes addresses the concerns of both groups. As a result of the wide metatheoretical nature of Rorty's approach, his engagements with critical social theory tend to touch on a variety of the most central and wide-ranging issues in these debates, including (but not limited to) modernity/postmodernity, the reason-imagination dichotomy, the relation of critical social theory to wider politics, the normative value of commonality and difference, and the comparative strengths of context-dependent versus context-independent approaches. Rorty's debates in critical social theory go to the wide issues of the proper role, ethos, and project for sociopolitical criticism in light of contemporary theoretical-political conditions.

AUTHORITY AND CONTEMPORARY SOCIAL THEORY

Critical social theory is united around the problematic of the relation between critique and normativity while being deeply divided over the forms of theorizing and type of politics needed. While a broad category, it can be given shape by distinguishing it from another major grouping in contemporary thinking, normative/analytical political theory. The latter separates the critical and the normative and does not concern itself with assessing existing social conditions. Rather, its analyses are "freestanding," guided only by "analytical rigor." In contrast, critical social theory "regards normative political reflection as being intrinsically connected to a critical social theory" (McNay 2008, 85). As a result, critical social theory, which includes traditions from hermeneutics and pragmatism to poststructuralism, Marxism, and Frankfurt critical theory, offers ethically oriented modes of reflection that critically assess existing sociopolitical arrangements in relation to some normative ideal. The latter at its widest point could be characterized as some explicit or assumed notion of "human flourishing" or idea of "the good society," which represents the normative goal of a context without the sociopolitical obstacle in question and is necessary to motivating the practice of criticism (Cooke 2005, 379–80; 2006, 1–8).

In spite of this broad agreement, there are deep disagreements within critical social theory. For example, Habermas, whose model dominates contemporary critical theory, rejects the continental tradition, which he alleges is based on normative vacuousness, a festishization of the world-disclosive functions of language and "others to reason," and a failure to address what David Owen has called the "guidance problem," the theoretical attempt to guide political practice through generating reasons that form the basis of norms of justice or legitimacy (Owen 2016, 174). Continental political thought's emphasis on "critique," the activity of critical reflection on our sociopolitical forms of reasoning and its treatment of our norms, practices, and institutions as critical objects rather than as constructions, illustrates a different relation both to reason, as a guiding category, and the critique-normativity nexus. Within debates in critical social theory, this continental focus has been a catalyzing issue.[14]

Much of the response from contemporary Anglo-American forms of continental thought falls within the weak-ontological frameworks I have reviewed. The strategic use of ontology as a background to critique and normative reconstruction is characterized by the attempt to balance the critical use of examining the ontological presuppositions of modern sociopolitical forms with the need to articulate the normative perspective from which they occur. Consequently, this literature has embraced a language of qualified affirmation, of examining both how "ontological figures structure ethical-political insight in specific ways" and how it informs normative reconstruction (White 2000, 16). This results in a balancing act between ontological normative guidance and the pullback of the mechanism of contestability, which attempts to find a middle ground between critical detachment and positive attachment (Connolly 1995a, chap. 1).

This places weak ontology and contemporary radical thought, which overlap significantly,[15] in tension with another fundamental dichotomy within critical social theory: the distinction between context-dependent and context-independent approaches. This is a distinction around the *status* of our normative intuitions, an important object for critical social theory, and the norms generated by critical theories. Is the validity of such intuitions confined to particular sociopolitical contexts and their systems of justification? Or can certain intuitions appeal to context-transcendent standards and desires common to humanity and its potentiality in a manner that gives them universal validity? Further, does critical social theory have a coherent project if the latter is not the case?

Rorty confronts both Habermas and critical theory, on the one hand, and radical thought, on the other, on these questions. As I argued in chapters 2 through 4, Connolly is committed to a theory of the ontological and theoretical *necessity* of contingency. Other sectors of weak ontology are also explicitly committed to this presupposition as a motivating basis of their critical theories. The self-declared consequences of this are extremely question begging. The claim of the necessity of contingency, as a result of the identification and priority of a distinct ontological realm of politics, is a "form of political ontology as *prima philosophia*" (Marchart 2007, 166). Beyond the previous theoretical concerns raised with such claims and their relation to the problems of justification and pluralism, this entails a context-independent critical and normative standard, raising all questions regarding radical thought, its critical-normative project, and its relations to other approaches in critical social theory.

Such questions are important because, at least on some interpretations, critical social theory is committed to antiauthoritarianism. For Maeve Cooke, the problem of justification raised by the linguistic turn and the notion of the subjectivity and partiality of ethical judgment require an antiauthoritarianism both epistemic and ethical. They must both reject any implicit or explicit assumptions of a neutral perspective outside history and particularity and recognize the contestability of the theorist's perspective (Cooke 2005, 382–83). There have been an intense series of debates about the appropriate response to the contemporary conditions of sociopolitical criticism. While there is a broad commitment to antiauthoritarianism across critical social theory, there is deep and sometimes ambiguous disagreement about these metatheoretical issues around the relation between normative and critical thinking and the compatibility of context-independent standards with authority.

UNIVERSALITY, RATIONALITY, AND SOCIAL CRITICISM

While Rorty's focus on these issues was persistent, there are important shifts during his career. As with his liberalism, he began his engagement with critical social theory through the lens of his public-private divide. Habermas is the archetypal "liberal without being an ironist." He asserts the superiority of liberal mechanisms and gestures toward their pragmatic justification. However, he ultimately slips back into foundationalism in his claims to universal validity and his commitment to Truth. Thus, Habermas represents the virtues and vices of public liberalism. Rorty generally approaches Habermas as a political ally whose differences are "merely philosophical," centering on questions of the role of rationality and the imagination in social criticism and the status of liberal norms. However, in terms of the aforementioned shift, Rorty and Habermas end up even closer than Rorty sought to portray, especially around questions of rationality.

The second, private, part of this reading is a critique of "radical thought."[16] In a series of discussions comparing Habermas and radical thought, Rorty selectively employed the latter's critique of postmodernity to identify in radical thought a similar demand for a philosophical validation of politics (Rorty 1998d, 1991c, 1991a). For him, radical thought misunderstands the consequences of its *theoretical* critiques of Enlightenment rationality as compromising the *political* ideals of modernity. It misunderstands normative authority and social change, and, like Habermas, continues to assume that philosophy represents the ultimate judgment for our social and political languages and practices.

In his earlier engagements of critical social theory, Rorty's public-private divide looms large not only within his actual readings but in the critical responses from these groups. For example, Thomas McCarthy identifies the divide, and its view of a "depoliticized theory and a depoliticized politics," as the central controversy between Rorty and critical theory: the question of the relation between philosophy and politics (McCarthy 1990, 358, 366). For him, this division is based on flattened notions of reason and truth that deprive them of any transcendence. The real issue is Rorty's rejection of the centerpiece of Habermasian critical theory, without which the latter loses all its critical and normative force: the context-independent nature of universal validity. For Habermas, the importance of the move from the philosophy of consciousness to the intersubjective paradigm is a continued (though modified) commitment to universality. Such universality does not come from a common human core but derives from the practices of everyday language use, which contain presuppositions that transcend those contexts. "Inasmuch as communicative agents reciprocally raise validity claims with their speech acts, they are relying on the potential of assailable grounds. Hence a moment of *unconditionality* is built into *factual* processes of mutual understanding" (Habermas 1987, 322). Rorty's rejection of universality leads McCarthy to deploy critical theory's most cherished critique: the charge of *performative contradiction*. Rorty both implicitly relies on the concept of truth and assumes the presence of truth in holding that social criticism can correct present problems. This tension between his ethnocentrism and linguistic revisionism means he calls for a form of social criticism he theoretically precludes. Further, Rorty fails to consider how central cultural presuppositions of universal validity are to Western political culture (McCarthy 1990, 646; 1996, 97–98).

These criticisms ignore the textual evidence I have provided in the preceding chapters. Rorty certainly has a strong sense of how normative reconstruction without universal validity can occur. Equal to this, he has a deep sense of the centrality of self-foundation to Western thought. In general, the early debate between Rorty and critical theory is characterized by a tendency to speak across each other. This superficiality resulted in a failure to understand the nature of Rorty's claims, or their status, and to identify substantive agreements. This is at the widest level a product of failing to read Rorty holistically through the lens of metatheoretical antiauthoritarianism. Habermas, in his only comment on Rorty from this period, lumps him in with the world-disclosive conception of language, ignoring the other aspects of his philosophy (Habermas 1987, 206–7).

In contrast, Rorty's strategy was to link himself to Habermas. In one sense, this is a deep understatement. Rorty and Habermas share very similar projects with respect to the history of Western thought and the project of modernity. In *The Philosophical Discourses of Modernity*, Habermas confronts the problem that modernity has created a unique justificatory problem: we can no longer justify in relation to our traditions. As a result, modernity must *"create its normativity out of itself"* (Habermas 1987, 7). This project mirrors Rorty's attempt at normativity without foundations and seems to resonate deeply with the reading of modernity we encountered in chapter 4 (self-assertion over self-foundation). Rorty and Habermas thus share the attempt to reconstruct modernity by more thoroughly carrying through the project of dedivinization and secularization, pushing our forms of justification away from tradition and inherited custom and toward the development of new practices and institutions (Rorty 1999d, 168; 1989, 45, 62).

Nuances in later engagements allow us to clarify the actual connections and differences between their frameworks, while illustrating how this overlap has increased. While they surely do differ on the issue of context-independent standards and universal validity to pursuing the reconstruction of modern normativity, the heart of this difference was not philosophical, about the nature of truth, but social, about the nature of justification. In fact, Rorty agrees with Habermas about the universal nature of truth (insofar as truth requires universality). He disagrees about the use of the concept and the connection between truth and the practice of justification. Habermas links contextual instances of justification to universal truth by claiming that justification is internally related to truth; it points to truth and hence also claims universal validity. Rorty dissociates truth from justification by claiming that the latter is a social claim to authority that does not necessarily refer to a neutral set of criteria for universal justification. In fact, for him, there is no sense to Habermas's claim that when we engage in justification, we implicitly take ourselves to be doing so universally (i.e., to all humans past, present, and future). Our various sets of linguistic practices are not *all* oriented in such a manner, and judging them according to that standard assumes it is a purpose they all share (Rorty 2000d, 57; 2000g, 7).

McCarthy fails to see that Rorty in no way argues that the goals of justifying ourselves to all humans (universal validity/context independence) are incoherent, irrelevant, or normatively undesirable. Rather, they are indeed significant parts of Western public culture. Further, the desire to justify (and thus engage in conversation) to ever more groups is the central normative value of Rorty's cosmopolitanism, one that links all periods of his politics in general and his engagements with critical social theory. At the beginning of his political theory, Rorty claimed that his model of cultural engagement requires "a culture which prides itself on constantly adding on more windows, constantly enlarging its sympathies. It is a form of life which is constantly extending pseudopods and adapting itself to what it encounters. Its sense of its own moral worth is founded on its tolerance of diversity" (Rorty 1991l, 204). In *PCP*, Rorty furthers this, arguing for a common cosmopolitan project that employs our thick regional moral identities to build larger thinner ones. To this end, he reconceptualizes the project of justice, sociologically, as the "offer of a new moral identity and thus a new and larger loyalty, a loyalty to a group formed by an unforced agreement between smaller groups" (Rorty 2007e, 52). On his recommendation, this project should be one of the central pieces of our public vocabularies.

However, the claim that there are neutral, transcultural, and transhistorical standards for validity within all language use that serve as the normative foundation of the cosmopolitan project is both unconvincing and authoritarian. Hence, while universal validity is an important project, one that can be achieved by intercultural engagement, it is not a philosophical necessity, the conditions for which are within language use. Conceiving it as a necessary condition repeats the problematic assumption of an appearance-reality divide in assuming that within all vocabularies there is a hidden core, a universal normative structure linking linguistic practice (Rorty 2000d, 57; 1990, 642). It is a bad way to describe what links all languages because the diversity of languages and their purposes/ways of making validity claims mean we cannot measure them against a single standard.[17]

Rorty's concern is with the *status* of the project of a cosmopolitan inclusive community. As with normativity in general, his emphasis is that this goal is *made rather than found*. There is no theoretical shortcut, no discovery of a common linguistic, rational, or human core that will provide a universal normative basis for why we should build such a community. There is only the hard work of building it from within our present identities by employing the normative resources of our present practices of justification in order to craft new, more inclusive, and wider linguistic practices and communities (which in the first instance will necessarily be thinner) through sustained intercultural engagement. This is not only less theoretically problematic, especially in relation to the problems of justification/pluralism, but it is more likely to succeed within the global context:

> If we Westerners could get rid of the notion of universal moral obligations created by membership in the species, and substitute the idea of building a community of trust between ourselves and others, we might be in a better position to persuade non-Westerners of the advantages of joining in that community.... One practical reason is that getting rid

of rationalistic rhetoric would permit the West to approach the non-West in the role of someone with an instructive story to tell, rather than in the role of someone purporting to be making better use of a universal human capacity.

(Rorty 2007e, 55)

As discussed below in relation to radical thought, inclusiveness, tolerance, and humility are the chief virtues of Rorty's theoretical framework for democratic engagement among difference.

However, this is not merely a difference of *status*. To be a difference worth mentioning for Rorty, it must *make* a difference. As contingent and fragile, this project must be pursued in a different manner than Habermas's discourse ethics; it is a different practice for sociopolitical criticism. In opposition to critical theory's context-independent standards, Rorty situates the cosmopolitanism ideal within existing communities and their norms. When there is no external vindication for our social practices (including those of truth telling and reason giving), there is no standpoint outside our practices for adjudication. As a result, pragmatists place normative authority within communities. In a sense, this is a politicization of normativity: all forms of authority become questions about the values and borders of a community. Matthew Festenstein is right to note that Rorty's practice-based view of normativity is wrapped up with the concepts of community, identity, norms, and purpose. He argues that against the usual charges of acquiescence and a lack of resources for social criticism, Rorty carves out an alternative form of situated sociopolitical criticism focused on the established norms and identity of a community (and the purposes its vocabularies and practices currently pursue). These can only be made from the standards "of some other particular community, and this latter 'community' may be real or imagined" (Festenstein 2003, 6). Rorty's focus on the community is not mere acquiescence. Communities are not homogenous, coherent wholes. Some aspects of their vocabularies and practices will contradict others. Further, in modern societies, we rarely have one exclusive identity. Such conditions provide for the possibility of critique (Rorty 2007e, 45).[18] However, like Cooke, criticism requires the normative ideal of a community, with which we can identify, that does not contain these objectionable elements. This "good society" does not have to exist currently and in most cases will be the imagined future of a present society. In its most extreme forms, it may require that we reject our present society in favor of some other. Thus, social criticism for Rorty is an interpretive and constructive activity in which critics assert what a community, and its traditions, is and should be.

This clarification contradicts the usual view of Rorty and his relation to consensus. He often invoked the democratic goal of seeking agreement and the consensual language of deliberative democracy. His use of "we liberals" is only the most flagrant example. Consequently, quite a bit of criticism derives from either his invocation of this standard (Laclau 1996b, chap. 7; Mouffe 1996b; 2000, 66–67) or his superficial understanding of it, more common to liberals. This resulted in the view that Rorty ignores normative disagreement within communities (Newey 2000, 199). The superficiality of this reading is its failure to link his politics to his metatheoretical antirepresentationalism. The notion of "merely appealing" to tradition or settled norms (i.e., consensus) depends on representing the truth of a tradition/community. That is, it would depend upon a logic of uncovering that Rorty rejects as reinstating an appearance-reality divide. No community is fixed, and he is painfully aware of their contested nature, especially regarding contemporary American society (Rorty 1999f, 1998b). His conception of criticism deploys consensus only insofar as every specific criticism, in invoking a norm, also implicitly or explicitly appeals to a community that has strong (not total) *present* agreement on that norm. Thus, contra Habermas's ideal of universal validity, for Rorty "the only ideal presupposed by discourse is that of being able to justify your beliefs to a competent audience" (Rorty 2000g, 9). This may not even involve a currently existing community. Even if it does, Rorty's fallibilism requires something to be taken as relatively stable. "In any particular inquiry, one or more of these [norms, identities, goals/purposes/projects] must be taken to be fixed, for inquiry or deliberation to get off the ground: as fallibilism insists, we cannot throw everything into question all at once" (Festenstein 2003, 8). Thus, when Rorty invokes consensus, it is an appeal to a temporary current agreement that he interpretively summarizes not to provide foundations but in order to encourage his particular alternative norm or practice (Bacon 2006, 867–69).

This speaks to the importance of identity in Rorty's approach to social criticism. His use of the "we liberals" label is predicated on the claim that communities and norms are linked via identities. "One's moral identity is determined by the group or groups with which one identifies—the group or groups to which one cannot be disloyal and still like oneself" (Rorty 2007e, 45).[19] Identities are contrastive and exclusive; they preclude taking up at least some other identities, and these relations are temporary and open to contestation. This is the real sense of his attempt in *CIS* to flag up the links between vocabulary and identity. The figure of the liberal ironist, "the person who has doubts about his own final vocabulary, his own moral identity," and the recoding of liberalism to refer to those who think "cruelty is the worst thing we do" are a reconstruction of current identities, via a change in linguistic practices, in a more reflexive and adaptable manner (Rorty 1989, xv, 186). It is the attempt to make them more ready to engage in social criticism.

Consequently, Rorty describes the cosmopolitan project, within his revised conception of justice, as *creating larger loyalties*. For him, we should not describe moral conflicts between our duties to immediate communities and more removed ones as conflicts between the demands of loyalty and justice, as is often the case in analytical political theory. These are better framed sociologically as conflicts between different levels of loyalty (e.g., family against tribe, regional against national). Smaller, more intimate groups *tend* to have thicker and more detailed narratives and norms (e.g., family histories). Larger group loyalties tend to have thinner, more abstract stories and norms (e.g., universal human rights). This means there is no absolute priority or authority between them. Rather, they are partially conflicting and overlapping "concrete webs of social practices" that, because of the contingent history of the international realm, largely summarize "the customs of contemporary liberal societies" (Rorty 2007e, 47).

This understanding largely removes any transcendental force from the cosmopolitan project. For Rorty, Habermas and his "discourse ethics" seek to identify in-built tendencies toward human convergence within the conditions of language. In contrast, as no inherent tendencies exist in his social model of justification, Rorty turns "to the question of how to persuade people to broaden the size of the audience they take to be competent, to increase the size of the relevant community of justification. The latter project is not only relevant to democratic politics, it pretty much is democratic politics" (Rorty 2000g, 9). This raises the question of how larger and thinner communities of identification are created. How does novelty at all enter into this social conception of social criticism? It is this question of the means of transformative social criticism where we find Rorty on shifting ground. While he is generally convincing when identifying problems for Habermasian social criticism and in indicating the social constraints of any actual form, his alternative has found few supporters. However, it is also where recent scholarship and his later work aid us.

The Rorty-Habermas debate over means centers on a disagreement about rationality and social criticism. In the first instance, they actually agree. Rorty generally endorses the reconstruction of rationality in intersubjective terms as "the internalization of social norms, rather than as a built-in component of the human self" and supports the claim that this is more appropriate to modern democratic politics (Rorty 1989, 62). Where he deviates is in Habermas's attempt to maintain "the critical force of reason." This concerns putting the sociality of reason together with a universal theory of the better argument (Rorty 2007c, 83). This debate circled around a set of overlapping distinctions between the strategic versus nonstrategic use of language, true versus false consensus, and rational argument versus ideology. For Rorty, these are the product of Habermas's commitment to a conception of justification pointed at truth (Rorty 2000d, 58).

In the first instance, these distinctions are central not only to understanding the Rorty-Habermas relationship but also the division between radical thought and critical theory more broadly. For the latter, the problem with radical thought's antifoundationalism, epitomized in something like Lyotard's "incredulity toward metanarratives," is its inability to offer one normative standard for the explanation of the corruption of all other standards. Without such a standard, whether it is lost through totalizing critique or Rorty's context dependence, any distinction between masked and unmasked, corrupt or not, ideology or theory cannot be maintained with any critical force (Rorty 1991c, 164–65). For Habermas, this results in ceding the idea of "critical reason," the notion of the rational developments of modernity, and any reliance upon the "force of the better argument." It also compromises our ability to identify and expose (i.e., unmask) distortions of sociopolitical reality that serve the interests of some and not others and thereby distinguish normatively justified consensus (i.e., truth) and false consensus (Rorty 1998d, 319–22; 2000d, 58–59; 2000g, 22; 1991c, 164–67).

Traditionally, critical theory has understood Rorty as flatly rejecting both these distinctions and the conception of reason undergirding them (McCarthy 1996, 95; Habermas 2000, 50–52). As Habermas argues, sociologizing justification and naturalizing reason change our norms to the point that "the standards themselves would no longer have any possibility of self-correction and would thus for their part forfeit the status of norms capable of being justified" (Habermas 2000, 51). This is a version of his argument that theories that eschew his communicative form of reason, in rejecting the previous subject-centered conception, besides engaging in a performative contradiction, end up normatively vacuous. They have no means of asserting better except through conservative appeals to the status quo.

This argument gets Rorty on rationality wrong on two fronts. First, it is unclear that Rorty is incapable of the sorts of distinctions Habermas wants, arguing for the better, or identifying "ideological" descriptions. Taking the latter first, Rorty has expressed skepticism about the category of *ideologiekritik*, his criticisms tending to repeat concerns about the authoritarianism of the appearance-reality divide. However, this does not mean he cannot accommodate distortion within his theory. "We do this by starting with such obvious differences as that between Socratic dialogue and hypnotic suggestion. We then try to firm up the distinction by dealing with messier cases: brainwashing, media hype, and what Marxists call 'false consciousness'" (Rorty 1989, 48). This bottom-up experimentalist way of thinking about ideology is thoroughly context dependent. Rorty rejects Habermas's claim that the intersubjective exchange of reasons is premised on the assumption that participants allow their positions only to be determined by the "force of the better argument." This claim presumes a natural order of reasons that our arguments must approximate. This ignores that reasons are always reasons for a particular group, constrained by the conditions of a situated context. In intercultural (or multicultural) contexts, "criteria for betterness of argument are relative to the range of arguments at our disposal, just as our criterion for betterness of tool are relative to the technology at our disposal. To describe someone as having come to a certain conclusion for bad reasons is simply to say that the reasons which convinced her would not convince us" (Rorty 2000d, 59).

For Rorty, distortion is measured contextually. Nonetheless, it distinguishes between a *reason* for a belief, that is, a claim that can be given in the flow of conversation, and a *cause* of belief, an external input that shifts belief. Rorty argues that in the contemporary democratic context, we have discovered a series of ways that belief can be negatively, externally shifted.

> "Free discussion" here does not mean "free from ideology," but simply the sort which goes on when the press, the judiciary, the elections, and the universities are free, social mobility is frequent and rapid, literacy is universal, higher education is common, and peace and wealth have made possible the leisure necessary to listen to lots of different people and think about what they say . . . but I do not think there is much to be said about what counts as "undistorted" except "the sort you get when you have democratic political institutions and the conditions for making these institutions function."
>
> (Rorty 1989, 84)

A theory of communicative rationality was necessary to none of these identifications (Bacon 2006, 873–74). Rather, each was a contextual process of understanding what, in the type of societies we have, can negatively affect democratic deliberation. This is why Rorty can both support Habermas's ideal speech situation as containing a series of conditions for democratic dialogue (e.g., openness, inclusivity, equal right to participation, etc.) while rejecting the idea that it is the regulative, metatheoretical ideal of all discourse. This can be summed up with his slightly glib claim that "if we take care of political freedom, truth and goodness will take care of themselves" (Rorty 1989, 84; 2006c). Essentially, Rorty is stating that the conditions we associate with democratic life are the current (yet revisable) prerequisites of a form of dialogical interaction that can, unencumbered, engage in the form of critical and normative transformation called for by critical social theory.

This does not mean there is no linguistic, theoretical work to do. However, it is not the universalizing project of finding democratic virtues that just happen to be contained within transhistorical structures. Rather, it is the situated task of finding new ways to speak about problems as yet realized, the creation and dissemination of new, needful reasons to be given in dialogue. I will provide an example of Rorty's own thoughts on this further along. Presently we must address the second way in which critical theory's charge of normative meaninglessness fails. While he did surely reject traditionalist conceptions of reason as a transhistorical faculty at the core of the human self and Habermasian notions of rationality as a transhistorical validity structure within all language use, Rorty did not reject rationality as such. Rather, there is strong textual evidence to suggest that while initially and often polemically skeptical,[20] Rorty reconstructed rationality in his later work as a series of virtues, or pragmatic ethos, given to reflexive learning. The important difference is that his model does not assume the convergence of human normative structures. Whereas Habermas sees undistorted communication as naturally convergent and this as evidence of rationality, for Rorty normative convergence of some sorts is desirable but ultimately the outcome of prolonged intercultural dialogue and luck (Rorty 1989, 67; 2000g, 17).

Rorty's reconstruction of rationality occurs within a series of considerations of the relation between reason and imagination. Interestingly, this potentiality in his work has been flagged up recently within critical theory. Both Maeve Cooke and Nicolas Kompridis have provided similarly motivated and balanced critical readings of Rorty and social criticism, centered on rationality and imaginative social transformation. Cooke flags up the strengths of Rorty's project to offer a new self-image for humanity without claims to universal validity and how this fits with the aims of antiauthoritarian critical theory (Cooke 2006, 28–29). Similarly, Kompridis highlights his attempt to frame sociopolitical criticism as a conflict between new and old linguistic practices, arguing that this opens the door for noncriterial forms of reason that avoid overly inflating or deflating it (Kompridis 2000, 279). Interestingly, both also soften Habermasian reason, moderating claims to universality (Cooke 2005, 393; Kompridis 2006).

In spite of this support, both Cooke and Kompridis highlight Rorty's hesitancy to reconstruct reason fully. While different in their accounts, they identify this hesitancy with a tendency to place practices of reasoning within established vocabularies and posit imagination as the fundamental mechanism for moving between them. The philosophical backdrop and some criticisms of Rorty's tendency to cloister vocabularies in this way were raised in chapters 1 through 4. In this chapter, it engenders Rorty's public-private divide, where public vocabularies work within shared intersubjective standards and private are those linguistic acts (exercises in autonomy) outside of shared contexts. Cooke argues that the dichotomies of public reason and private imagination, absolute universality or radical contextualism, and weak and strong reason, as wrapped up with each other, lead to a series of tensions in Rorty's social criticism and a hesitancy to carry through that reconstruction of reason, leaving criticism solely immanent, circular, and without reflexive relations for normative transformation. For Kompridis, these same tensions prevent Rorty from seeing that "an enlarged, 'non-criterial' interpretation of reason may allow us not only to connect reason to transformation, but to show that reason is continuous with transformation" (Kompridis 2000, 277).

Cooke and Kompridis both highlight strong textual resources to play up these tensions. Without contradicting their accounts, my strategy goes further not by flagging up Rorty's real and limiting hesitancy but by highlighting the moments of daring and pushing them further. I claim that they both miss the significance of Rorty's later shifts. Importantly, these changes in his conception of rationality and its relation to the imagination also do important corrective work in relation to his public-private divide in a manner that speaks directly to their reformulations of critical theory.

PRAGMATIC RATIONALITY: AVOIDING GRANDEUR AND PROFUNDITY

In later writings, Rorty moved closer to an intersubjective, dialogical, and educative understanding of reason. This conception pushed against previous tendencies to place reason in opposition to imagination in public and private respectively, occurring within an antiauthoritarian conception of metatheoretical practice oriented against two tendencies to reinstitute authority in contemporary sociopolitical criticism. He dubbed these tendencies *grandeur* and *profundity*. Many claims to authority within contemporary theory operate on metaphors that posit either a higher-order standard (whether epistemic, ontological, or metaphysical) that conditions all elements therein or an essential core, deep down, that determines the nature of humanity, social life, and the political structures governing them. Grandeur and profundity represent these respectively; they are also the most developed forms of his criticism of metaphors of height and depth as authoritarian forms of social justification that claim their authority from supposed contact with external conditioning structures. Rorty links them in a common claim that runs the gambit from "the universalist metaphor of ascent to an overarching framework that transcends the merely human to the romantic metaphor of descent to the very bottom of the human soul" (Rorty 2007c, 80). Grandeur and profundity are his succinct typologization of two manners of pursuing external authority and the approach of positing levels (epistemic, ontological, or metaphysical) to establish it.

Rorty originally tried to moderate these tendencies in a public-private split that would contain romantic depth, an epidemic among romantic poets and philosophers, and control public grandeur (i.e., claims to universalist reason) through public pragmatic ironism. The result, as Koopman argues, is his "high modernist contrast between reason and imagination" in *CIS*, which suggested the complete distinction between these two dispositions and projects (Koopman 2007, 49). However, this division was in tension with the imaginative social project of cosmopolitan inclusivism that, as I argue here, sits at the center of Rorty's politics:

> In my utopia, human solidarity would be seen not as a fact to be recognized by clearing away "prejudice" or burrowing down to previously hidden depths but, rather, as a goal to be achieved. It is to be achieved not by inquiry but by imagination, the imaginative ability to see strange people as fellow sufferers. Solidarity is not discovered by reflection but created.
>
> (Rorty 1989, xvi)

Despite continued invocations to replace metaphors of height with width and his continued invocation of a public-private divide, the romantic framing of this moral project only increased (Rorty 1999d, 82). Importantly, this romantic framing of the cosmopolitan project, which assumes a strict reason-imagination divide, never disappears and is clearly present in writings contemporaneous to his analysis of grandeur and profundity (Rorty 2007i, 2007j).

However, in that analysis, Rorty distances his pragmatism and romanticism in a way designed to split the difference between the latter and universalism. In characteristic Rortian fashion, he identifies these two themes as the dominant impulses of the last few centuries of European thought. The trouble with both "universalist metaphors of grandeur" and "romantic metaphors of depth" is a shared suggestion that sociopolitical proposals "can gain strength by being tied in with something that is not, in Russell's words, merely of here and now—something like the intrinsic nature of reality or the uttermost depths of the human soul" (Rorty 2007c, 86). Both simply assume that normative authority descends or ascends to humanity from extrahuman powers. However, instead of dividing reason, as intersubjective consensus, from imagination (his usual strategy), Rorty emphasizes reciprocal balance, suggesting mutual roles:

> Pragmatists who find this . . . banality sufficient think that no inspired poet or prophet should argue for the utility of his ideas from their putative source in some other to reason. Nor should any defender of the status quo argue from the fact of intersubjective agreement to the universality and necessity of the belief about which consensus has been reached. But one can still value intersubjective agreement after one has given up both the jigsaw-puzzle view of things and the idea that we possess a faculty called "reason" that is somehow attuned to the intrinsic nature of reality. One can still value novelty and imaginative power even after one has given up the romantic idea that the imagination is so attuned.
>
> (Rorty 2007c, 87)

We need to balance the need for consensus and novelty, rationality and imagination. Rorty's views here require changing his view that the imagination is the only mechanism of normative transformation. This view, which is tied to his Kuhnian account of paradigm change that sees frameworks as distinct and paradigm changes as comprehensive and sudden, provides a way to reread later comments on rationality that give much more shape to his reconstructive, reflexive vision.

This reconstruction is not systematic. Nonetheless, it speaks to the preceding concerns over the project of inclusive cosmopolitanism and the role of reason and imagination in normative change there and in sociopolitical criticism generally. Thus, it is particularly oriented to the conditions of pluralism and the social nature of justification. Rorty's reconstructed view of rationality flows from his moral ideal of solidarity, discussed in chapter 1. That conception of inquiry understood it as aimed at solidarity, seeking as much intersubjective agreement as possible, to subject our claims to linguistic challenge reflexively. In later writings, he similarly turns reason outward, as an intersubjective *disposition*.

Rorty first raised this possibility in a dialogue on pluralism with critical theory. In "The Ambiguity of 'Rationality,'" he filled out his recurring claim that "rationality is just a preference for persuasion over force: you are rational insofar as you would rather argue than fight, rather use words than blows" (Rorty 2001c, 42–43). This rather glib formulation obscures the real project. Rorty distinguishes the epistemic and moral notions of rationality. The former is the cognitive attempt to surmount appearance, get to rationality, and achieve universal validity. The latter is an ethical relation between speaking parties. Thus, what Rorty is interested in is rationality as a certain disposition to conversation partners.

More importantly, it is a disposition toward *new* conversation partners that establishes reflexive equality between them. "The only notion of rationality we need, at least in moral and social philosophy, is that of a situation in which people do not say 'your own current interests dictate that you agree to our proposal,' but rather 'your own central beliefs, the ones which are central to your own moral identity, suggest that you should agree to our proposal'" (Rorty 2007e, 52). In contrast to Rawlsian minimalism, Rorty appeals to thick engagements with the moral identities of others to build new and thinner loyalties. This is an important shift because of the role of narrative in his thought. For Rorty, political imagination (i.e., normative transformation) is linked to the narrative self-understandings of communities (Rorty 1991c, 184). The upshot of this is a conception of rationality not as the threat of incorrectness but as the offer of inclusion in a new moral identity:

> Being rational and acquiring a larger loyalty are two descriptions of the same activity. This is because any unforced agreement between individuals and groups about what to do creates a form of community, and will, with luck, be the initial stage in expanding the circles of those whom each party to the agreement had previously taken to be "people like ourselves."
>
> (Rorty 2007e, 53)

This is rationality not as authority but as a willingness to engage in intersubjective construction, in deeper, reflexive relations with others. Rationality is a "continuum of degrees of overlap" (Rorty 2007e, 53). Finally, situated within our moral identities, intercultural engagements, and real linguistic practices, this is an embedded view of rationality as a form of educative and imaginative normative transformation that splits the difference between grandeur and profundity (Rorty 2007c, 78; 1991c, 175).

Chris Voparil has convincingly argued that this is the center of Rorty's thought, linking his social conception of justification to his democratic ethics. The moral and political significance of fallibilism is the need to shift the normative source of our sociopolitical criticism from objectivity to solidarity. To "take other human beings seriously" in democratic inquiry is to situate normative justification in sociopolitical contexts in a framework that prioritizes our ethical relations to other groups in the game of giving and asking for reasons (Voparil 2014b, 83). We saw in chapter 1 how this ethicized inquiry. In sociopolitical criticism, it prioritizes the normative project of recognizing others. For Voparil, this illustrates the noncriterial view of rationality implicit in Rorty's ethos. When rationality is the responsibility to larger and more diverse communities, it concerns the ability to take on new vocabularies, to grow reflexively.[21] This emphasizes that rational justification always involves the ethical choice of which terms and vocabularies to employ and whom to speak to. Further it broadens our communities of justification (Voparil 2014b, 91–93). Importantly, this outward focused nature provides important resources for critique, something Rorty is consistently accused of lacking. By necessitating the engagement of different normative frameworks, he requires us to view our own language and practices from the lens of another. Thus, this conception, contra Cooke and Kompridis, is clearly a context-dependent but critical approach to rationality and sociopolitical criticism. Presently, we must shift to radical thought.

RADICAL THOUGHT: AUTONOMY AND TOTAL REVOLUTION

This critical reconstruction provides several insights into Rorty's reading of radical thought. It, like Habermas and critical theory, is a fundamental critical interlocutor that consistently appears in Rorty's writings. The main difference is that while Habermas was a liberal without being an ironist, Foucault, the paradigmatic radical thinker (also the one Rorty is most ambivalent about), was an "ironist without being a liberal." While not a problem as such, this characterization illuminates the general weakness of radical thought: its failure to engage normatively with the present and its persistent attempt to escape, rather than transform, the practices of contemporary sociopolitical life. This reading has been quite contentious, and not for unfounded reasons. However, it is also not without insight; in fact, while one might argue that Rorty's readings of radical thought attack a straw man, that straw man does appear within some contemporary versions of ontological political theory, especially in terms of their readings of Foucault and the attempt to ontologize his critical genealogical method.

Initially, Rorty also read radical thought through his public-private divide as a paradigmatic private vocabulary. For him, its refusal to speak within the public vocabularies of Western liberal democratic life and its tendency to experimental linguistic innovation were perfect examples of the quest for *autonomy*, for freedom from the constraints of collective, social life. In this, radical thinkers are *ironists* through and through. However, they also have an implicit demand for their autonomy to exceed themselves, for their autonomy to rupture the given stasis. For Rorty, this changes the status of their linguistic interventions: "They want the sublime and ineffable, not just the beautiful and novel—something incommensurable with the past, not simply the past recaptured through rearrangement and redescription. They want not just the effable and relative beauty of rearrangement but the ineffable and absolute sublimity of the Wholly Other; they want Total Revolution" (Rorty 1989, 101). This demand relapses into foundationalism in a similar though opposed direction to Habermas. Where the latter seeks the authority of universal validity, radical thought seeks it through a total eclipse of the present social universe.

Rorty's critique of radical thought is dependent on Bernard Yack's *The Longing for Total Revolution*. This somewhat forgotten work of historical critique identifies a covert demand for radical social transformation within one trajectory of European philosophy. This is the desire to exceed the social, to overcome an oppressive set of conditions often understood as inherent to modernity and our current sociopolitical universe. These conditions somehow pervert our humanity, which is affected by some malignant form of degradation.[22] Through readings of Rousseau, Hegel, Nietzsche, and Marx, Yack identifies two assumptions within this longing. First, that modern humanity is somehow lacking and unable to achieve itself. Second, that the cause of this limitation is fundamental to modern social conditions. The longing for total revolution develops out of an analysis of these obstacles within modernity. Importantly, this tradition identifies these obstacles in some fundamental subpolitical sphere (e.g., ontological) of social interaction that shapes humanity and society. Removing this condition requires a total revolution, "which transforms the whole of human character by attacking the fundamental sub-political roots of social interaction" (Yack 1986, 9). For Yack, these two assumptions are problematic. The first assumes it is possible not to be fully human, that there is a human essence we can fail to achieve. The second assumes the underlying unity of the social: that when institutions do not provide for the full realization of our humanity, they dehumanize us. It demands that institutions match our humanity, which we should realize within social conditions. For Yack, this is the ultimate source of the longing and its self-contradiction. By defining human freedom in terms of the individual's ability to resist external conditioning, it invalidates the entire project of realizing our humanity in the social world. With such a definition of freedom, *all* social conditions will be dehumanizing. The error of this thinking is in positing the unity of the social in a single spirit that characterizes social interaction. This necessitates a revolution from the present. Once it is understood that these analyses are constructions, that they are particular vocabularies, there is no obstacle to social change. Thus, "partial reform and, indeed, partial revolution regain meaning and importance" (Yack 1986, 369). Rather than rejecting it, Rorty's initial solution was to privatize this revolutionary impulse.

This was a problematic solution. However, this does not minimize the real concern that this sort of theorizing misses the nature of social justification and assumes freedom as outside the social. Interestingly, in his privatization of romantic novelty Rorty seems to repeat this assumption. However, he rectified this in a later response to Robert Brandom, where he accepted the latter's "friendly amendment" that *every* use of a vocabulary, every application of a concept in making a claim, *both* is answerable to norms implicit in communal practice—its public dimension, apart from which it cannot mean anything (though it can cause something)—*and* transforms those norms by its novelty—its private dimension apart from which it does not formulate a belief, plan, or purpose worth expressing.

(Brandom 2000b, 179)

To use a vocabulary is to change it normatively. Beyond clarifying how language is different from other tools, this weakens the public-private divide to merely a heuristic distinction of emphasis in language. They are no longer distinct vocabularies (with agreement and creativity as their respective aims) but different dimensions of *every* vocabulary. Consequently, every act of critical normative transformation must both speak to and against existing norms. There is no way either to reinforce or transcend the present fully. On this understanding, language use gains a unique significance in political critique not merely because of its capacity to reinforce but because "subjecting oneself to constraint by the norms implicit in a vocabulary at the same time confers unparalleled positive freedom—that is, freedom *to* do things one could not only not do before, but could not even *want* to do" (Rorty 2000e, 187–89; Brandom 2000b, 178).

In contrast, Rorty diagnoses in radical thinking the assumption of an inner human core free from socialization. However, in his view of normativity, the conditions of possibility of social action are set by (and continually changing because of) semantic world disclosure. Thus, there is no access to, and thus no such thing as, an essential humanity to be emancipated. There is no set of social relations more distorted or obscured than another. Because norms transform in use and justification occurs within the claims of shared sets of linguistic practices,

> every form of social life is likely, sooner or later, to freeze over into something the more imaginative and restless spirits of the time will see as "repressive" and "distorting." What is wrong with these forms of life is not that they are "ideological," but just that they have been used to justify the systematic administration of pain and humiliation.
>
> (Rorty 1998d, 320)

Radical thought ignores that all discourse is coerced insofar as it is limited to the terms and practices of a given community at a given moment. It rebels against this condition and, through a series of concepts similar to Habermas's ideal speech situation and domination-free discourse (e.g., ideology, dehumanization, emancipation etc.), assumes the possibility of a nonsocialized human essence (Rorty 1991c, 167). As soon as emancipation is dissociated from a particular instance of oppression, as soon as it is given a general sense, it relies upon some understanding of the nature of an unoppressed human. For Rorty, the fallacy is the desire to speak anew, outside of the public vocabulary of the present, outside of terms meaningful to it. This attempts to transform norms without reference to current linguistic practices. It takes a system of meaning only significant for it and subsumes the contemporary world underneath its conceptualization. This is a powerful desire, one that promises affiliation with a higher power (profundity), disclosure of a hidden reality, and the possibility of total autonomy. The desire for autonomy (freedom from all social limitations) becomes a claim to external (nonhuman) authority. This produces the notion that theoretical critique without a concrete normative alternative of some form necessarily has political consequences. For Rorty, this assumption stands behind a diverse range (both politically and philosophically) of continental thinkers who repeat the quest to map the political from the theoretical.

Where radical thought and Habermas seek emancipation, Rorty emphasizes *tolerance* as the virtue of his pragmatic social criticism. In contrast to penetrating appearances down into reality, tolerance has a reflexive capacity to engage in normative transformation internally, by using old terms in new ways, and externally, by adding new claims through linguistic innovation and normative comparison with the practices of others real and imagined. It does not oppose incommensurable frameworks of analysis (e.g., by trying to get outside the present of politics). Its logic creates the possibility of reflexive development both between different frameworks in the moment and between different periods. For Rorty, in this disposition, his method is inclusive of new experiences, situations, norms, and practices. It "constantly changes to accommodate the lessons learned from new experiences . . . [This is a] program of constant experimental reformulation" (Rorty 1991a, 219). This is tolerance not as a political virtue (though Rorty would not exclude this) but as a theoretical disposition to normative change.

Rather than relying on the aforementioned distinctions between ideology-nonideology, humanizing-dehumanizing, and emancipation-oppression, it emphasizes a single political distinction between force and persuasion. For Rorty, this distinction is nontheoretical. It is merely the difference between communication that is systematically distorted and communication that embraces the cosmopolitan brand of inclusive, reflexive engagement among an evolving set of empirical conditions of freedom.[23] This allows no other authorities than the public. In Rorty's antiauthoritarian pragmatism, social criticism becomes empirical and contextual. It offers concrete alternative norms, practices, and relations, not the analytical exposure of a hidden dynamic (Rorty 1989, 84). For Rorty, offering an alternative social world *is* social criticism. It is a piecemeal process of suggesting concrete alternatives, gradually confronting established habits and institutions with new dynamics and situations. Thus, the imperative is a kind of Rawlsian reflective equilibrium

> between our old moral principles (the generalities we invoke to justify old institutions) and our reactions to new developments, our sense of the desirability of various recently disclosed possibilities. . . . So there would be continual social criticism, but no radical social theory, if "radical" means appealing to something beyond inherited principles and reactions to new developments.
>
> (Rorty 1998d, 322)

Criticism is gradualist. It explicitly works from the present universe of meaning (vocabulary) and engages in normative transformation from that base. We cannot doubt everything at once and so cannot attempt to shift that base radically. The problem with radical thought is that it does not speak to the present. "Adopting a new vocabulary only makes sense if you can move back and forth, dialectically, between the old and the new vocabulary" (Rorty 1991a, 221). Radical thought tries to shift too much too fast. It wants to change the language of the present dramatically, to revaluate the existing conditions with no positive use of the present understanding. In this, for Rorty, it ignores the social basis of the political. It ignores how social practices actually change.

Rorty's strategy here is familiar. He does not argue against the substantive analyses of radical thought. Rather, he sociologically circumvents those critiques. Like his treatment of analytic thought, he treats radical thinkers as a social group who share a cultural demand for total revolution. He circumvents many of their specific ideas by viewing them primarily as a linguistic community with a certain relation to normative transformation. This is his unique strength. He does not pick theoretical holes but illustrates that their whole approach to normative transformation misunderstands the way groups actually change their linguistic and social practices. Further, he *does not* preclude the productive use of their particular analyses. Instead, Rorty critiques the self-described status and implied normative consequences of radical thought on its own terms. As a set of vocabularies with particular critiques, these frameworks can be included within Rorty's cultural politics. They are only inappropriate as meta-accounts of theoretical practice.

FOUCAULT, NORMATIVITY, AND ONTOLOGY

The significance of this general critique is not yet clear. To those suspicious of radical thought, it may be an insightful diagnosis. To those who are not, it is a straw man only true of the weakest elements of the literature. To flesh this out, here I address Rorty's relationship with Michel Foucault. Foucault and Rorty share much.[24] This analysis focuses on their divergences, which center on the status of social criticism and the nature of normative change.[25] While Rorty and Foucault do speak across each other in terms of the broad aims of their theoretical frameworks, which in the end are not subject to rational arbitration, Rorty's criticism does expose a problematic trend in contemporary ontological readings of Foucault.

As with all his continental sources, Rorty's writings on Foucault are structured by a division between the good and bad, the living and the dead, a good critique of foundationalism and a bad alternative. Where the pattern diverges is in a tension around the source of Foucault's weaknesses. This tension is problematic because it involves a series of criticisms and claims that he never systematized. This is despite that Foucault is fundamentally important for him. Rorty's engagements with

Foucault are mainly from the 1980s and early 1990s, during the heyday of American postmodernism, which centered on readings of Foucault and Derrida. Because of Rorty's own antifoundationalism and his temporary positive use of the label of postmodernism, he was taken as "an attractive, homegrown version of American deconstructionism" (Voparil 2006, 125). However, while he was surely much more well disposed to Foucault's work than most American philosophers, Rorty was always deeply hesitant about the political implications and lack of social hope in Foucault's work (Rorty 1982d, 1982e). This led to the usual narrative, which Rorty himself propagates, that their relationship was characterized by philosophical similarities and political differences.

This assumption dominated even the most insightful analyses of Rorty's accounts of Foucault,[26] obscuring the real theoretical disagreement at the heart of his political criticisms. As ever, these focus on the question of the *status* of Foucault's accounts of power and the self. In his only article dedicated solely to Foucault, Rorty begins:

> Does Foucault give us a sketch of, or a basis for, something like a new theory of knowledge? Or should we perhaps conceive of his "archaeology" as a sort of successor discipline to the theory of knowledge, or perhaps a supplement to it? . . . My own hunch is that, whatever he may want, he has set things up so that he cannot *have* such a theory.
>
> (Rorty 1986a, 41)

Rorty thinks Foucault is fundamentally ambivalent on this question. When the latter attempts a theory "of how objects constitute themselves in discourse," for Rorty all this can mean is pointing to the social context of linguistic practice and the fact that the way we speak about things both can create new things and change our relations to them. However, he knows that Foucault would reject this deflationary view of the notion of "constitution" because along with his emphasis on his accounts as histories, Foucault appeals to the aim of a "general theory of discontinuity" (Rorty 1986a, 43).[27] The source of this tension is Foucault's Nietzscheanism, his attempt not merely to write a history but to undermine all claims to historical progress and introduce "chance, discontinuity, and materiality" into the roots of thought. For Rorty, this attitude precludes the possibility of theory building. It results in Foucault's accounts being mere redescriptions of past events, hints about how *not* to do history; they are solely negative maxims against problematic assumptions.

The problem emerges only when Foucault goes beyond these constraints to offer two types of normative conclusions. Wojciech Małecki has usefully typologized Rorty's readings on this point. On the one hand, there is the more limited claim that Foucault's analyses are regional; they are focused on exposing the manner in which bourgeois democracies are an inherently oppressive form of social life along a specific series of dimensions. On the other hand, there is the larger claim, a general critique, that all structures of social life are inherently oppressive and that contemporary democracies are just one form of this oppression. Unsurprisingly, Rorty has problems with both claims, to different degrees. In terms of the former, smaller claim, the problem is mostly normative and only a bit theoretical. For him, Foucault's lack of a theory means that his histories have no way to distinguish between good and bad forms of power. This leads to a certain "dryness produced by a lack of identification with any social context, and communication" (Rorty 1991c, 173). Rorty glossed this as the lack of any "we" in Foucault's writings. In this instance, the problem is that Foucault draws such drastic normative conclusions from his descriptions. These conclusions focus on the oppressive nature of the liberal-democratic power relations creating the aforementioned tension. "Foucault's work is pervaded by a crippling ambiguity between 'power' as a pejorative term and as a neutral, descriptive term," between power as simply the possibilities afforded through social life and power as an alien and repressive force. Consequently, he used a "pejorative term like 'discourse of power' to describe the result of *any* social compromise, any political balancing act" (Rorty 1991i, 195–96).

The problem with the larger claim is mostly theoretical and only a bit normative. Rorty acknowledges that Foucault explicitly rejects the Rousseauian conception of all social life as oppressive of a true human nature (Rorty 1981, 3). However, he also participates in a common continental assumption that the philosophical justification of a social order equals its justification. Without a human core as a stable reference point, Foucault thus assumes that *no* justification is possible. For Rorty, this lands him squarely in the Platonic tradition of assuming "society as

Man writ large" (Rorty 1991i, 197). While Foucault repudiates that claim, he remains stuck in its system of possibilities. In contrast, Rorty takes the metatheoretical view that a theoretical justification of a given sociopolitical order is not the sufficient condition of whether, normatively, we should continue to have that order. As we saw above, all social structures enable and disable certain ways of speaking and being. Further, all can be reinforced or undermined. This means that a necessary part of any justification of social change must be an indication of the normative order that corrects the perceived wrong. Thus, reviewing *Herculine Barbin*, Rorty claims,

> Foucault urges that the structures of power have made life pretty well impossible for somebody whose sexual organs are intermediate. So they have: but that seems like saying that they have made life almost impossible for somebody who is deaf and blind. One is not going to feel the force of either remark unless one can think up some structures which wouldn't have this effect.
>
> (Rorty 1981)

Rorty argues that pointing out the constraints of a system, that is, critical disclosure through a genealogy of the present, has no critical thrust unless you can offer a system in which that constraint would be absent. Further, rejecting this project has disastrous consequences in Foucault. As a result of maintaining his normative repudiation of the "normalizing power" of all social institutions, he turns to the desire for sublimity as an implicit normative base for his critiques. This results in all the problematic assumptions and goals and ultimately the inappropriate role of sublimity as a normative base for public political thought. In this manner, for Rorty, Foucault's work is confused about the status of his analyses, the normative conclusions he can draw, and the nature of social life.

Most sensitive critics of Rorty are aware that he slips indistinguishably between critiques of Foucault and of his American interpreters. This is for the simple reason that Foucault was so influential on what Rorty called "the Cultural Left" that they soon became conflated (Rorty 1998b). However, while my purpose is not to make an argument about Foucault, this perspective ignores Rorty identifying a problematic *tendency* that, while perhaps not totally undermining Foucault, at least raises important questions. This is borne out by Foucault's response to Rorty's "we-accusation":

> But it is also necessary to determine what "posing a problem" to politics really means. R. Rorty points out that in these analyses I do not appeal to any "we"—to any of those "we's" whose consensus, whose values, whose traditions constitute the framework for a thought and define the conditions in which it can be validated. But the problem is, precisely, to decide if it is actually suitable to place oneself within a "we" in order to assert the principles one recognizes and the values one accepts; or if it is not, rather, necessary to make the future formation of a "we" possible, by elaborating the question.
>
> (Rabinow 1984, 385)

Foucault attempts to hold the question and the problem prior to the "we." He attempts to articulate his diagnosis without any normative reference, to problematize without assuming any system of norms. On the face of it, this is a noble ambition to open up normative reconstruction in a way unbounded by any assumptions.

However, for Rorty and pragmatism, it is deeply problematic. Any first-year student of politics has the inextricability of the normative and the descriptive drilled into them. There is no description without normative assumptions and prioritizations. Equally, there is no normative claim without a descriptive account of the context assumed. We simply do not have this type of *autonomy* from the present. The questions this raises are: What is Foucault valuing here? What is his standard? Contemporary debates on Foucault have struggled with these questions around the status of Foucault's work (as theory or analytic tools) and the presence of normativity. The substance of Rorty's challenge is that, in taking this approach yet also making normative claims, Foucault misunderstands the relation between critique and normativity and the way norms actually change in sociopolitical life. For our purposes, what is interesting is the contemporary trend in continental ontological political thought to ontologize Foucault's work as a way of filling out its normative base.

William Connolly provides some of the canonical work. In two articles in particular, he attempted to provide an ontological account of Foucault and a consequent ethical sensibility for contemporary democratic politics (Connolly 1985, 1993a). The latter will be left to chapter 6. The former illustrates the consequences of Foucault's normative reluctance. For Connolly, Foucault's genealogies "support an ontological thesis with political implications" (Connolly 1985, 365). Specifically, Foucault claims that discourse, linguistic practice with its inevitable norms and exclusions, is "a violence we do to things" (Connolly 1985, 368). Thus, his accounts of various social practices are all intended to incite the experience of discord and to pull us out of those established frames of meaning and practice. The motivation behind this, for Connolly, is theoretical; "every such settlement [social order] involves imposition even while it may enable life to be in particular ways." As every set of norms is imposed, one can legitimately assume that every set of norms must be resisted.

> Freedom, in this perspective, is not reducible to the freedom of subjects; it is at least partly *the release of that which does not fit into the moulds of subjectivity and normalization*. This is what Foucault means when he says that "the soul is the prison of the body" and when he supports the "insurrection of subjugated knowledges" that speak, although imperfectly and indirectly, to that which is subjugated by normalization.
>
> (Connolly 1985, 371)

It is unsurprising that Connolly's criticism of Rorty then focuses on how he ignores the violence in socialization and the deep consequences of contingency (Connolly 1990, 105, 107). In contrast, for Rorty, this is the illegitimate jump. The contingency of norms and practices is not, *in and of itself*, a reason to oppose them. Further, it is not even a reason to assume its existence. To value as free that which does not fit into current normalization is to assume the exact human core Rorty accuses Foucault of holding. This is why we can't critique in isolation. Contingent as both our social orders and criticisms thereof are, the practice of critique requires situating those accounts within the present and a normative alternative. Otherness as an abstracted generalization is not sufficient. And for Connolly, this seems exactly how alterity in some form can provide a normative base for criticism. Critiques only in other vocabularies, without an alternative referent, are theoretically interesting but, unless they can speak to present languages, practically meaningless.

While there is a deep question about whether this is true of Foucault, Rorty's basic claim is only that the tension that elicits this reading is present. If not, Foucault could not claim that "the freeing of difference requires thought... that accepts divergence; affirmative thought whose instrument is disjunction; thought of the multiple—of the nomadic and dispersed multiplicity that is not limited or confined by the constraints of similarity" (Foucault 1980, 185–86). While Habermas and critical theory overvalue agreement and convergence, and although pointing this out is a key value of theorists like Foucault, passages like this indicate a continental overvaluation of divergence and discontinuity. *Neither exhausts the political.* For Rorty, the only way to split this difference is through a healthy nominalism that understands every description, even ontologies, as under a description (Rorty 1986a).

PRAGMATIC INCLUSIVITY BETWEEN UNIVERSALIZING AGREEMENT AND REIFYING DIFFERENCE

My preceding analysis situated Rorty between the approaches of critical theory and radical thought. His criticisms, accurate or not, clarify his own method of social criticism. Once again a later comment proves useful. For him, "it is as pointless to prize diversity as to prize unity" (Rorty 2000g, 17–18). Neither is appropriate as a metastandard for sociopolitical critique or reconstruction. Rorty is as anticonvergence, as against the assumption that some universalism ensures the conjunction of human ethical life, as he is antiotherness, in the sense of seeing diversity, fracturing, or rupture as a metajustification of the priority of critique. As I will discuss in chapter 6, these two characterizations of the political, the context transcendence of critical theory prizing the pursuit of agreement and the critical ruptures of radical thought prizing disagreement, both essentialize sociopolitical life and fail to understand its diversity.

They both fall into essentialism because they continue to ask the ontological question "what are we?" while ignoring the social nature of justification that entails that we are, incidentally and fortuitously, self-shaping beings:

> We are much less inclined to pose the ontological question "What are we?" because we have come to see that the main lesson of both history

and anthropology is our extraordinary malleability. We are coming to think of ourselves as the flexible, protean, self-shaping animal rather than as the rational animal or the cruel animal.

(Rorty 1998f, 69–70)

As self-shaping, only humans authorize the transformation of our norms through the expansion of our linguistic relations. However, what this means may be opaque, and so this chapter closes with an examination of an article that has recently received attention in Rorty scholarship, as it is in tension with Rorty's earlier problems and illustrates the critical and normative potential of his theory to address the problem of our relations with others (Voparil 2011b; Kompridis 2000; Cooke 2006, chap. 2; Koopman 2007).

In "Feminism and Pragmatism," Rorty confronts one of the central problems of contemporary difference for radical thought, "the problem of speaking for others." This is the problem, powerfully identified in the works of postcolonial theorists like Spivak and Said, of Western discourses of emancipation identifying the conditions of oppression and emancipation for silenced others. As Voparil argues, this is Rorty's most sophisticated treatment of politics, and it breaks with many of his earlier weaknesses. Drawing on feminist scholarship, he outlines a pragmatic process of normative transformation that can be employed by marginalized groups. The motivation here is clear: "If you find yourself a slave, do not accept your masters' descriptions of the real; do not work within the boundaries of their moral universe. Instead, try to invent a reality of your own by selecting aspects of the world that lend themselves to the support of your judgment of the worthwhile life" (Rorty 1998c, 216). This steps away from the conception of social change in *CIS*, where the metaphoric and often private redescription of poets is the sole agency of normative change. Instead, he understands "linguistic innovation in collective, political terms, thus paving the way for broad-scale social movements to struggle against dominant constellations of meaning" (Voparil 2011b, 122). However, linguistic innovation in this argument is not solely a process of imagination but of the transformation of practice and the identity of a group. On this understanding, "To get such [semantic] authority you have to hear your own statements as part of a shared practice. Otherwise you yourself will never know whether they are more than ravings, never know whether you are a heroine or a maniac" (Rorty 1998c, 223). Such projects require community as the forum for the intersubjective development of distinct norms and vocabularies. That is, such groups need the opportunity to speak and act differently.

Only once this communal work is done can this kind of shared inclusive engagement even be attempted with the hope of reciprocity and reflexive development. Rorty's insight is to consider seriously the problem of "a voice saying something never heard before" (Voparil 2011b, 123). For him, the task of sociopolitical criticism in this context can only be one of an underlaborer removing the social obstacles and normative barriers "for those who have visions of new communities" (Rorty 1998c, 215). Philosophy as cultural politics, in this instance, reveals its true antiauthoritarian and democratic colors.

CONCLUSION

The deepest contribution of Rorty's sociopolitical criticism is to illustrate how a social, pragmatic, and nominalist conception of justification and normative transformation changes our goals and approaches. For him, the nature of normative authority requires community and identity in a way both radical thought and critical theory ignore—Habermas is wrong that justification in modernity needs universal validity, and radical thought is wrong in its disproportionate focus on critique and refusal of normative alternatives. The point is not that you can't create coherent vocabularies that place normative authority solely in either universal validity structures or engaged critiques but that such vocabularies are only taken up and employed through some group speaking a language, however loose, and finding their criteria convincing based on a complex set of relations between the new vocabulary and the old. This requires both a narrative of what has gone wrong and an image of its correction. The fortunes of languages are not, at the metalevel, determined by how true or critical they are. These are particular criteria humans, within languages, have argued as important and necessary in a variety of ways. Imposing any one of them at the metalevel risks taking one regional standard as the ultimate arbiter for the diverse things humans might want languages to do in present and future societies. Thus, at that metalevel, the best (not true!) way so far conceived to speak of linguistic diversity is as diverse sets of practices attempting to do diverse things. This is best only because it seemingly allows us to speak about languages in a way that does not place any above the others according to an absolute standard while allowing us to engage in the normative transformation of current linguistic practices and stand aside when new ways of speaking and new claims to being silenced are made.

Thus, Rorty's point is metatheoretical. Both critical theory and radical thought are built on faulty pictures of the theorist and the role of theory in sociopolitical life. From the heights of universalist grandeur to the depths of romantic difference, he instead calls for a return to the situated nature of sociopolitical life and its primary context in the vocabularies and practices of individuals and groups. These alone are where authority resides.

6

HOW PRAGMATISM CONSTRAINS AND ENABLES POLITICAL THINKING

Perhaps the writer who has done the most in the latter half of the twentieth century to disseminate and defend a broad cultural reorientation towards practice and away from theory and structure is Richard Rorty. He has encouraged us to dispense with the great metaphysical and postmetaphysical theories associated with different forms of human organisation and value spheres, as well as with post-modern critiques, and to abandon the attempts to discover large-scale underlying processes or conditions of possibility that determine our thought and action behind our backs. Look instead on forms of human organisation, from science to politics, as intersubjective activities of exchanging reasons and redescriptions among the players involved. . . . In short, activity is prior to theory.

—JAMES TULLY, PUBLIC PHILOSOPHY IN A NEW KEY

Political theory is a reflective discipline. Beyond offering theories of democratic institutions, justifications of political orders, or critiques of oppressive norms, a significant part of its practice is a reflexive self-criticism of how it proceeds in these tasks. It is at this level that Rorty is significant. He does not provide grounded norms for democratic institutions or uncover the oppressions of contemporary society. For Rorty, theoretical claims about the nature of knowledge, reality, or human individuals and social life have no *necessary* political consequences. This does not mean they cannot have large particular consequences on our vocabularies and practices in situated contexts but that theories are not algorithms for political life.[1] At most, they provide frames to proceed within, not blueprints to follow. Rorty's significance is found in the metatheoretical frame for political thought within his work, clarified by his later emphases and the set of methodological maxims I will describe in what follows.

This approach overcomes one of the central difficulties of reading Rorty as a political theorist: that of reconciling his negative antitheoretical positions with his positive pronouncements. On the one hand, it is impossible to dissociate absolutely his affirmations from the theoretical fallacies he attacks. Rorty often seems equally obsessed with the ideas he rejects. Overly dependent on a negative logic, his alternatives can seem thin and underdeveloped (Bernstein 1986, 47; Voparil 2006, 124). I have followed alternative approaches that meet this weakness by explicating a deeper positive project in Rorty, one both theoretical and political. However, this study goes further by not only focusing on positive values but also on a series of methodological maxims for metatheoretical political thinking in Rorty's work that has great potential to address two of the central problems in contemporary political theory: the problems of (theoretical) justification and (political) pluralism. Further, I have also sought to connect these back to this set of values, offering a robust Rortian framework.

In this chapter I finish elaborating this Rortian frame. After systematizing his dispersed account of philosophy as cultural politics and the methodological maxims introduced in the preceding chapters, I engage two questions in contemporary political theory, divided between theoretical and political debates. The first is dispersed and largely inchoate, concerning the methodological question of how diverse political theories should relate to one another, especially when working across traditional barriers, and still go about making critical and normative claims. The argument is that Rorty's metatheoretical "vocabulary of vocabularies" and his understanding of normativity among difference are invaluable for intermethodological engagements across recalcitrant divisions in contemporary political theory. The second, implicitly connected, concerns democratic politics among difference, confronting contemporary agonistic theories of democracy. This section argues that pragmatism has much to contribute to agonism, specifically around one of the central divisions in that literature: the use of ontology in critical and normative theorizing. Such an engagement is presently lacking and is fertile ground for considering the problem of pluralistic democratic engagement.

RORTY, CULTURAL POLITICS, AND METHODOLOGICAL MAXIMS

The concept of cultural politics has underwritten much of the current critical reconstruction. However, its exact sense requires systematic articulation to clarify Rorty's positive approach for political theory. I now turn to this task, arguing that cultural politics is Rorty's framework for inclusive public dialogue. It is a public vocabulary for understanding the engagement of plural languages in a horizontal, nonhierarchical manner. It should be understood to occur firmly within the pluralistic ethos discussed in chapter 5, which argued that Rorty's politics is defined not by a problematic justification of liberalism or a regressive public-private divide but an ethos for contemporary pluralistic democracy that takes inclusion beyond the quasi-foundational approaches of liberal proceduralism, Habermasian universal validity, and the reification of difference in radical ontological thought. It splits the difference between these approaches by shirking universalism and neutrality while retaining the cosmopolitan inclusive community within a different narrative and disposition toward others. Cultural politics is the conception of public dialogue within this ethos. It is the positive metatheoretical (metapolitical) vocabulary that enables intercultural critical and normative exchange (i.e., pluralistic sociopolitical criticism).

CULTURAL POLITICS AS PUBLIC DIALOGUE: RORTY AND THE POLITICAL

Many recent pragmatist readings of Rorty have focused on teasing out the centrality of cultural politics and the cultural-critical task to Rorty's thought. This study has further developed this. The present task is not further explication but to illustrate how the vocabulary of cultural politics is a metatheoretical frame oriented to enabling egalitarian engagement across linguistic-normative difference. Importantly, this vocabulary embodies all the methodological maxims and virtues discussed so far.

Rorty's later turn to cultural politics examines the specifically political questions around the issues of authority, normativity, community, identity, and critique that pervade his work. It represents the last articulation of his conception of theoretical political practice as a form of sociopolitical criticism. There are two important dimensions. First, this entails a turn within philosophy and theoretical disciplines to social and political issues, that is, a politicization of theory. While this might be surprising for some, this analysis has argued that his reconstruction of theoretical practice, and its strategy for avoiding the problems of epistemology and ontology, has been a reorientation to the project of "enlarging human freedom" (Rorty 1982a, 69). Cultural politics sharpens this emphasis by *widening the notion of political* to everything open to sociopolitical contestation, to include all discourses about "humanity's ongoing conversation about what to do with itself" (Rorty 2007h, ix). As discussed in chapter 1, in *PMN* Rorty offers conversation as a description of inquiry that flattens out the hierarchical distinction between it and other forms of linguistic practice. It does this through a sociological perspective that emphasizes the hermeneutic and holistic nature of language use, as conversation. In *PCP*, Rorty repeats this, casting political thought within a wider history of cultural-political conversation. "Interventions in cultural politics have sometimes taken the form of proposals for new roles that men and women might play.... Sometimes they have been sketches of an ideal community.... Sometimes they have been suggestions about how to reconcile seemingly incompatible outlooks" (Rorty 2007h, ix–x). The category of cultural politics expands the scope of the political to the type of wide linguistic interventions characteristic of theoretical disciplines: new uses of words, new vocabularies enabling new criticisms and normative claims, and suggestions of what words to begin or stop using. Thus, central to this "turn to the political" is a conception of theory as a linguistic practice within a society about what vocabularies, terms, and topics to employ.

Second, cultural politics politicizes theory in its imperative to engage with the present sociopolitical-cultural matrix as the site of critical-normative political reconstruction. "The progress of this conversation has engendered new social practices, and changes in the vocabularies deployed in moral and political deliberation. To suggest further novelties is to intervene in cultural politics" (Rorty 2007h, ix). Cultural politics is the sociopolitical process of justification where we contest the current context in terms of which languages, categories, and objects to employ. The point of this conception of theoretical contestation in political theorizing is that political exchange cannot, *at the metalevel*, be understood as rational argument or ontological questioning. Rather, it can only be understood as *interpretive intervention* into existing sociopolitical discourses. Such interventions modify our languages and resulting conceptions of who we are, what we are doing, and what is important, altering both our purposes and the practices we use to achieve them (Rorty 2007k, ix–x). This means that self-consciously engaging other languages in imaginative redescription is the only way to avoid the unproductive methodological impasses of the past. We play off one approach against another, finding particular points of contact and divergence in order to offer new vocabularies that might build on aspects of each.

The intended scope of application of this conception is important. When and where is this understanding operative? Does it govern all political discussions? The answer is clearly *no*. Rorty was not sanguine about the capacities of most citizens to be sufficiently ironic to balance detachment and belief. However, it is also for him a necessary metadisposition in the context of two crucial conditions, deeply embedded in contemporary conditions of politics: contingency and pluralism. Rorty conceives of both as broadly limiting our capacities for justification, especially at the level of intervocabulary exchange. It is exactly here where Rorty's frame, his vocabulary of cultural politics, is operative. Intervocabulary exchange is a context of normative disagreement, where there is an absence of any significant shared interpretive horizon. This does not entail no overlap, as there must, and usually will be, enough for conversation to take place. This means that cultural politics is about situations of abnormal politics, moments when established standards are up for grabs (Voparil 2013, 111). Some would argue that such conditions pervade contemporary "late-modern" politics and its tendencies to speed and complexity (Connolly 1995b). Rorty's cultural politics does not depend on such an account. For him, the metaconditions of intervocabulary engagement do frame our particular contributions. So while we may, at any given moment, be firmly linguistically acting within one reasonably stable set of linguistic practices, there is always the possibility of new speakers (of different vocabularies) and using new words (or old words in new ways). Thus, cultural politics does provide a kind of reflexive metalimit on normative stability. Current trends toward pluralism and complexity in contemporary politics only reinforce his point.

As discussed in chapter 4, Rorty fundamentally questioned the approach of universality, of "putting everything into a single, widely available, familiar context" (Rorty 1991f, 95). Such an approach ignores the source and nature of normativity. As a result, he argued that the Western tradition of political thought needs a new way to speak about such engagement. The foundationalist project of the Enlightenment, which Rorty pried apart from self-assertion, was built on different purposes, designed to shore up secular authority in the face of deep conflict with traditional authority (Rorty 2007c, 73). However, we do not face such a conflict today. Rather, we face how Western rationalism has, over the course of that previous conflict, in fact excluded most other vocabularies, where the "appeal to rational acceptability by the standards of the existing community" is precisely what sets the boundaries to be questioned (Rorty 1998c, 214).

Rorty's conception of *logical spaces* is crucial to how the discourse of cultural politics addresses this problem. For him, every sociopolitical context contains a plurality of "logical spaces"; some are shared by a variety of perspectives, others overlap to some extent, and some find very little resonance with others. All have their sets of criteria, or "canonical designators," for argument and normativity. That is, they have their own rules for what types of claims can be made and what types of purposes are assumed. At this level, these spaces, even the relatively inclusive language of liberal-democratic politics, are closed off from one another and only have the criteria that results from their respective cultural politics to employ in any engagements. This changes as vocabularies can be shared by groups who may themselves have subvocabularies that are not shared or that share other vocabularies with other groups. In fact, this is a dynamic increasing in our interdependent world, though perhaps not at the pace some would claim. In any case, shared discourses, as logical spaces of cultural politics, open up the possibility of cultural-political relations between groups (Rorty 2007b, 21).

As mentioned in chapter 5, this alters the nature of sociopolitical change. For Rorty, changing social practices involves the expansion and/or adaption of the logical spaces we inhabit to include others or change our relations to others. "Debate about the utility of such logical spaces and about the desirability or undesirability of uniting them with, or disjoining them from, one another is the substance of cultural politics" (Rorty 2007b, 22).[2] Rorty's reframing of communities in moral/ethical terms rather than epistemic or ontological ones is central to this conception. Chapters 1 and 5 attempted to explicate this reframing through his theory of inquiry and conception of sociopolitical criticism. This resulted in a conception of knowledge and political engagement as functions of moral communities of identification. This is why Rorty's theory is so attuned to the problem of exclusion, to "borderline cases" (Rorty 1998f, 168). The conception of political engagement on cultural-political terms and the language of logical spaces allows for expanding our realms of conversation partners, which Rorty argued was crucial to "taking other human beings seriously." It achieves this by neither privileging nor rejecting the standards of the speaking community. As situated and finite beings, we only initiate such dialogues from within present networks and identifications. Single, universally authoritative frameworks for commonality become impossible. Rorty's claim was that this model more effectively engages those with whom we share no normative horizon. He offers it as a metavocabulary of intervocabulary normative exchange in the absence of agreed-upon criteria and without reference to an external source of authority. By expanding the logical spaces we inhabit to include new groups and languages, Rorty places an important agonistic constraint that opens up existing standards and consensuses (Rorty 2007b, 19–20).

THE NORMATIVE FOUNDATION OF CULTURAL POLITICS

Before systematizing this method for the critical reconciliation of diverse ways of speaking, it is necessary to discuss the other positive political role for theoretical practice Rorty discusses. Cultural-political theory plays an important normative role in supporting a *politics of social hope*. This addresses one of the continuing challenges to pragmatic and Rortian sociopolitical criticism: that it is politically acquiescent and normatively vacuous. Once again, this misunderstands the nature of Rorty's normativity. Concerned with the metatheoretical, where abnormal conditions persist, Rorty's focus is the mood in which social change is pursued by diverse vocabulary holders within internormative engagement. He attempts to provide a *general governing ethos for the cultural-political realm* that allows the pursuit of common social change among cultural-political diversity: commonality among nonhierarchical difference.

The shift from the eternity to the future, in terms of where we find normative authority, is crucial for this opening up and deauthoritarianizing sociopolitical criticism (see chapter 4). An indeterminate social future, the shape of which is exactly the subject of cultural-political contestation, comes to take the normative significance of immutable standards, and sociopolitical criticism becomes about culturally-politically shifting our language to address present tensions and enable future practices. This conception focuses on "the need to replace a human self-image which had been made obsolete by social and cultural change with a new self-image, a self-image better adapted to the results of those changes." It "mediate[s] between the past and the future" and "weave[s] together old beliefs and new beliefs, so that these can cooperate rather than interfere with one another" (Rorty 1995a, 198–99).

Rorty's later work claims that an ethos of melioristic hope can be the motivational successor to truth, certainty, or radical contingency in other conceptions of social change. The recent literature in pragmatism has focused on the melioristic mood central to pragmatist politics in general and Rorty specifically. The strength of pragmatist meliorism is its distinctive combination of pluralism, the assumption that we inhabit diverse justificatory systems, with humanism, that humans make distinctive contributions (not mastery) to these contexts, amid a mood of general optimism (not necessity). For pragmatists, this is fundamentally democratic. "Meliorism ... focuses on what we can do to hasten our progress and mitigate our decline. As such, meliorism resonates with the central ethical impulse at the heart of pragmatism: democracy. Democracy is the simple idea that political and ethical progress hinges on nothing more than persons, their values, and their actions" (Koopman 2006, 107). Such meliorism follows cultural politics as a *situated* form of sociopolitical change that simultaneously accepts its context, by treating it as the site of cultural politics, while criticizing it. This relation to authority established in cultural politics allows more open and flexible normative relations in a politics of social hope. This enables more diversity in the moment and more change in the future: commonality and change among diversity.

While Rorty failed to theorize social hope fully, in a symposium on Charles's Taylor's *Sources of the Self* he hints at how it provides a shared normative standard appropriate to contemporary conditions. In that book Taylor identifies a tension within modernity between moral universalism and romance, specifically between the social demands of equality within the former and the desire to differentiate oneself in the latter, and argues that this tension indicates the insufficiency of moral motivation in modernity (Taylor 1989). Rorty argues that Taylor fails to see a possible reconciliation between these two aspects that addresses the problem of motivation and grounding in contemporary politics. A pragmatic antiauthoritarianism and situated practice of sociopolitical criticism can provide the political grounding (or "hypergood") Taylor desires:

> This is to say that human beings are, indeed, self-interpreting beings, and consequently not Cartesianly apparent, while insisting that their self-interpretations are at their best when they are social. . . . Why should not the *social creative imagination* be a hypergood?. . . [Why cannot] The Glorious Social Future, the one in which the procedural morality of the Enlightenment has made possible the spiritual flourishing of everyone rather than just the happy few, do the work that God, or some other version of The Objectively Existent Good, used to do?
>
> (Rorty 1994, 199, my emphasis)

In spite of modernity's tensions, politics can be grounded in our social capacity to hope and imagine. Our capacity to engage in cultural politics (i.e., normative transformation) can be the source of hope that motivates such change. For Rorty, our ability to employ cultural politics to dissociate current forms and imagine visions of our society different and better than the present reconciles moral universalism and romantic differentiation (see chapter 5). It allows us to dream a collective and glorious social future that acts as a normative and critical standard against the present. Further, it resolves the motivational deficit within modernity and the eschewal of particularistic perspectives necessary in contemporary politics (at least at the metatheoretical framing level). While this account remains broad, it is fundamental to Rorty's inclusivity and strength. Social hope as a normative foundation of cultural-political change continues his pursuit of inclusive commonality within horizontal internormative engagement. This is the goal of an overarching thin commonality, based in a narrative and vocabulary and built within the domain of cultural politics. As discussed below, this has important points of linkage and contrast with agonistic forms of democratic ethos.

MAXIMS AND VIRTUES: HOW TO PHILOSOPHIZE WITH A TOOL

In un-Rortian fashion, this section systematizes the methodological virtues and maxims that have arisen in this investigation. While this may be problematic from a Rortian perspective, it is helpful for contemporary methodological discussions. The following tracks the various maxims of Rorty's theoretical model and its particular approach to political theory, cultural politics, as a way of speaking about internormative exchange. All of these have been addressed in one form or another. Subsequent discussions use this account as a basis for identifying similar trends in contemporary political theory and summarizing the critical account of ontological trends in continental, ontological political theory.

First, the main metamaxim of Rorty's pragmatic political thought is *antiauthoritarianism*. This theme has recurred frequently throughout this analysis and is a growing framing in the recent literature on Rorty (Rorty 2006a; Rondel 2011; Bacon 2006; Koopman 2011b; Curtis 2015). In chapter 1, I argued that his framework seeks to "set aside *any* authority save that of a consensus of our fellow humans" (Rorty 2006a, 257). In his early work, Rorty criticized the epistemological and ontological projects as quests for certainty, "desire[s] for a constraint" (Rorty [1979] 2009, 315). Such constraints would resolve the persistent ethicopolitical and social contingency of human practices and vocabularies: the fact that we could always speak and act differently, which necessitates continual scrutiny of our practices.

Rorty's vocabulary of vocabularies operationalizes his antiauthoritarianism, delimiting its intended scope and context. It is proposed for the metatheoretical level, where vocabularies interact and where there are no neutral shared criteria. Further, this way of speaking suggests that we can understand the dynamics, limits, and opportunities of this sphere through the model of *the social*. Chapters 1 and 2 explicated this "ontological priority of the social," arguing it is ideal for assessing the interaction of distinct normative frameworks and their claims to authority. Its focus on social practices, linguistic and otherwise, avoids positing standards of judgment through reference to either epistemic or ontological status and focuses solely on the lived consequences of a language. This entails a series of emphases that all focus on the practice and intersubjective aspects of language use as ways to understand authority/normativity in terms of linguistic practice: conversation, solidarity, identity, community, etc. I also discussed how Rorty glossed this focus as on the use/purpose/utility of a vocabulary.[3] This is a focus on social practices, which is more appropriate to the social conditions of pluralistic authority; "attention to the implications of beliefs for practice offered the only way to communicate across divisions between temperaments, academic disciplines, and philosophical schools" (Rorty 2006a, 260). Here, practices (especially linguistic) provide a common object and context for discussion: which ways of being, speaking, and relating are enabled or precluded by our frameworks of authority?

With this initial focus, Rorty turned to the issue of theorizing how internormative engagement could be pursued under antiauthoritarian constraints. As I argued in chapter 2, his antiauthoritarianism is structured around both *antifoundationalism* and *antiskepticism*, seeking normativity without foundations. This resulted in a longstanding concern with theoretical practice as a form of sociopolitical criticism that led first to hermeneutics, then to pragmatism, and that framed Rorty's engagements with continental thought. The concern throughout was how sociopolitical criticism could facilitate the type of engagement he thought appropriate to metatheoretical conditions. In chapters 1 and 2, we encountered two initial virtues: fallibilism and nominalism.

Fallibilism turns linguistic justification toward other humans and away from the external standards that have dominated political thought (truth, the rational, human nature, the real, divine will, etc.). "Many previous communities have betrayed their own interests by being too sure of themselves, and so failing to attend to objections raised by outsiders" (Rorty 2000g, 4–5; Voparil 2014a, 392–93). As such, it involves a particular *intellectual, ethical, and social relation* to our normative claims that understands their partial relevance to today's world and their, in principle, future revisability. For Rorty, pursuing the difficult project of justifying among such difference pretty much is the substance of democratic politics (making the initial connection between normativity and politics). Fallibilism focuses us on our relation with others by imposing constraints and preventing the reification of knowledge (and external sources).

Nominalism performs a similar function with language. In chapter 2 I argued that Rorty's critique of Heideggerian theory and the political thought indebted to it is that it reifies language and/or contingency into something with a nature (however broad) and necessity. In contrast, Rorty, through his social-practice-based tool account, keeps his understanding of language nominalistic. Nominalism respects the contingency of language by locating that contingency in *use rather than in the essence* of terms. It dissociates our vocabularies from language in the abstract, which, however broad in its dynamics, can serve as some kind of normative standard for change. However, it is not any less pervasive. While Rorty often paired nominalism with historicism (Rorty 1989), he also consistently advocates Wilfrid Sellars's "psychological nominalism" that "all awareness is a linguistic affair" (Rorty 1982a, xxxvi; Sellars 1963b, 160). This does not mean that language *constitutes* the world but that all experience is experience under a description. All of these reflections resulted in a focus on social criticism and a series of developing frameworks for this, climaxing in cultural politics.[4]

Together, fallibilism, nominalism, and a conception of theoretical practice as sociopolitical criticism facilitate the respective disposition and focus of internormative engagement. This only entails the claim that, at the widest metatheoretical level, these conditions and standards hold, which for Rorty is a virtue rather than limit. Thus, it only has implications for vocabularies that take the metatheoretical mantle and speak about the range of human practices and frameworks for thinking. Rorty in no way undermines any particular regional vocabulary in terms of its internal relations. His concern is always with the metatheoretical and thus mainly with frameworks that claim validity there.

Chapters 3 through 5 developed the antiauthoritarian lens in naturalism, historicism, and Rorty's mature model of social criticism. The former two are linked by the second main metamaxim: *holism*. Naturalism is "the view that anything might have been otherwise, that there can be no conditionless conditions" (Rorty 1991v, 55). On the one hand, this is an antitranscendent *negative methodological injunction* to avoid reference to external critical or normative standards. Within sociopolitical thought and the question of normativity, this means descending to the level of social practices and the languages that enable and preclude them. On the other, this is a *methodological imperative to holism*. We can only criticize linguistic practices by reference to other linguistic practices and the consequences of each. We thereby judge our assumptions about humanity in relation to some practice by how that accords with other areas of behavior (chosen and deployed for certain sets of reasons). Beyond this, Rorty suggests the vocabularies of subject and Darwinian naturalism as supplements to the vocabulary of vocabularies, deepening pragmatic linguistic practice. These vocabularies, as sets of terms and concepts, frame and enable such a level of discourse within his naturalistic injunctions. They are designed to enable political critique and normativity while avoiding essentialism, metaphysics, and foundations. As I argued in chapters 3 and 4, these are tied to Western traditions of philosophical and political thought and are not intended for language users outside those communities.

The other side of Rorty's holism is *historicism*. The previous injunction to holism entails that sociopolitical criticism occur through engaging linguistic and social practices with other *past and present* practices. Rorty mandates placing discussions of whatever element of contemporary life within a narrative of its development, while acknowledging the contingent, interpretive, and "redescriptive" nature of such accounts. They not only provide the necessary critical distance from our practices but enable the transformative normative capacity of vocabularies, whereby new uses of norms and new contexts transform them. Thus, the injunction to holism is also an imperative to *comparison*, to avoid reified external standards by using the normative possibilities of narrative redescription and imagination. Theory at the broad level of intervocabulary engagement, to be inclusive, cannot pre- and proscribe much. This comparative push is part of Rorty's broad account of theoretical sociopolitical criticism as "seeing similarities and differences between great big pictures, between attempts to see how things hang together. He [the social critic] is the person who tells you how all the ways of making things hang together hang together" (Rorty 1982a, xl). The historicist approach is exactly attuned for argument at the level of attractiveness of vocabularies, not individual propositions, and thus to metatheoretical conditions.

Together, Rorty's naturalism and historicism constitute a methodological injunction to holism.[5] This holism is *methodological rather than metaphysical*. It is not a positing of unity, like new materialism, but a mutual enabling and limiting. Naturalism "grounds" us in our present purposes, removing external standards, and situates us within the present nexus of languages and practices. It, necessarily, does come with a vocabulary of social practices that is not without links to the natural sciences. This entails a set of assumptions, as well as a history, that can be framed in ontological terms (e.g., as mastery). As a language with a history and a context, this is unavoidable. There is no view from nowhere. However, historicism, in turn, pushes us beyond this framework by emphasizing the contingency of our present and enabling us to frame new ends. Naturalism and historicism together give us the capacity to intervene critically and reflexively within our present sociopolitical worlds.

This raises the most important and controversial metamaxim this reading argues for, *reflexivity*. It is important to clarify again that this is not Rorty's term. However, this study has claimed that it is the goal of much of critical social theory and that it summarizes the main methodological value of Rorty's framework. In fact, it unites all the previous maxims and constitutes the main possibility in his work (implicit though never realized) for fulfilling the project of normativity without foundations.[6]

Rorty's reflexivity focuses on changing our relation to the critical and normative standards by which we engage in justification. This is true across the spectrum of norms (epistemological, ontological, ethical, political, etc.), which are equally subject to the conditions of the social at the metatheoretical level. As a result, in chapter 1, where Rorty criticized the foundationalist conception of inquiry and offered his sociological rendering, he argued for a reflexive form of communal inquiry and cooperation. The fallibilistic relation to knowledge and the naturalistic understanding of practice as communal coping serve this reflexive end. He reframed inquiry as aimed at solidarity, not at truth or objectivity: the goal being as much intersubjective agreement as possible and to subject our claims reflexively to as many linguistic challenges as possible. In chapter 2, I further argued, in contrast to the Heideggerian model and its contemporary manifestations, that the chief virtue of embedding reflexivity in the social (particularly in language), is that it operationalizes this *methodologically rather than metaphysically*. Rorty's claim is not that language holds a privileged viewpoint, as Heidegger argues, but that starting from language explicates our forms of normativity without appealing to foundations.

In chapters 3 and 4, naturalism and historicism illustrated this comparative strength further. Rorty's naturalism, with its previously discussed injunctions *and* its enabling vocabulary, explicated the methodological conditions for reflexivity. The latter languages additionally illustrated how a substantive and embedded language, with long historical development, could come to understand itself in a manner that didn't necessarily prioritize its own normative criteria. This is not the only way such a thing could occur, but it is an important historical example.

In chapter 4, the analysis of reflexivity came to a head. I argued that one of Rorty's later essays could be read as a reconstruction of *rationality as critical reflexivity* that provides an invaluable resource for his model of sociopolitical criticism. Further, expanding on Rorty's points about naturalism as a contingent language of a particular development, he identified resources for this reflexivity in a reading of modernity that rejected its project of self-foundation in favor of the goals of self-assertion and a notion of sufficient rationality possible, not necessary, in historical development. Together these ideas recognize the social origin of normative authority: that it is something *we do*. It also exposed that the modern recognition of the social origin of normative status results in the project of establishing a mode of assessing, judging, and critically developing these normative statuses we ascribe, so that our practices are subject to reflective guidance rather than the authority we have already inevitably invested somewhere (Brandom 2013, 24–29). Thus, the priority of the social requires a certain form of mastery: the methodological acceptance of fallibility and incompleteness, that we always have and continue to revise our standards, and contingency, that our present set of standards are the product of a series of decisions taken, possibilities pursued, and alternatives discarded. This can provide the possibility of reflexivity.

This reading of modernity and its resources for progressive sociopolitical development is the basis of, as discussed in chapter 5, Rorty's commitment to the inclusive cosmopolitan project of the Enlightenment, despite his agreement with continental criticisms. The result was Rorty's antiauthoritarian conception of the inclusive democratic project as a process of linguistic-cultural expansion. While Rorty clearly thinks reflective techniques possible, his engagements with critical social theory (critical theory and radical thought) are mainly negative contrasts; only in his final discussions of cultural politics does this project become clear. For Rorty, there is no clear set of reasons that either posits a better normative alternative or a convincing argument against this ideal. Further, the necessary inclusivity can be built through reflexive social change that creates broader identities and larger communities through the piecemeal process of creating larger loyalties. Such internormative engagement must not prioritize the normative standards of any particular participant, which is its great difficulty. Further, it must be broadly critical. Rorty's response to this problematic unites his social conception of normativity with his democratic politics; his later reconstruction of rationality posits it as a pragmatic series of virtues, or ethos, given to reflexive learning. Thus, *rationality is an ethical relation among groups*—a disposition toward new and existing conversation partners that frames their engagement in reflexive equality. Each is subject to the critical perspectives of others, but none is privileged from the outset. Rationality is no longer authority but a willingness to subject ourselves to intersubjective construction, to deeper and reflexive relations with others. It is a "continuum of degrees of overlap"—or reflexive growth (outward from the situated present). Inclusive commonality is a piecemeal and pragmatic process of common norm building situated in present communities, practices, and norms but striving beyond them through sociopolitical conversation across difference.

All of this contributes to Rorty's theorization of the positive culturalpolitical role of an *ethic of tolerance*. Along with the orientation of reflexivity (in relation to our practices and others), this ethic is the main lesson of his approach. While the former attempts to provide for the continued possibility of critique and normativity, the latter democratizes and pluralizes political discourses by establishing a certain way of relating between groups. Both together operationalize the methodological constraints and imperatives previously discussed.

The ethos of inclusive tolerance, as discussed in chapter 1, began as Rorty's sociological response to the problem of normative diversity within language use. It offered a model of dialogical engagement intended to enable inquiry that lacked agreed-upon criteria. Initially framed within the tradition of hermeneutics, this ethos offered a governing metatheoretical frame for human inquiry. It was *not* a set of precepts for conducting inquiry in any particular area but a metaphilosophical understanding of inquiry as social practice. Rorty's rejection of hermeneutics for this "vocabulary of vocabularies" resulted from its tendency to exceed this, placing language in an essential, rather than practical, relation to human existence. This demonstrates the "freestanding" nature of this ethos, its pragmatic status as a contingent social practice and tool.

This tension was repeated in Rorty's use of pragmatism for this ethos, which led to a tense relationship of reconstructive appropriation with Dewey. Beyond this, it provides the main language for his social-practice-based approach. Its strength is how it demonstrates how any theoretical framework is ultimately dependent on normative authority derived from the social; they are communal activities involving ethical values about individual interaction. This frames theoretical controversies in moral-relational terms. However, it also suggests a way to proceed through an appeal to moral virtues of engagement. This is the keystone of Rorty's work. He seeks to derive ethicopolitical insights only from the social and relational context of human life. In this manner, Rorty's antiauthoritarianism is tied to a positive ethicopolitical moral project that reveals the origins of the central sociopolitical strategy of Rorty's method. "Tolerance for a plurality of non-competing descriptions, descriptions which serve different purposes and which are to be evaluated by reference to their utility in fulfilling these purposes rather than by their 'fit' with the objects being described" (Rorty 2006a, 262). By framing epistemological and ontological debates in social terms, switching attention from the demands of the object to the practices and relations a language enables,

Rorty *politicizes* inquiry. This fundamentally levels different descriptive and normative frameworks, which now exist along a horizontal set of distinctions around purpose rather than along a vertical one around certainty.

This strategy became central to Rorty's political thought. As discussed in chapter 5, Rorty offers a democratic ethos for sociopolitical thinking among abnormal conditions of pluralism that takes inclusion beyond the quasi-foundational approaches of both liberal proceduralism and the radical ontological reification of difference. Importantly, it does not junk the language of tolerance on the usual critical grounds. Rorty's ethic is self-consciously partial. It is the contingent and strategic product of a particular community facing a particular political context. Such is the nature of cultural politics, and Rorty uses this language to emphasize that a relation to others (who are tolerated or included) is something done by a particular group of language users from within their identity and practices. For this reason, criticisms of Rorty's "we-focus" are unconvincing (Voparil 2011b, 123–25). It may be a limitation that he mainly focuses on rendering inclusive our Western liberal-democratic conversation. However, it is not a limitation anyone has convincingly argued we can exceed. Inclusion *as such* is not an implementable ideal. Inclusion is always done by some group of language users, and his point is that there are very good reasons to culturally-politically attempt to get Western democracies engaged in quite of bit more of that.

This ethic also motivates the theory of reflexivity and reconstruction of rationality previously discussed. In turn, Rorty's implicit reconstruction of rationality as noncriterial is the premise of his ethos. When rationality is responsibility to larger and more diverse communities, it is the ability to take on new vocabularies, to grow reflexively. Where critical social theory seeks emancipation, Rorty emphasizes *tolerance* as the virtue of his pragmatic social criticism. In contrast to penetrating appearances down to reality, it reflexively engages in normative transformation internally, by using old terms in new ways, and externally, by adding new claims through linguistic innovation and normative comparison with the practices of others, real and imagined. Its logic creates the possibility of reflexive development between different frameworks in the moment and between different periods. This emphasizes that rational justification always involves the ethical choice of which terms and vocabularies to employ and whom to speak to, furthering the previous politicization. In this sense, the ethical project in Rorty must be understood in ultimately political terms. With this, it is appropriate to turn to Rorty's relation to contemporary political theory and two questions of pluralism.

RORTY IN CONTEMPORARY POLITICAL THEORY: TWO QUESTIONS OF PLURALISM

Contemporary political thought confronts pluralism along (at least) two dimensions. First, there is the *methodological* question of how inquiry should proceed within a discipline characterized by theoretical diversity on basic epistemological, ontological, and sociological presuppositions that stand behind critical analyses and normative prescriptions. This is the problem of methodological plurality: how do we engage frameworks with very different vocabularies, questions, and priorities in common conversation/inquiry? Second, there is the *political* question, which has dominated postwar Anglo-American political thought: how can democracy respond to and cope with the multifaceted pluralism that characterizes contemporary societies?

HOW TO PRACTICE PLURALISTIC POLITICAL THEORY

The fact of methodological plurality raises a methodological question: how do we structure a common conversation for divergent approaches that avoids implicitly prioritizing one set of concerns/conceptions? Rorty's significance is his direct confrontation of this and capacity to foment intermethodological work. This capacity stems from his nonhierarchical vocabulary of vocabularies that purposely prevents appeals to external normative standards as a means of raising one vocabulary above others.

There are several virtues to Rorty's conception of language as social practice and politics as cultural-political intervention. First, the former provides a detailed justification of why, at the metatheoretical level, a language cannot be measured by another (nonlinguistic) standard. A focus on language as practice removes the idea that it is justified by that relation, that it must be adequate to something else. Rorty's version of the linguistic turn allows us to be antifoundationalist and antimetaphysical *and* retain normative authority within our linguistic practices. Further, by shifting our methodological focus to the actual languages employed by human groups, it does this methodologically rather than metaphysically. Rather than hypostasizing language into all there is, as reductive versions of the linguistic turn have, it only claims that language "offers a privileged point of departure for philosophical work that seeks to explicate our forms of normativity without appealing to foundations" (Koopman 2011b, 70). In this, it manages to emphasize the contingency of our languages, relative to purpose as they are, without making contingency a universal condition. This is a thorough dedivinization of our thought and acknowledgment of finitude.

Second, the resulting *status* of languages in cultural politics more productively provides for intervocabulary relations within the situation of linguistic and methodological pluralism. A common criticism of liberal norms for the public sphere is that they implicitly assume the neutrality of their categories. In various forms (e.g., Rawlsian public reason, Habermasian communicative rationality) they claim a neutrality that excludes other perspectives. Importantly, this compromises their critical reflexivity, by obscuring real assumptions that privilege their perspectives and delegitimize others. Rorty's model retains this reflexivity by leveling the discursive field and normative authority. For him, even the language of cultural politics is a move in the game of cultural politics. He does offer us a vocabulary with which to speak about the many linguistic frameworks that exist. Yet, as I argued in chapter 2, operationally this is thoroughly *pluralistic* and *democratic*. When critical engaging discourses is approached on the model of assessing tools more or less useful for certain purposes, the present and future contingency of those purposes follows. It acknowledges the multiplicity of goals and solutions without erecting a universal standard to judge either. That is, the tool-based account allows for flexibility in both the standards and forms of practice within communities. This means that while purpose is *not* a neutral category, it *is* a horizontal one. It allows a variety of normative standards and ends without predisposing any finally to triumph on the field of cultural politics. As discussed, the language of purpose (utility or use) is not a functionalism. Rather, it denotes that linguistic practices always enable certain sets of practices and goals while disabling or discouraging others. Thus, vocabularies have a clear and practical impact on political forms of life. Applied to intermethodological exchange between contemporary analytical and continental political thought, this model enables *situated* pluralistic and democratic exchanges that are no more neutral than previous pretenders. They are only uniquely *useful* for intermethodological engagement.

Recent work spanning pragmatism and genealogy indicates how this might be operationalized.[7] Colin Koopman's "genealogical pragmatism" is an archetype of how such engagements can advance methodological debates. Beyond establishing specific connections between pragmatists and genealogists, he has attempted to articulate a wider project of a genealogical and pragmatist political methodology. While he has not explicitly systematized his method for achieving this, it occurs through several steps. First, Koopman establishes broad thematic connections between pragmatism and genealogy, each of which he has undertaken extended studies of (Koopman 2009, 2013b). For him, they are linked in a shared historicism and model of philosophy as a form of "transformational cultural critique," where critique is a situated practice addressing a particular context. Second, Koopman illustrates how their different emphases in conceiving historical critique both explain recurrent criticisms of each tradition and provide for the possibility of methodological alliance. As mentioned previously, pragmatism is repeatedly accused of acquiescence, of the inability to distinguish good from bad in politics. Contrariwise, Foucault and genealogy are criticized for lacking normative resources considered imperative to the task of critical thought.

Rather than being cause for rejection (for which they are often employed), these concerns are the product of different emphases within a common prioritization of the practice of critique. "But whereas the pragmatists practiced critique as a reconstructive problem-solving activity, Foucault practiced critique as an act of problematization" (Koopman 2009, 215). The result is that, while pragmatists have a detailed method of meliorative reconstruction, theorizing how to recreate problematic social practices, they lack sufficient mechanisms for identifying problems to reconstruct. Equally, while genealogy has established an important method of problematization, of disclosing practices as oppressive, it underthinks normatively reconstructing those practices. In this manner, building on the identification of shared emphases, Koopman establishes productive relations for a common benefit between these two traditions, to advance a new methodology that utilizes their strengths and rectifies their weaknesses.

My concern is not the accuracy of Koopman's readings of genealogy and pragmatism but his project. He follows Rorty in understanding pragmatism and genealogy as methodologies rather than theories. In naturalistic terms, they are webs of concepts, ideals, and approaches whose significance is relative to the purposes they enable. This changes the *status* of their respective emphases and the critical and normative standards contained in each without affecting those actual standards. This allows Koopman to *integrate* these two "phases of thought," Foucauldian problematization and pragmatist reconstruction, to advance a critical project neither is capable of alone. This philosophical and historical integration focuses on the specific connections and diverging *purposes* and goals within both approaches to move them forward. The claim is not that pragmatists and genealogists say the same thing but that they say things that, taken together, importantly contribute to contemporary debates in critical political methodology (Koopman 2009, 229). Following Rorty's prioritization of language, the advantage of this reconciliation is that it occurs only at the methodological (not metaphysical) level. It is not a philosophical synthesis, which always risks reducing methods to their common denominators or rendering one framework into the other's terms. It is "a more modest retail combination of the methodological strengths found in each tradition" (Koopman 2013b, 222). Koopman develops Rorty's naturalistic approach by illustrating how to advance conversations that have stagnated in divisions between approaches unable to justify beyond the confines of their particular perspectives/criteria. By naturalizing our understanding of languages and approaches, as Rorty theorizes, we move beyond unproductive absolutist conceptions of theory.

This is not to say that Rorty's engagements with his diverse sources always lived up to these insights. Many of his discussions of continental thinkers (and others) were accused of willful misreading. In chapter 1, I attempted to justify his reading strategy. Given Rorty's focus on use and tools, texts for him are not exegetical objects but sites for redescription.

His concern is always with what is "living," with the fruitful legacy of a thinker. As such, he reads mainly in light of contemporary problems. In this, Rorty similarly foregrounds the role of contingent choice, by reading figures in relation to present needs and debates. That is, he politicizes interpretation by making it reconstructive intervention.

This reading strategy raises questions. Particularly, is this strategy and Rorty's commitment to intermethodological engagement in conflict? Can one read a tradition against itself and still engage it reflexively? While I cannot treat this issue at length, I do not see these two elements, reconstructive reading and horizontal intermethod engagement, as *necessarily* opposed. Reading a tradition against its own terms can reframe assumed debates. Further, it can aid mutual understanding by clarifying how another perspective views one's own. This is the basis of the focus on the productive dimensions of conflict in agonistic democratic theory. This is not to say that agonism is *sufficient* to engagement either. Rorty also undertook more overt bridging mechanisms of creating new, inclusive (larger-loyalty) categories. For example, he recast the analytic-continental divide as one between analytic and *conversational* philosophy. This reconstructs the central division of Western theory around the issue of foundations and the resulting role of philosophy in human life. Analytic thought assumes "there is something that philosophers can get right" (Rorty 2007a, 124). Conversational philosophy is the wide category united by rejecting this image. It includes that broad swath of theories that think complete agreement in philosophy and politics impossible. Rather, on some understanding, they acknowledge that we only ever engage in "cultural politics," in "suggesting changes in the uses of words and by putting new words in circulation—hoping thereby to break through impasses and to make conversation more fruitful" (Rorty 2007a, 124). Such a reconstruction is illustrative of the fact that, as we have seen, Rorty also consistently linked pragmatism to analytical and to continental thought, while attempting to split the difference between liberalism and radical thought similarly. Conflictual *and* inclusive redescription seem two parts of a single strategy for engaging difference. This dual emphasis is repeated in his democratic theory.

PLURALISM AND AGONISM IN DEMOCRATIC THEORY: ONTOLOGICAL ETHICS VERSUS PRAGMATIC VIRTUES

Rorty's framework can also contribute to current debates in agonistic democratic theory. This should not be surprising; there are many intuitive connections between his work and agonism. For example, both attempted substantial theoretical and methodological reconstructions of the practice of political theory. Both drew on noncanonical sources, including continental political thought. Both are intensely critical of the rationalistic and universalist assumptions of much of liberal political thought and their methods. Finally, politically, they both significantly revise liberalism, while arguably remaining within its general framework. However, the details of these commonalities push Rorty away from some agonists, particularly those who employ ontological approaches. Below, after briefly considering the agonistic literature, I examine Rorty's relation to the nonontological, social-practice-based agonism of James Tully, subsequently comparing their frameworks for engaging difference to Connolly's democratic ethos. The latter has been a recurrent voice; this final discussion clarifies the particular *political* consequences of the theoretical and methodological differences discussed previously.

Agonism, similar to Rorty, rejects the foundational project of normative political theory in the Western tradition of grounding their accounts of politics in substantive accounts of some external standard: human nature, the good life, the patter of history, moral theories like consequentialism, and the currently dominant political liberalism that holds that we can establish agreement on constitutional essentials through analytic methods and the public use of reason, bracketing off comprehensive and controversial beliefs (Wenman 2013, 6, 13). In this manner, there is a basic methodological claim at the heart of agonism about the connection between theoretical practice and political ideas. Like Rorty, it is a broadly antiessentialist one, emphasizing the situated nature of theory and the inevitable mix of description and prescription. Unlike Rorty, agonism tends to fit within postfoundational viewpoints that do "not attempt to erase completely such figures of the ground." Instead they attempt to "weaken their ontological status" by revealing not the absence of grounds, as such, but "the impossibility of a final ground" (Marchart 2007, 2). Thus, like Connolly, agonism tends to circle around the question of grounds as necessary but ultimately and necessarily contingent and incomplete.

While there is significant contestation over agonism, this shared critical object means that there are general features. "A consensus has emerged amongst post-foundational theorists that democracy must emphasize contestation of basic principles, conflict between citizens, respect for difference, and attention to the informal operations of power. Agonistic democracy describes this constellation of commitments" (Wingenbach 2011, vii). Agonism centers around these themes of "pluralism, tragedy and the value of conflict" (Wenman 2013, 4) and, thus, envisions democracy as a "continual contest among incompatible visions, identities, and projects" in which no view can dominate or assume hegemonic status for long (Wingenbach 2011, 21).

To prioritize conflict/contestation, agonism combines several themes from pluralism and republicanism, with the result that they emphasize democratic contestation over the liberal-constitutional emphases on the rule of law and the protection of individual liberties.[8] The degree is contested. Tully, for example, holds to the "equiprimordial" and "reciprocal interrelation of the two primary principles," seeing agonism as a rebalancing of these to equals, where deliberative and liberal theory has always prioritized the latter, seeing democratic practice as restricted to consensus (Tully 2005, 251). Others, in contrast, argue for the supremacy of the democratic over the constitutional.[9] The result across agonism is an emphasis on the need to open—and to keep open—political spaces in which opposing groups can engage in democratic contestation. For Mark Wenman, this *agonistic pluralism* is focused on the constituent power of democracy. Importantly, stemming from its views of the impossibility of a ground and the consequent uncertainty of political form, agonists emphasize the constituent power of humans to create new forms of life, ways of being in the world, and new sets of relations and practices, in a manner similar to Rorty's views on normative transformation. They then translate this capacity for freedom into the view that democracy, rather than a determined form of government, is the "founding moment" of innovation and authorizing. To varying degrees, and this is the real difference with liberalism, they accord some level of explanatory and normative priority to this "pre-juridical moment of political freedom that initiates and composes concrete social and political forms" (Wenman

2013, 7). As a result, in varying forms and to varying degrees, all agonists hold to some notion of the *constructive* nature of democratic agonism that seeks to question or engage in such founding.

The relation between ontology and agonism is a central ambiguity in the literature. Wenman, for example, identifies agonism with the ontological turn (Wenman 2013, 13). However, this defines that group more by its Connolly-Mouffe pole than by others, like James Tully and Sheldon Wolin, who theorize it with no mention of ontology. This tension raises the question of where the theorization of conflict originates. What backs the claim that conflict is an essential attribute of political life? McNay's focus on the distinction between politics and the political seems to catch more of the literature. For her, agonism is part of a wider turn to the question of the political, its conditions and nature, as a sphere. Conceived in this manner, the political (separate from politics, which refers to the everyday world of institutions, elections, and government) refers to the underlying shape of political life, the "very essence of political being" (McNay 2014, 2). In this, it becomes an autonomous realm with its own unique logic and dynamics.

This, of course, can be framed in ontological terms. Mouffe, for example, directly maps the politics-political distinction onto Heidegger's ontic-ontological distinction (Mouffe 2005, 8). However, it need not be, as it is not in Rorty and Tully.[10] Nonetheless, in the ontological account, the political becomes the main realm of justifying the primacy of disagreement within practical democratic politics. Mouffe, again, is a key source:

> By "the political" I mean the dimension of antagonism which I take to be constitutive of human societies, while by "politics" I mean the set of practices and institutions through which an order is created, organizing human coexistence in the context of conflictuality provided by the political.
>
> (Mouffe 2005, 9)

For her, the political-ontological is defined by a fundamental antagonism, which manifests in a basic friend-enemy distinction constitutive of political life and which *conditions* the everyday life of practice. In this manner, for the ontological variant of agonism, the conflict, which is liberalism's myopia, is identified within an ontological account of the fundamental nature of the political.

Much of agonism contains a similar impetus to ground the prioritization of conflict in some manner. As discussed in chapter 2, Connolly bases this in an ontological account of the necessity of contingency and the dynamics between identity and difference. As I will argue here, this leads to a pluralization of politics in his particular form of agonism. This is the key feature of agonism: the manner in which conflict is articulated in the political strongly affects the type of agonism suggested to alleviate it, something we will see between Rorty and Tully, on the one hand, and Connolly, on the other.

As discussed in the introduction, agonistic readings of Rorty generally accuse him of ignoring how conflict is *constitutive* of the political. However, these fail to understand how complexity and conflict are either already implicit within Rorty's framework or at the very least compatible with his overall thinking. Further, from a social-practice-based perspective, there are also deep concerns with the ontologization of the political, its essentialization as conflict, and the language of constitution used to make this claim. To make these points, I bring together Rorty with the nonontological agonism of James Tully.[11]

As clearly illustrated in the epigraph to this chapter, for Tully Rorty is a preeminent thinker of the turn to social practices, to the view that activity and *praxis* is prior to theory. He places Rorty at an instrumental point in his own intellectual history of "public philosophy" (Tully 2008, 17–18).[12] However, their theoretical links extend beyond this history to a series of shared methodological concerns and a strikingly similar account of agonistic democratic engagement in the context of diversity. The base of this is a shared antiauthoritarianism. For Tully, Rorty is central to this wider practice turn, "a move away from the search for an essence hidden behind human activities to the surface aspects that give them meaning and significance" (Tully 2008, 136–37). Here, the focus of political theory is on practice, rather than on some purported determinative level beneath/within/above.

Tully claims that Rorty's "revolutionary insight" goes to the heart of one of the most important, if ignored, methodological debates in political theory: the relation between political theory and other vocabularies within contemporary democratic political culture. For Rorty, as cultural politics, political theory cannot be considered hierarchically separate from other political languages or practices; that is, it cannot be raised above the general level of democratic activity. For Tully, four linked assumptions in the history of Western political thought have perpetuated this hierarchy: (1) there are hidden, determinative causal processes of historical development; (2) there are universal, unchanging normative principles that determine the correct action for citizens and the proper shape of democratic states; (3) there are background norms and goods implicit within democratic practices that prescribe democratic activity; and (4) there are "canonical institutional preconditions" that ground democratic activity. By holding to one or more of these assumptions, theorists have claimed a privilege over the rest of democratic activity by assuming that there are "background conditions of possibility for democracy" that the theorist uncovers. Rorty's significance is in revealing how all claims to authority are "internally related to and reciprocally shaped by the everyday activities of democratic citizens, not separate from and determinative of their field of freedom" (Tully 2008, 9). Reciprocally engaged in the practical activity of actual struggles, political theory is not different in kind to other citizen activity. Rather, it is only "the methodological extension and critical clarification of the already reflective and problematized character of historically situated practices of practical reasoning" (Tully 2008, 29). For Tully, this is both democratizing and enabling. Bringing philosophy down into *conversation* with democratic culture and citizens, it also frames our problems in a more tractable manner. "For while we are still *entangled* in conditions that constrain and enable, and are difficult to change, we are no longer *entrapped* in background conditions that determine the limits of our foreground activities, for none is permanently off limits" (Tully 2008, 9; see also Festenstein 2003, 15).

As a result of this basic difference, Tully revises the normative project of political theory and negotiates between liberal universalism and radical critique similarly to Rorty. Rejecting the task of a normative theory of justice or democracy, Tully's public philosophy is premised on the antiauthoritarian idea that "any rule (law, norm, right, principle) would always be open in principle to the challenge and negotiation of agents (individuals and groups) who are subject to it through the exchange of public reasons" (Tully 2005, 250). There is no, *in principle*, privileged center to cultural politics. In this manner, he similarly reconstructs liberal norms without their foundationalist backing. In a recent exchange with Michael Blake, Tully's pragmatism is dramatically apparent under the essentialist charge that it does not adequately protect against exclusion by ring-fencing certain foundational assumptions (e.g., the moral equality of persons). Blake charges Tully with failing both to protect minorities and to support liberal political principles (Blake 2005, 231). Tully responds that this concern misses the point of fallibilistic agonistic criticism. The capacity to *in principle* question any norm does not in any one moment mean that every norm, institution, or tradition can be questioned. "The exercise of freedom with respect to a contested rule would itself have to be exercised through the latest rules of law protecting individual and minority rights . . . even though these rules in turn could be challenged on another occasion" (Tully 2005, 251). As in pragmatist fallibilism, while everything is open to doubt, we cannot doubt everything at once.

While his debate with liberalism represents the difference between an ideal and social view of norms, like Rorty, Tully is at odds with radical theories of critique.[13] Their main criticism focuses not on the model of public philosophy or the method he employs but on his use of the conventional language of liberal-democratic politics. Mirroring continental critics of Rorty who were baffled by his wedding of postmodernism and liberalism, Bonnie Honig, for example, claims that Tully's use of the language of "reasonableness" implicates him in liberal myopias around conflict and power (Honig 2014, 72–74). However, Tully disagrees with the assumptions this claim makes about language and political change. Shirking the language of liberal-democratic politics (the language of freedom, citizenship, governance, etc.) renders one unable to shift and move its present interpretation and the uses and purposes it enables. Such "self-marginalization" and its often implicit claim to a deeper "radical" language that authentically reveals the political are incompatible with a democratic ethos. Further, this language is itself the site of agonistic struggle because it is often the subject of appropriation and abuse by a series of forces/actors central to contemporary power politics. To cede it is to surrender its normative value, which runs deeply throughout Western political culture, to their interpretations and the practices they enable. Finally, methodologically, Tully knows no other option. Expanding on his fallibilism, he notes: "No matter how deep philosophical questioning goes, it will always rest on uses of language that cannot in the circumstances be in question . . . there is a diverse world of political thought and action between total revolution and unthinking conformity" (Tully 2008, 52–53).

This Rortian balancing leads to a horizontal conception of political theory, making it only a participant, rather than arbiter, of political thinking. Tully describes his public philosophy as a practical, critical, and historical approach, a "way of living" that focuses on the practices of governance experienced as problematic in the present" (Tully 2008, 16). It attempts to establish the conditions of possibility of a specific practice by critically surveying the languages and practices within which struggle arises and the current options for addressing this issue and by providing a genealogy of the historical formation of these languages for comparison. Tully emphasizes several aspects here. First, such methods are strategic. Genealogy, for example, should only be understood as a "toolkit" rather than as a full-fledged theory, and, as such, it does not come with a developed normative ideal. Second, this is a *redescriptive* practice that "seeks to characterise the conditions of possibility of the problematic form of governance in a redescription (often in a new vocabulary) that transforms the self-understanding of those subject to and struggling within it, enabling them to see its contingent conditions and the possibilities of governing themselves differently" (Tully 2008, 16). This emphasizes that it is a mode of *interpretive critique*, but not one where interpretation is seen as foundational or constitutive of human and/or political being.[14] Rather, his method strategically redescribes a practice to illustrate the *how*, not just the *that*, of its contingency to expose the nature of the present set of limits and open up alternative manners of collectively organizing that form of cooperation.

The point of this approach is critical detachment, to stand back and "see the practices and their forms of problematisation as a limited and contingent whole" (Tully 2008, 16). This *holism*, like Rorty's, enables the comparative dimension of critique. Public philosophy is inherently comparative, conducting its surveys and genealogies to offer a Foucauldian history of the present *and* enable its comparison with possible alternatives.

This places the current struggle, and its object, within a broad field of possible responses, allowing a narrative to emerge about causes and solutions, one that is thoroughly situated:

> This is not a critique from the vantage point of a transcendental standard or procedure of judgment, for as we have seen such standards are internally related to the language games they purport to transcend. Rather, it is a non-transcendental yet transcending critique of the horizons of our practices and forms of thought by means of reciprocal comparison and contrast with other possible ways of being in the world.
>
> (Tully 2008, 35).

This pluralizes along two dimensions. Not only does it open up opportunities for change within a community in relation to a particular struggle, but it also enables dialogue between diverse social groups (in terms of language and practices) by offering new descriptions of the whole of some aspect of sociopolitical life. Importantly, it also fills out Rorty's own undertheorized imperatives to comparative holism while clarifying why he identified it as critical. In fact, Tully fills in the gaps of Rorty's theory of sociopolitical criticism.

The primacy of linguistic social practice lurks behind this account. Tully employs a Wittgensteinian account of language: it is a pragmatic and intersubjective activity performed by members of language games. This is crucial to his theory of democracy: Tully attempts to set up linguistic practice as both nondeterministic *and* conducive to intersubjective democratic justification. He follows Wittgenstein in thinking of this process as best described by the analogy of a game. Language users in any political dispute over a practice are engaged in the process of exchanging reasons over the various articulations of descriptive and normative concepts used to characterize the practice in question. Importantly, this exchange is a complex mix of communicative and strategic claims, and it can extend to contestation over the use of background framing concepts, for example, as to what constitutes a "reasonable" contribution. For Tully, this contests the assumptions that political concepts are discovered (theorized) and then applied to specific contexts and that the application/use of such criteria is algorithmic. The rules of linguistic practice, especially in political contexts, are loosely structured and open to many possible revisions in any moment. Like Rorty, he argues that linguistic practice is not defined by applying a rule but by the plausible *use* of a term, and use is always *relatively* open to a plausible set of practices that relate to one another in various ways. The language of games is meant to indicate this: that the criteria for the application of a term are not ultimately set but that there are areas of vagueness and room for revision. There are always "reasonable re-descriptions" (Tully 2008, 26–28).

This has methodological and political consequences. First, it further explains the aforementioned antiauthoritarianism, clarifying public philosophy's fundamental reciprocal relation to the present, an "on-going mutual relation with the concrete struggles, negotiations and implementations of citizens who experiment with modifying the practices of governance on the ground" (Tully 2008, 17). It is not different in kind to other citizen activity but is "the methodological extension and critical clarification of the already reflective and problematized character of historically situated practices of practical reasoning" (Tully 2008, 29). This is not to say, as discussed below, that there are no practical differences between the practice of criticism and citizen activity but that they are reciprocally and horizontally equal. This democratized shift in the *status* of theory removes barriers between it and everyday political activity.

The value of Tully's framing of linguistic engagement and Rorty's naturalized model of language and cultural politics is this intellectual democratization, removing barriers between theoretical frameworks. They provide both a way of understanding the contemporary intellectual matrix that avoids privileging one perspective/criterion and an understanding of the nature of normative authority and how it changes. Thus, like cultural politics, public philosophy offers *reflexive authority*, by enabling political agency without predetermining its form through recourse to theories of foundational rationalism or revolutionary uncovering. In this, both are best understood as metatheories of sociopolitical discourse, pragmatic "vocabularies of vocabularies," ways of speaking about and understanding the diversity of linguistic and normative claims without immediately offering criteria for assessment that would trump democratic engagement. They cannot claim neutrality. They are just as contingent, just as much a product of a certain set of factors (a history), as any other. They are simply the best option to satisfy antiauthoritarian norms.

Tully's detailed understanding of agonism and democratic engagement, I argue, formalizes many of Rorty's insights around the interaction between diverse-vocabulary-using groups in democracy.[15] Taking the linguistic framework above, Tully inserts agonism by understanding politics on the model of the game. As discussed above, on this model anything is in principle open to revision even though much has to be assumed in any one moment. This introduces an important element of freedom into political practice, via the inevitable vagueness in political norms and the ever-present potential, in principle, to transform a norm in use. This constitutes an "agonistic dimension of games" in politics that is different from a conception of politics under the ideal of consensus. On this model of democratic dialogue, opposed to deliberation, "no agreement will be closed at a frontier; it will always be open to question, to an element of non-consensus, and so to reciprocal question and answer, demand and response, and negotiation." Further, the process of challenging the rules of languages and practices, using old words in new ways or inventing new words, is "itself an agonistic game of freedom: precisely the freedom of speaking and acting differently" (Tully 2008, 143). This broadens the field of agonism out to any activity or language game in which the constraints are potentially open to contestation and recodes freedom not just as a relation between individuals, one another, and the state but as the relation between citizens and the formal and informal constraints of their political universe.

Like Rorty, Tully's account is not only focused on disagreement but on how it supports democratic and pluralistic *reasoning*. Thus, Honig is correct to cast Tully's model as "between the worlds of dissidence and governance" (Honig 2014, 71). Anthony Laden observes that this is the product of Tully's two contributions to contemporary political theory, his horizontal model of thought and his sense that the value of democratic dialogue (or negotiations in Tully's language) lies not only in the agreements they might produce but the activities themselves. This significantly revises the deliberative end of the dialogical turn by understanding deliberation/negotiation/engagement not "as a morally constrained form of bargaining, but as a species of a wider genus of conversational interactions that call for responsiveness" (Laden 2014, 13). This illustrates the wider sense of reasons and reasoning within Tully's work that harkens back to Rorty's reconstruction of rationality. Reasoning is a particular way of interacting with others that builds relations around the values of reciprocity, mutual respect, and recognition. Importantly, Laden characterizes it as a kind of "inviting" and "responsiveness," bringing it close to Rorty's language of inclusion. Tully's key insight is that reasoning in this manner is not episodic or sporadic, that is, deployed in distinct moments of deliberation. Rather, such dispositions to others are a background to shared life and constitute a space of reasons. While this already sounds decidedly Rortian, Laden goes further:

> I situate the activity of reasoning within the broader category of *conversation* . . . conversation has no natural termination point or goal, and thus succeeds precisely insofar as it is ongoing. If, then, we can re-orient our conceptual maps so that the activity of reasoning, and in particular the kinds of reasoning together that form the heart of democratic political interaction, can be seen as a specialized form of conversation rather than a joint exercise in decision-making, then we will be in a position to appreciate Tully's lesson in full.
>
> (Laden 2014, 15–16)

As an ethos of interaction, democratic conversation is characterized by the norm of *audi alteram partem* (always listen to the other side). For Tully, this is an immanent (to democratic conversation) rule of reciprocity that reveals that democratic political engagements are calls for recognition[16] and democratic agency within a context. For Laden, this can be drawn out to two key norms: all participants must offer one another reasons they, in good faith, understand to be reasons others can understand, and all participants must be properly responsive to the way their invitations are received. While the first is only a minor revision to key deliberative norms, the second argues that real engagements involve an openness to transformation *and* that "our conversation must leave appropriate space for the reasonable rejection of proffered reasons to affect the further course of the deliberation" (Laden 2014, 19). Conversion and disagreement can be a product of these norms. Nonetheless, they are inclusive in Rorty's sense. Offering reasons in such contexts is so important to democracy because it constitutes an invitation to inhabit a shared space of reasons. "In order to engage with others, each of the participants must work to offer reasons to the others on the presumption that these are reasons they can share, what might be called 'we'-reasons" (Laden 2014, 20). On this understanding, the reasonableness of engagement is not about its commitment to the end of consensus but to remain engaged whether common ground is discovered or not. It is for this reason that Tully explicitly places reasonable disagreement above consensus as an end (Tully 2005, 254).

Laden keenly observes that Tully, like Rorty, is motivated in this model by the question of how to bring diverse perspectives together without hierarchy in their norms. Further, Tully's answer is also about agonistic inclusion. The value of *audi alteram partem* is that it repeats the pragmatist political maxim, taken up in deliberative theory, that all those affected by a practice should be acknowledged and have real agency in the negotiations surrounding it. Importantly, this has inclusive larger-loyalty-building attributes. Tully argues that agonistic engagements

> provide stability and a sense of belonging for the right reasons.... Negotiations open to citizens and trusted representatives provide a new or renewed norm of recognition that is stable because the people who must bear it have had a say in its formulation and have come to see that it is well supported (even when they do not all agree with it). They identify with it. This is the sense of belonging appropriate to a democracy.
>
> (Tully 2008, 176–77)

This is not to suggest there are no weaknesses or gaps in either Rorty or Tully. One common criticism of both theorists is that their models cannot be general for politics (e.g., McNay 2014, 194–203), that the generality I argued for in terms of Rorty's model of intermethodological exchange in political theory is not matched by an equal generality in political life, because democratic engagement is just one of many political questions. This is why critics of both Rorty and Tully tend to focus on how their frameworks can't adequately explain, expose, or analyze some particular set of political problems (e.g., power, inequality, etc.). But this misreads their significance. They provide a forum for the interpretive engagement of diverse analytics that can make such claims with respect to some set of issues and problems. While this can be general at the level of political theory, it obviously cannot in politics. No political theory can provide a unified frame that adequately addresses all the problems of political life.

To demand that they should is to repeat the quest for certainty, correspondence, and the union of justice and truth.

In terms of diverse democracies struggling with groups separated by vocabularies and social practices, Rorty and Tully provide a viable frame for intergroup engagement and language for contemporary forms of identity politics. Critics are surely right that the capacity of their analytics to think some issues (e.g., unemployment) may be minimal. But such is not a coherent demand. What their theories can do is provide an understanding of the relation between claims and analyses that would allow democratic actors and thinkers concerned with such issues to bring their frameworks to the agonistic level of contestation, in the hopes of shifting structure and practice in their respective issue area.

CONNOLLY'S AGONISM AND PRAGMATIC PUBLIC PHILOSOPHY: THE QUESTION OF AN ETHOS

This discussion examines some of the consequences of previous analyses of Connolly for his attempt to offer a democratic ethos attuned to the same political problem as Rorty and Tully: the question of the shape and spirit of a common democratic sphere in a context divided along identity-related lines. For Connolly, this problem is both methodological and political. Consider:

> Where method, faith, and problems are loosely intertwined and where no single problematic has yet proven itself to be dispositive to all reasonable parties, what is the most admirable ethos to negotiate between contending problematics? And how is such an ethos to be fostered by those who themselves are also partisans to the disputes?
>
> (Connolly 2008, 90)

> My thinking, in fact, revolves around a fundamental tension that helps to constitute ethico-political life . . . between the partisan orientation to ethical life an individual or constituency adopts, and the larger ethos of politics they pursue with those embracing alternative sources.
>
> (Connolly 2004b, 168–69)

His pluralistic response constitutes the normative core of his democratic theory, which is similarly concerned with preventing intensive, dominating minorities; providing in agonism a system of partisan mutual adjustment; and, like Rorty and Tully, keeping the space of contestation open rather than offering definitive rankings of democratic values (Wenman 2013, 118–20). This last point is especially important. Like Tully and Rorty, Connolly highlights how the existing matrix of democratic discourse can preclude claims framed in new vocabularies, by new groups with new voices, that is, those "subsisting below the public register of justice" (Connolly 1995a, xvi; 1999b, 10).

Connolly's main mechanisms for addressing this are his ethos of engagement/cultivation and its two constituent parts, the civic virtues of *agonistic respect* and *critical responsiveness*. The former ethos "cultivates presumptive appreciation for a protean diversity of being" along the lines of his immanent naturalist ontology (Connolly 2004b, 169). He is distinctly aware of the irony that his ethic of cultivation, offered as a general ethos for the public realm, is framed in and motivated by his own particularistic ontology. Thus, enacting his own second movement of contestability (chapter 2 and 3), he claims only to "propel it onto the public register as one among a series of contestable orientations to public ethics" (Connolly 2004b, 169). Its presence, along with its noted contestability, is the basis of fashioning an interdependent ethos between groups both unlikely to drop their particular views nor convince others. Such an ethos for Connolly can grow "out of reciprocal appreciation of the element of partisanship in each orientation to public ethics, alongside concerted efforts by numerous parties to overcome existential resentment of this very condition" (Connolly 2004b, 169). Such a "general ethos" is central to the process of translating social antagonisms into egalitarian democratic assemblages.

Connolly's two virtues schematize the ethical dimension of contemporary democratic life to cope with this tension adequately. Agonistic respect, similar to liberal tolerance, is a relation between groups *already recognized* to some degree. Unlike tolerance, it is not a private diversity but an inclusion of those particularized elements within a mood of forbearance. For Connolly, it fundamentally involves the ontological articulation of contestable moral sources in public. The purpose is cultural, to "negotiate oblique connections across multiple lines of difference," thereby creating the possibility of new connections and groups (Connolly 2004b, 176). Critical responsiveness, in contrast, concerns the public ethos to *new* claims to inclusion. It constitutes a "presumptive generosity" to groups struggling for recognition on the register of justice, recognizing the insufficiency of established justice to new democratic claims. Both civic virtues require intense efforts at cultivation and negotiation. Given his theories of sensibility and affect, Connolly argues that much of this work must take place on "the lower affective registers of being" and the "visceral register of self-identity" (Connolly 2004b, 177). For him, such "micro-politics" is crucial to achieving agonistic but not violent democratic engagement (Connolly 2004b, 178).

On first glance, Connolly's agonism goes through similar motions to Tully's, addressing diversity in light of the problems with liberal approaches and with a clear focus on normativity lacking in much of the rest of agonism.[17] However, closer reflection reveals several problems with this normativity and the role of political theory. As discussed in chapters 2 and 3, Connolly's pluralistic ontology of immanent naturalism has a problematic relation to his method. By combining strong articulation with a moment of contestability, Connolly's theory is simultaneously too strong and too weak, overdetermining his sociopolitical analyses *and* inadequately prefiguring his normative judgments. This dynamic also affects his politics.

First, Connolly's ethos of engagement is inadequately motivated. By refraining from articulating a method of democratic normative engagement *and* construction and by relying on ontological motivation, he fails to offer plausible reasons why diverse communities would engage in general ethos building. For example, he claims that a common ethos of engagement can grow out of reciprocal appreciation of the tension between partisan ontologies and general ethos (Connolly 2004b, 178). However, this way of viewing contemporary democratic conflict is exactly what will differ across participants. This *tautology* is one instance of the general weakness of employing a contestable ontology as the main normative resource of a democratic political theory. Connolly fails to provide critical and normative resources other than ontological standards, which are themselves the very subject of democratic contestation on his account (a claim giving too much significance to purveyors of ontology). This has led to concerns around the role ethos plays in his political strategy. For Connolly, particular constellations of political forces should employ persuasive ethos to counter the dominant right-wing "evangelico-capitalist resonance machine" (Connolly 2008). For Inder Marwah, the ontological dimension of this claim is the source of two problems with the democratic viability of his use of ethos for negotiating diversity. First, situated in Connolly's naturalistic ontology of affect (see chapter 3), his account assumes that visceral sensibility is hierarchically primary in relation to reasonable reflection. Beyond reinforcing a separation he wants to undermine, this is not merely the claim that it is *also* important but that it is somehow *more* important, that it exists beneath conscious reflection conditioning it regardless of our whims (unless we engage in protracted micropolitics). Second, the affective strategy is normatively nonsensical, asking democratic agents to make conscious choices to contradict affective imbued prejudices while simultaneously claiming that the latter are determinative of their political actions (Marwah 2015, 10). Further, normatively, this conception of democratic politics as affective manipulation is undesirable. It fails to treat citizens as democratic agents while also ignoring any virtue to dialogical politics (e.g., increasing self-reflection, creating new communities, improving reasons) (Livingston 2012, 284–86). It thus lacks any acknowledgment of the desirability of reciprocal linguistic relations. As I argued in chapter 3, this set of tropes in his work is also increasingly dominant. This stands in opposition to both Tully's and Rorty's methods, which employ an ethos only to maintain critical engagement among diverse vocabulary users (Tully 2008, 37, 83, 151). It further contrasts with the former's democratic method of recognition, which illustrates that participation both leads to increased recognition and agency and to increased motivation for further engagement through we-belonging (commonality).

Second, Connolly's ethos is analytically overdetermined. As discussed previously, his method tends to assume a natural order/hierarchy to reasons with ontology/affect/sensibility/faith at the top and argument/dialogue/reasons at the bottom. This is the product of a common jump in reasoning. Connolly and White rightly point out that every political theory comes with some built-in ontological presuppositions. There is, of course, a real question whether those assumptions are necessarily there or merely that said political theory can be described with and in terms of some ontology. However, taking it for granted, this intuitive truism then assumes that this means ontology is both unavoidable for political discussion and normatively determining for the strength of a democratic theory. They jump from unavoidability to analytic primacy. Hence why, for Rorty, ontology is a rhetorical power grab in the realm of cultural politics (Curtis 2015, 197). By placing ontology in a privileged position to actual democratic discourse, Connolly and others exacerbate the normatively undesirable consequences of this approach while failing to provide sufficient reflexivity for their framework to remain critical of its own presumptions.

The root of this is a reification of the category of *the political*. Connolly links a contestable ontological indeterminacy, which he variously codes as contingency, pluralism, fragility, or becoming, to a characterization of the political as inherently pluralizing and thus riven by fundamental *ontological* disagreement. As a result, micropolitics and ethos building become the primary locales of politics, rather than actual democratic engagement among diverse participants, designed at building common democratic decisions. As a result, his view of the political bypasses democracy and productive engagement in disagreement, precluding the possibility of reasonable provisional agreement.

This is problematic theoretically *and* politically. Theoretically, the prioritization of disagreement over agreement both analytically, in terms of questions of the nature of politics, and normatively, to argue against the value of agreement, is as reductive as seeing the political only as the pursuit of consensus. In contrast, Rorty explicitly and Tully implicitly highlight the dangers of casting either harmony or disharmony as the essence of political life. Rorty's cultural politics widens the political (similar to the ontological turn and agonism) by bringing more within the realm of contestation, but without either politicizing everything or essentializing the political. This acknowledges that politics is about both agreement and disagreement, the balance being a product of circumstance. Agonism importantly argues that democracy should not be understood as overcoming disagreement. However, equally, we must avoid overemphasizing the political as only disagreement, conflict, creativity, and contingency (or seeing more authenticity in these). Stability, agreement, and consensus are also aspects of political and democratic life. Rather, the political is not harmonious in any sense—neither as harmony nor the lack of it.

Politically, this understanding of the political discourages democratic engagement. In Connolly the project of a general ethos does not, on his terms, result in a call for reciprocal, reflexive engagement. Rather, engagement becomes ontological exposition: each group speaking their own ontology but not listening to others, in an attempt to convert, where we "forge a relation of agonistic respect with us, even while each of us tries, within reasonable constraints, to convert the other" (Connolly 2008, 90–91). Analytically, such an imperative to normative articulation in an ontological vocabulary tells us nothing about how normative transformation actually occurs or how to have democratic versus nondemocratic versions of it. Essentially, Connolly doesn't answer the question of how we can have horizontal democratic engagement—only mandating ontological expression moderated by respect. There is no conception of democracy as providing any sense, however thin, of a larger unity. While the reasons are ultimately unclear, his assumptions of the necessity of contingency, the violence of all social life, and the paradoxical nature of politics seem the root. Further, without the project of greater democratic unity, Connolly locks us within regional ontologies and repeats the classic problem of diversity politics: reifying groups and their "cultures" to the point that they are incapable of changing, integrating, and, eventually, becoming something totally different. He ignores the normative transformation that characterizes social life.

This suggests a basic flaw in the question of "the political," which assumes its autonomy from the other dimensions of human life. It thus relies on a desire to purify our analyses from the messiness of the social and those other spheres and accord analytic and normative primacy to a distinctly political set of relations that are understood to be discrete from other areas. For examiners of the political it "is accorded its own distinct logic that not only renders it autonomous but also gives it primacy over other social realms. The rise of the political can be said therefore to be accompanied by a corresponding retreat from the social" (McNay 2014, 3–4). This reflects a similar move to hierarchy in order to posit an analytic and normative authority to a perspective that both misunderstands the social origin of authority and fails to democratize either its framework or its resulting politics (both of which are stated aims). Further, it also reveals a confused image of the role of the political theorist in democratic discourse.

Once again, the ontological conception of political theory ends up either too weak or too strong in relation to the plurality of social and political vocabularies within wider democratic culture. On the weak side, as demonstrated in Connolly it has a tendency to conflate the practice of theory with political judgment. As Colin Koopman notes, there is

> a crucial distinction for any reflexive political theory: a distinction between the work of *critique* and acts of *judgment*. When the political theorist formulates their work as a set of judgments, or as a recognizable political *position*, this work loses the force of the distinctive *politicizing* contribution that philosophy can make to politics. Philosophy's contributions ... do not consist in giving us true answers to deep dilemmas. Rather, philosophy's contributions involve a reflexive work of critique that would enable us to begin conceptualizing possibilities for emergent political forms that are not yet positions on our extant political chessboards.
>
> (Koopman n.d., 2)

This does not suggest that political theory is analytically superior to the *demos* but only that as a distinct practice and set of vocabularies, it has a unique set of purposes and uses to offer public discourse. Thus, it has its own distinctive contribution to make to democratic culture, one that does not exist in a relation of authority. On the other hand, as we have seen, in its authoritarian mode, ontological political theory ends up too strong. This fails to maintain the complex balance of reciprocity and reflexivity that I have argued are central to Rorty's and Tully's method and politics. In the end, this is the special type of agonism that Tully and implicitly Rorty offer: an agonism not constrained by ontology and thus enabled in its reflexive critical capacity in relation to contemporary democracy.

CONCLUSION: THE LIMITS AND USES OF RORTY FOR POLITICAL THEORY

Rorty does not theorize either a robust set of principles for liberal democracies or a critical method for uncovering the violences of contemporary norms/institutions. Rather, his significance occurs at the metatheoretical level of the interaction of diverse normative frameworks. Rorty illustrates the constraints on and opportunities for normative transformation, in a manner that does not run afoul of the problem of justification and that does not render reflexive normative development unreachable, though he perhaps does overemphasize the barriers over the opportunities at certain moments. Further, he examines the consequences of these insights for both the interaction of political discourses, which in contemporary democracies are similarly marked by this plurality, and for the practice of political theory and sociopolitical criticism. For Rorty, political theory can only be understood as a form of sociopolitical criticism, if these conditions are recognized, and this practice's best goal is the reflexive engagement/development of critical linguistic practices.

In these ways, Rorty provides a series of important methodological imperatives and proscriptions for political thinking. This chapter summarized them, related them to his mature framework of cultural politics, and drew out its implications for political theory. The center of these insights is the possibility of maintaining a rationally reflexive approach among both the contemporary pluralistic conditions of inquiry and social conditions of normativity. For Rorty, reflexive theory doesn't need stark proceduralism, shedding substantive views, nor "dwelling in the paradox" of contingency/being/pluralism. Instead, it is the product of certain social relationships, established through an understanding of the status of languages as collective practices, the metatheoretical vocabulary of vocabularies, and the horizontal relations between such sets. Rorty's cultural politics is not a universal framework but one situated in specific traditions (Western and Anglo-American) that, at best, can offer an instructive story to others. Importantly, these do not answer the question of why to value difference, as such; they only offer (situated) reasons to value difference now and suggest how to render our current cultural-political contexts more inclusive.

This project and its methodological frame reinforce contemporary social-practice-based political theories like James Tully's, while extrapolating his agonistic approach to intervocabulary engagement in diverse societies. This is fundamentally important for the practice of contemporary political theory. However, it also requires an important caveat: it does *not* necessarily preclude languages that have the type of authority that Rorty rejects at the metalevel. Such an application would exclude many current cultural, religious, political, and academic vocabularies. Further, we will often have good reasons to ascribe such an authority *within* such languages because this enables important sets of practices and relations or prevents altogether horrible ones.[18] Thus, the argument here is not that much of the practice of political theory will change resulting from this reading of Rorty—many already are commonsensically antiauthoritarian and pragmatic. Rather, this argument's relevance to contemporary political theory is its capacity to alter relations along two dimensions: between theories and between itself and wider democratic discourses. In both, a more horizontal nonauthoritarian model of speaking is necessary.

While the political significance has been emphasized above, there are also clear benefits for social-scientific analysis. "Pragmatism is probably best thought of as providing us with an ethos for reconceptualising social science; that is, with some minimal direction and sensibility" (White 2004, 314). For Stephen White, pragmatism's inclusive ethos can address the methodological ferment in the contemporary social sciences by confronting the conditions of inquiry that elicit this diversity: the inescapability of a plurality of perspectives, the social character of the self and scientific inquiry, and the ultimate entanglement of a scientific community of inquirers with the broader public. Its strength is that it is problem driven rather than focused on theoretical lines between groups. Hence, its primary question is what we want a language/theory to do and which practices it should enable/disable. Paradoxically, we must speak from within a framework, with its implied purposes, even to ask this. As a result, while we do not have total reflective control, this conception captures a degree of reflexive agency at the metatheoretical level by engaging our diverse methods of inquiry.

Finally, the secondary project of this study on Rorty's relation to continental thought clarified his reading strategy and the recurrent shape of his engagements with this tradition. This analysis has exposed how Rorty employs this continental thought to illustrate the flaws of an ontological approach to the problem of justification. When this problem is framed in terms of necessity or impossibility, it becomes a negative version of the same foundationalism it undermines. Rorty's criticism of most of his major sources (Dewey, Heidegger, Gadamer, Foucault, Habermas, etc.)

illustrates that the temptation to fall back into foundations is strong, hard to avoid, and easy to rationalize. For him, this was especially true of continental critical social theory's goals of emancipation. Understanding this makes Rorty's approach useful as a cautionary voice against reifying sociohumanisitic limits into metaphysical ones. The political problems of justification and pluralism are not ontological but based in the different ways of speaking and acting that diversity entails. Equally, this reading systematized Rorty's approach to this diversity at the level of theoretical difference within the Western tradition. His traversing of the major divisions in philosophy and political theory illustrates several methodological insights about combining traditions. On the one hand, he offers an inclusive ethos for fusing diverse horizons. On the other, he provides important lessons for remaining critical through contrasting purposes at the metatheoretical level.

All of this contributes to Rorty's unique and misunderstood significance for contemporary political thought. He provided new possibilities for some of the broadest and most pervasive problems for political thinking and democratic engagement. Perhaps, it is because of the intractability of the problems he addressed and the radicality of the manner in which he did so that he has elicited great attention and ire in equal measure—fittingly, as fomenting such conversation was his only *end*.

NOTES

INTRODUCTION. THEORY AND METHOD: RECONSTRUCTING RORTY

1. These groupings represent selective clusters of similarities rather than defined traditions. They are selective in that the similarities emphasized and the differences ignored are useful for the present study. However, they also have reality; their common dynamics are not imposed but represent similar approaches.
2. E.g., there is the tendency to conflate postfoundationalism with poststructuralism/postmodernism in general (Marchart 2007; Silverman 1993; Butler 1992).
3. This distinction is problematic as most of the prominent names of this school are in fact Europeans. However, "continental philosophy" tends to refer more to thinking within the broad lineage of Nietzsche and Heidegger. What is meant here by this term will be clarified later.
4. Bernstein is part of a group challenging the traditional eclipse narrative (Ralston 2011; Talisse 2007). Rorty is central to this pragmatizing narrative. He not only identified a emergence of pragmatic trends in midcentury analytic thought, as already discussed, but argued that pragmatism was waiting at the end of a road much of continental thought was currently traveling (Rorty 1982c, xviii).
5. Dewey's use in debates in deliberative democracy is a good example (Honneth and Farrell 1998).
6. A glance at the edited volumes on Rorty confirms this (Brandom 2000a; Guignon and Hiley 2003; Peters and Ghiraldelli 2001; Pettegrew 2000; Malachowski 1990, 2002; Festenstein and Thompson 2001).
7. Charles Taylor also makes this point (Taylor 2003, 175–76; 1990, 271).
8. As we will see, their readings are also compromised by the disproportionate desire to defend continental philosophers from Rorty's appropriations (Critchley 1996; Norris 1989; Derrida 1996; Dooley 1999; Caputo 1983).

9. I discuss this "situated turn" in Chin (2016a).
10. White only briefly engages Rorty's alternative to weak ontology, noting the power of its critique but failing to respond to it in any detail (White 2000, 15–17).
11. The charge of acquiescence will be moderated to a hesitancy in Rorty around examining the unique capacity of theoretical practice within contemporary political life. In his urge to resist authoritarian conceptions of theory, he pulled too strongly in the other direction, undermining the potential role of reflective political thinking.
12. Because of the limits of a single work and the need to fit diverse readings together, I have had to engage in some omission and smoothing. For example, I say little about Rorty's relation to several continental figures he frequently discussed, Jacques Derrida and Gianni Vattimo being the two most egregious. I avoided substantive discussions of these for several reasons. First, these interpretations do not *as* directly relate to the methodological reading of Rorty offered here. His engagements with Vattimo focus more on the question of religion, an issue Rorty vacillated on substantially in his career (Rorty 1999e; Rorty 2006b). While their discussions of "weak thought" do relate to the issues of foundations, Rorty's views in these moments chime more with other dynamics in his work around postmetaphysical thought and the need for a public-private divide that this reading has rejected (Zabala 2005). Similarly, Rorty's reading of Derrida, while relevant to the issue of the relation between philosophy and politics, is the keystone of this problematic division. It focuses on justifying why Derrida is *not* a public thinker and why he is an example of private thinking par excellence.

1. THE AUTHORITY OF THE SOCIAL: A PRAGMATIC ETHOS OF INQUIRY

1. *PCP*, for example, still contains substantive discussions of analytic philosophy.
2. Rorty cites Platonism as the main target of his work (Rorty 1999f). However, he identifies Platonism with the assumption of a single authoritative framework, a master discourse, for philosophical authority. This is much the same as his critique of analytic epistemology. For recent critical accounts that chime with my own, see Brandom (2013) and Habermas (2000, 31).
3. Similar debates have characterized the history of both political theory and the social sciences (Shapiro, Smith, and Masoud 2004).
4. One particularly important tension he identifies is between approaching language as something to be described or reformed. This difference represents the respective pull of the science and the arts on philosophy (Rorty 1967, 38).
5. As Neil Gross points out, in this volume Rorty is much more on the side of linguistic analysis than subsequently. He in fact goes as far as to argue that it is a fundamental turning point in the development of systematic philosophy, a claim he repudiated (Gross 2008, 184; Rorty 1967, 33).
6. Neil Gross argues that Rorty's focus on the philosophy of mind was a strategic (in terms of his academic career) vehicle for his real metaphilosophical interests (Gross 2008, 177–91).

1. THE AUTHORITY OF THE SOCIAL 249

7. It should be noted that Kant is also a key figure in this narrative. In one sense, he is the most important, as his transcendentalization of these assumptions is the main source for their contemporary forms, playing a key role in the professionalization of philosophy, which has made the discipline unwilling to question this authority structure (Gutting 2003, 42–43). On the other hand, Kant also largely repeats these assumptions in an inverted form that does not alter their problems (Rorty [1979] 2009, 160–61). In the interests of brevity, I have omitted his particular reformulations.
8. The cause-justification conflation takes a particular form in contemporary analytic philosophy, a detailed examination of which is beyond the present study. What is key to note is that, for Rorty, both of these claims are made. Both Quine and Sellars make half a move toward this position but remain unwilling to give up the other distinction. See Koopman (2011b, 66–67).
9. Rorty's invocation of behaviorism should not be confused with behavioralism in political science. The latter's claims to unbiased, neutral forms of explanation should be indicative of the obvious contrast. In fact, behavioralism is often credited with beginning the push to understanding political science as a neutral, value-free social science. In contrast, Rorty's thought gives us ways to reorient that often assumed view, which has strong implications for the practice of political theory.
10. This becomes more obvious in his later work, where Rorty alters this language to be more a matter of "playing ideas off against each other."
11. Rorty subsequently endorsed Brandom's account (Rorty 2000e, 187–88).
12. That is why Rorty is not a skeptic. He does not take structures like the mind to be nonexistent. With Nietzsche, Rorty would say Cartesian minds are real, but optional, and that there are better ways to describe us that allow us to retain the aspects we like (e.g., agency) without the problematic dualism it has engendered (Brandom 2000, 157; Ramberg 2004b, 5).
13. This chronology is intricate and not the object of this discussion. This comment is only meant to forecast the discussion that Rorty turned first to hermeneutics and then to pragmatism in response to a common issue. See Gross (2008, chaps. 7–8).
14. Further, most of this applies to his use of Gadamer and his entitlement to the label of hermeneutics rather than his actual relation to the field. See Warnke (2003) and Guignon (1982). For a notable exception, see Ramberg (2013).
15. I follow Koopman in employing the term "method" for Rorty's approach, though he rejects it himself. Koopman (2011b) flattens this out to a general notion of the way we proceed in theoretical practice. In doing this, I agree with him, Ramberg (2002), and Festenstein (2003) when they argue that Rorty should have been more open to the positive appropriation and reconstruction of terms like method, rather than shrinking from them, as was his tendency.
16. Rorty, being a close colleague of Kuhn at one point, was all too aware that the latter did not endorse his reading of him.
17. For a valuable analysis of the distinction between edifying and systematic philosophies in *PMN*, see Ramberg (2013).
18. James Tully similarly warns that while interpretation should be important, it should not be essentialized (Tully 2008, 62–64).

250   1. THE AUTHORITY OF THE SOCIAL

19. As a central figure in the tradition and the most important one for Rorty, his relationship to Dewey is a microcosm of his relation to pragmatism generally. Rorty acknowledged the rise to prominence of Dewey in his work (Rorty 1991k, 16).
20. For selections from phase 1, see Campbell (1984), Edel (1985), Brodsky (1982), and Kolenda (1986). For phase 2, see Bernstein (1987), Shusterman (1994), and Topper (1995).
21. See, for example, Koopman (2006), Rondel (2011), and Bernstein (2010, chap. 9).
22. Interestingly, Dewey may have come to this conclusion late in life, or at least this is what a posthumously published set of papers and their critical commentary seem to suggest (Dewey 2012; Gronda 2013). The introduction to this volume and the articles in this special issue identify a cultural naturalism that replaces his metaphysics of experience.
23. For a representative selection on the major positions and aspects of debates, see Hildebrand (2014).
24. This anticonvergence theory of inquiry will provide the theoretical base for us to question and reformulate the much maligned role of consensus in Rorty's politics in chapter 5.
25. He does the same thing with the concept of rationality. See chapter 5 and Rorty (1991k, 36–37).

2. THEORIZING AFTER FOUNDATIONS: ONTOLOGY, LANGUAGE, AND HEIDEGGER

1. Only a particular period and aspect of Connolly's work is employed here. Specifically, this analysis draws on his core articulations of ontological method and his resulting critique of Western thought. It does not substantively draw on his work after the 1990s and thus does not engage with his explicit work on pluralism nor his turn to Deleuzian analyses of micropolitics. It remains within his earlier Nietzschean-Heideggerian-Foucauldian period. The purpose of this circumscription is to illuminate specific dynamics in Rorty while also clarifying his major contribution to the ontological turn in political theory in that period (White 2000).
2. This common set of philosophical sources is important. As argued throughout this study, their varying interpretations of Nietzsche, Heidegger, and Foucault (among others) reveals the competing possibilities within this tradition. Despite weaknesses, Rorty illustrates another possibility within these figures that has not been the dominant way of interpreting their works.
3. This latter concept has been at the center of recent pragmatist work on Rorty, especially around this question of its resources for sociopolitical criticism (Gröschner, Koopman, and Sandbothe 2013; Castro and Ghiraldelli 2011).
4. It should be clear that Rorty's discussion is primarily oriented toward the analytic sense of ontology, where it is understood as the existence of particular things in the world. This is different from the Heideggerian sense of the term as the general revelation of being. However, as addressed subsequently, Rorty does extend this critique and his rejection to the Heideggerian usage as well. For example, see his contributions to Mouffe (1996a).

5. This is also a blind spot in the recent literature on Rorty.
6. Connolly has noted the power of Rorty's critique of analytic epistemology (Connolly 1987, 116–19).
7. For a criticism that Connolly does shift between these two incompatible options, see Digeser (1995, 134). For a dissenting view, see White (2000, 114).
8. Rorty is aware of the drawbacks of this analogy in its implication of mastery. However, he thinks it has the advantage of suggesting that language is ultimately a practice, the justification of which is dependent on what it does (Rorty 1982c, xix).
9. It is important to clarify these terms. While "continental philosophy" periodically denotes the entire tradition, Rorty most often uses it in relation to a finite list of post-Nietzschean authors: Hegel, Heidegger, Derrida (and Derrideans), Foucault (and Foucauldians), and Lyotard. Rorty does not comment significantly beyond these particular thinkers, and it is unclear whether he thinks his characterizations extend to other "continental" thinkers. While awkward, "radical critique" is Rorty's term for the temptation these thinkers succumb to (to varying degrees). As discussed in subsequent chapters, it is the desire for autonomy: to speak anew, entirely outside the vocabulary of the present. For Rorty, this ignores the nature of normative and social change. These two categories thus come to mean much the same thing.
10. Connolly's criticism of Rorty and pragmatism, introduced below and developed in chapters 3 and 4, repeats this claim. For Connolly, pragmatism assumes that truth is one; that there is a single, best (i.e., nonmetaphysical), and stable manner to relate to the world (Connolly 1993b, 10).
11. He even claims that pragmatism sits at the end of the road continental theory is currently traveling (Rorty 1982c, xvii).
12. See also Connolly (1985). While there are a few references to Foucault in Connolly's earlier work, this article represents a significant step in bringing continental and ontological frameworks to the fore in his methodology.
13. There is a similar balancing act of Nietzsche and Heidegger in Rorty and Connolly. For both, Nietzsche is the more determinative. However, while in Rorty he lurks behind the scenes, as we will see in chapters 3 and 4, for Connolly, Nietzsche is an overt source. For a comparison of their readings, see Ansell-Pearson (1994, chap. 8).
14. Connolly wrote this soon after the publication of *Consequences of Pragmatism* (1982). Many of the critical resources identified here have only been identified recently in pragmatist scholarship.
15. Hegel also had a distinct influence on Rorty; see chapter 4.

3. RECONSTRUCTING NATURALISM: PRAGMATIC OR ONTOLOGICAL?

1. Brandom also makes this point (Brandom 2000b).
2. For a wider discussion of materialism and the significance of the relativity of vocabularies on this debate, see Rorty (1997, 14–17).

3. This term is problematic. Identifying a methodological approach rather than political framework, the sense in which it is "liberal" is wholly unclear. Nonetheless, it does identify an important cluster of perspectives reconstructing naturalism in light of the critiques of its scientific form over recent years.
4. For a similar definition, see Rorty (1999g, 94).
5. There is a strong relationism in Rorty's naturalism that is usually ignored (Rorty 1999a).
6. It is important to keep this question in view. Any particular vocabulary will always have its own set of normative and critical criteria, but the only way to engage them together or ask questions about the strength of the language on the whole, say in the context of the possible change to a new one, is to turn to what uses and purposes this vocabulary serves.
7. Because this is an increasingly large and influential dynamic in contemporary political thought, I will spend some time laying out its key features and only then elaborate them in Connolly's work.
8. Jane Bennett's recent work is a good example of this (e.g., Bennett 2010, x).
9. In a slightly different form, this criticism also occurs in the speculative realism of Quentin Meillassoux. However, there the criticism is not so much of the Cartesian image as it is the Kantian and Heideggerian shift of philosophy away from the world, as such, to a sole fixation on the human relation to that world (Bryant, Srnicek, and Harman 2010; Meillassoux 2008).
10. The consistency of terms in Connolly's work is impressive: this phrase makes it into the title of his most recent work (Connolly 2013).
11. This is crucial to placing Connolly within contemporary continental political theory. This cluster of perspectives is often divided between those who are said to endorse either immanence or transcendence (Tonder and Thomassen 2005, 8).
12. These two chapters constitute the most detailed methodological statements of this phase of his career.
13. Interestingly, he approximates this term to a "metaphysic" (Connolly 2008, 69–70).
14. Examples: Connolly (2008) on the evangelico-capitalist resonance machine, Connolly (2011) on contemporary time, and Connolly (2013) on neoliberalism.
15. Several connected weaknesses concern this analysis. First, as many note, there is a strain of skepticism in Rorty about theory and the rhetorical role it occupies. As a result, he often pulls back from the reconstructive project and from the language of argument, rationality, and inquiry, failing to give as much backing to his methods as is available. This further causes him to ignore considering the details and consequences of his theoretical and political prescriptions. As we will see, Rorty was often brief on how his mandates would look in a concrete set of relations, practices, and/or institutions (Voparil 2014a; Ramberg 2002; Bernstein 2014). All of this amounts to a certain *theoretical conservatism* within Rorty, one that this reading will push against, expanding and extrapolating where needed and acknowledging limits where he needs to be superseded.
16. Ramberg makes this point when he claims that the naturalistic vocabulary functions as a metatheoretical "base-line stricture on any vocabulary" (Ramberg 2002, 41–42).

17. Perhaps the clearest image of the difference between pragmatism and weak ontology is this connection between metaphysics and normativity. As previously noted, Connolly employs James's pluralistic universe to fill out his ontology. However, James firmly divided his pragmatic method for cultural critique from his radical-empiricist metaphysics. For a strong account of this that deploys James criticism to criticize the ontological method, see Koopman (n.d.)
18. It is important to recall that the question of how to structure/guide such intermethodological and intercultural contexts is exactly the question Rorty's framework addresses. Connolly's model explicitly rejects such an approach and mandates ontological articulation moderated by ethical virtues of engagement. That is why I claim he offers no particular resources, beyond vague ethical maxims to critical responsiveness and agonistic respect, for this task.

4. HISTORY AND MODERNITY: SELF-ASSERTION AND CRITICAL REFLEXIVITY

1. While Bernard Williams and Rorty are usually understood as opposed thinkers, such as around issues of truth (Sleat 2007), there is a similar turn to history to enable cultural criticism in their work. See Chin (2016b).
2. A similar process to his reading Heidegger, discussed in chapter 2, where he read him without the category of Being
3. In this same essay, Rorty clarifies his overlap and differences with Skinner and Foucault, two key historicists (Gross 2008, 214–15).
4. Interestingly, Williams has also been accused of this overemphasis (Koopman 2013b, 65–73).
5. Festenstein's previously cited article remains the best account of this. For another view, see Chin (2015).
6. Though he did not initially frame it in these terms, Rorty enthusiastically accepts this account (Rorty 2000e). Chapter 5 examines the consequences of this in detail.
7. Jonathan Allen's article is one of the best versions of this criticism (Allen 1998). For an account and rebuttal of this general critique, see Bacon (2006).
8. While it is not often framed as such, the development of modern thought is a central concern for pragmatism (Gutting 1999). Rorty in particular is usually framed in terms of postmodernism. This argument takes into account his later rejection of that language (Rorty 1999b), focusing him around a reconstruction of modernity.
9. *CIS* is both a justification of this upward-narrative approach and an example of Rorty's own particular version. Through narrative, this work justifies the development of Western civilization toward Rorty's own vision of pragmatic liberalism.
10. Mostly ignored in the critical literature around Rorty, this review is of special interest because it occurs much earlier in his career than the overt turn to sociopolitical criticism and turn to theories of reflexivity.
11. This is a reference to Robert B. Pippin's seminal work (Pippin 1991).

12. Again, a very similar point to Williams (2005a, 37).
13. The similarity of this account with Heidegger's critique of enframing is apparent (Heidegger 1977b). These connections only buttress the argument of chapter 2 that Connolly's ontological model and critique of modernity, which stem from his initial ontological turn of the 1980s and 1990s, are structured by Heideggerian categories.
14. Interestingly, Rorty cites this as a pragmatic text (Rorty 1991g, 2).
15. Pragmatism is not usually thought of as sharing this insistence with Nietzsche. However, as briefly discussed, Rorty embraced Bacon's version of pragmatism, where knowledge is the power to shape the world for human works (Rorty 1999a, 50).
16. Nathan Widder directs this charge specifically at Rorty, Blumenberg, and the self-assertion of humanity (Widder 2000).
17. Of course, reflexivity will never be total, but it seems sufficient to respond to the implied criticism that more is clearly better in this case.
18. This approach is particularly telling as it is to these themes, especially vitalism, that Connolly is drawn. In fact, the single aspect of pragmatism that Connolly, and much of new materialism, draws on is the radical empiricism of James's pluralistic universe (Connolly 2005b, chap. 3).
19. Again, a very similar point to Williams (2005a, 36).
20. This should recall chapter 2's point that Rorty's framework does not proscribe ontological languages but only argues that they are inappropriate for mediating intervocabulary relations.

5. PRAGMATIC POLITICAL THINKING AND CONTEMPORARY CRITICAL SOCIAL THEORY

1. The single most obvious example of Rorty toeing the liberal line can he found in Rorty (1998a).
2. Its most overt form presently is around discussions of public reason. See Elkins and Norris (2012).
3. This is not to suggest that it is not criticized by liberals but only that it is not their main focus (Conway 2001).
4. Whether this is the best way to frame public purposes will be considered in the discussion of Rorty and agonism in chapter 6.
5. The point is not that Rorty is incorrect that some forms of self-creation are in tension with public goals. It is rather that he ends up reading all modes of self-creation through that lens because of idiosyncratic concerns with particular literatures. In contrast, Rorty would seemingly admit that the private is only incommensurable from the public if you define it as requiring liberation from public—but self-creation does not necessarily require that. For an account of the rise and fall of "literary criticism" within his thinking, see Koopman (2013a, 95–98).
6. Further, in the private context this would violate Rorty's defense of Wittgenstein's argument against private languages.

5. PRAGMATIC POLITICAL THINKING AND CRITICAL SOCIAL THEORY 255

7. This same tension emerged in the possibility of reading Rorty's pragmatism about norms in two manners; see chapter 1.
8. David Owen (2001) links Rorty to Rawls's criterion of public reason and criticizes him for its exclusion of religious reasons a citizen might have for a particular political position.
9. Rorty responded to this critique with the claim that Rawls's criterion wouldn't require actual exclusion but just an ethos of how seriously we take such claims (Rorty 2001a, 111–13).
10. This is the strategic/pragmatic point that not calling them liberal is more inclusive.
11. While Rorty's politics is ethnocentric, it is also universalist in its project, though not its method. See Bacon (2003).
12. This is a recurring phrase in Rorty's work, e.g., Rorty (1991t, 185).
13. While there is a critical literature on Rorty's conception of social criticism within Anglo-American liberal theory, it does not take the form of sustained engagements with Rorty's work but rather brief dismissals. For these reasons, it is not the primary locus of this discussion. For example, see Allen (1998), Taylor (2003), Kymlicka (1989, 65), Lukes (2003, 36), and Macedo (1990, 34). For a pragmatist defense of Rorty, see Bacon (2006).
14. The analytic-continental typology cuts across the critical theory–radical thought divide within the category of critical social theory. However, continental political theory, for the broad purpose of establishing the shape of the literature and its debates, can roughly be equated with radical thought. This does leave critical theory out presently, but we will return to its placement in this nexus. For an account of its placement in the analytical-continental divide in political thought, see White (2016). For a paradigmatic debate, see the Foucault-Habermas debate (Ashenden and Owen 1999; Habermas 1987).
15. As a result, I use these terms somewhat interchangeably here depending on context. Generally, weak ontology should be understood as a subset of radical thought. Rorty's purposes tended to extend to the latter as a whole, which does well to set up the more specific subsequent discussion of weak ontology.
16. This is an awkward and indistinct term that Rorty uses to refer to a broad group of theorists and identify a common set of dynamics and weaknesses. Though not without its problems, it does allow Rorty to approach the question of the broad metatheoretical orientation of this group.
17. This develops Rorty's point about objectivity discussed in chapter 1.
18. Such conditions are why Rorty holds that modernity and its social relations are generally more capable of reflexive critical development than other societies (Rorty 1991d, 46–47). Bernard Williams (2005b) makes a similar point.
19. This point is agnostic about whether "we liberals" was a prudent way to appeal to such a social consensus. The main claim is only that, as such, it is not an incoherent pathway to social criticism.
20. See, for example Rorty (1998d, 326).
21. Rorty explicitly claims this much earlier in *PMN* (Rorty [1979] 2009, 318).
22. This recalls White's reading of continental thought (see chapter 4).

23. Rorty posits this as the key division between him and radical thought (Rorty 1991a, 214).
24. For an account of Rorty's positive views of Foucault, see Malecki (2011, 107–110).
25. My concern here is not the accuracy of Rorty's account, though this is a persistent background question, but the role of this account in Rorty's larger political thinking, his relation to continental political thought, and its insights for contemporary uses of Foucault.
26. Most accounts tend to fall into the "defend Foucault from Rorty" trend we have seen repeated in other continental literatures on Rorty. See Koopman (2011c).
27. In chapter 1, we saw Rorty's opposition to this language of constitution in hermeneutics. Constitution connotes a causal relation. Language does not cause objects to exist, though it may condition how we think of them, what we say about them, what we do with them, and what we try to do in the future.

6. HOW PRAGMATISM CONSTRAINS AND ENABLES POLITICAL THINKING

1. This nuance is one that Rorty sometimes forgot in his polemical moments (Voparil 2006, 26).
2. This widens and politicizes his account of vocabularies and notion of logical spaces discussed in chapter 2.
3. This was problematic, but only insofar as it raised too many specters of utilitarianism and consequentialism for a body of theorists often skeptical of these labels and ready to link pragmatism to their perceived faults.
4. The development of this has been addressed at length already (chapters 1 and 5).
5. This mixing of naturalism and historicism, while unique, is not without parallel. As I argue in a recent article, Bernard Williams's political thought is characterized by a similar mixing (Chin 2016b).
6. The argument here is not that some close textual reading reveals this fundamental position within his thought. Such a strategy would be decidedly un-Rortian for the simple reason that there is no core sense of a text. Rather, it is that when you put together many of Rorty's metaphilosophical conclusions regarding the nature of inquiry, the limits of human social change, and the possibilities within the Western tradition of sociopolitical criticism, there are a series of substantive methodological insights that productively extend existing debates within contemporary political thought. Thus, this critical reconstruction does beat Rorty into a bit of a shape, but for the ultimately practical purpose of contributing to the self-understanding of the practice of sociopolitical reflection. This is a very Rortian project.
7. There has been a recent surge of work on genealogy and pragmatism generally (Koopman 2011c; B. Allen 2009; Colapietro 1998; Stuhr 1997).
8. For recent accounts of agonism's connection to these traditions, see Wenman (2015) and Khan (2016).

9. Sheldon Wolin (1992) is a good example.
10. Recent debates around "New Realism" similarly emphasize the autonomy of the political without ontology (Galston 2010).
11. In spite of the following links, there is very little on their relationship (Curtis 2015, 83–87; Festenstein 2003, 9, 15; Mendieta 2014, 35–37).
12. This way of approaching the history of thought, through alternative traditions, bears remarkable similarities to Rorty's approach and how he places himself in an ignored tradition of pragmatists, historicists, and antifoundationalists. There are several similarities in their reading strategies. Not only does Tully broach similar theoretical divisions to Rorty, but he also reconstructs and redescribes his sources. For example: his combination of Rawls and Foucault (Tully 2008, 74).
13. For example, Mark Wenman criticizes his exclusive focus on the politics of augmentation over revolution (Wenman 2013, 162).
14. Tully distinguishes himself from both Habermas and the hermeneutics of Charles Taylor (Tully 2008, 62–63, 67–68). This mirrors Rorty's own tension with this literature. Further, Tully broadly endorses Rorty's, and Quentin Skinner's, claim that much of political thought has implicitly operated with this approach (Tully 2008, 55).
15. I am not alone in claiming this. Eduardo Mendieta calls Tully's civic freedom and agonistic citizenship eloquent articulations of Rorty's prescriptions for a postphilosophical culture (Mendieta 2014, 37). Matthew Festenstein claims that Tully's view of social-political criticism bears a remarkable resemblance to Rorty's (Festenstein 2003, 9). Tully also agrees, noting that Rorty's broad shift requires specification (Tully 2008, 139).
16. This account has focused primarily on Rorty's and Tully's methodological and political similarities. There are also real differences. Primarily, while the concept of recognition is central to Tully's model, Rorty was very skeptical of the rise of recognition politics (Rorty 2000c). I would argue this rejection is in tension with his later cultural politics.
17. E.g., he criticizes Mouffe for underthinking ethics in pluralist democratic politics (Connolly 1995b).
18. E.g., see Rorty on human rights (Rorty 1998f).

REFERENCES

WORKS BY RICHARD RORTY

Rorty, Richard. 1961a. "Recent Metaphilosophy." *Review of Metaphysics* 15 (2): 299–318.
———. 1961b. "The Limits of Reductionism." In *Experience, Existence, and the Good*, edited by L. C. Lieb, 100–16. Carbondale: Southern Illinois University Press.
———. 1965. "Mind-Body Identity, Privacy, and Categories." *Review of Metaphysics* 19 (1).
———. 1967. "Introduction: Metaphilosophical Difficulties with Linguistic Philosophy." In *The Linguistic Turn: Essays in Philosophical Method*, edited by Richard Rorty. Chicago: University of Chicago Press.
———. 1970a. "In Defense of Eliminative Materialism." *Review of Metaphysics* 24 (1).
———. 1970b. "Incorrigibility as the Mark of the Mental." *Journal of Philosophy* 67 (12).
———. 1980. "A Reply to Dreyfus and Taylor." *Review of Metaphysics* 34 (1): 39–46.
———. 1981. "Beyond Nietzsche and Marx." *London Review of Books* 3 (3): 3–4.
———. 1982a. *Consequences of Pragmatism*. Minneapolis: University of Minnesota Press.
———. 1982b. "Dewey's Metaphysics." In *Consequences of Pragmatism*. Minneapolis: University of Minnesota Press.
———. 1982c. "Introduction Pragmatism and Philosophy." In *Consequences of Pragmatism*. Minneapolis: University of Minnesota Press.
———. 1982d. "Method, Social Science and Social Hope." In *Consequences of Pragmatism*. Minneapolis: University of Minnesota Press.
———. 1982e. "Nineteenth-Century Idealism and Twentieth-Century Textualism." In *Consequences of Pragmatism*. Minneapolis: University of Minnesota Press.
———. 1982f. "Overcoming the Tradition: Heidegger and Dewey." In *Consequences of Pragmatism*. Minneapolis: University of Minnesota Press.
———. 1983. "Against Belatedness." *London Review of Books* 5 (11).

———. 1986a. "Foucault and Epistemology." In *Foucault: A Critical Reader*, edited by David Couzens Hoy. Oxford: Basil Blackwell.
———. 1986b. "Introduction." In *The Later Works of John Dewey*, vol. 8, edited by Jo Ann Boydston. Carbondale: Southern Illinois University Press.
———. 1987. "Posties." *London Review of Books* 9 (15): 11–12.
———. 1989. *Contingency, Irony, and Solidarity*. Cambridge: Cambridge University Press.
———. 1990. "Truth and Freedom: A Reply to Thomas McCarthy." *Critical Inquiry* 16 (3): 633–43.
———. 1991a. "Cosmopolitanism Without Emancipation: A Response to Jean-François Lyotard." In *Objectivity, Relativism, and Truth*. Cambridge: Cambridge University Press.
———. 1991b. *Essays on Heidegger and Others*. Cambridge: University of Cambridge Press.
———. 1991c. "Habermas and Lyotard On Postmodernity." In *Essays on Heidegger and Others*. Cambridge: Cambridge University Press.
———. 1991d. "Heidegger, Contingency, and Pragmatism." In *Essays on Heidegger and Others*. Cambridge: Cambridge University Press.
———. 1991e. "Heidegger, Kundera, Dickens." In *Essays on Heidegger and Others*. Cambridge: Cambridge University Press.
———. 1991f. "Inquiry as Recontextualization: An Anti-Dualist Account of Interpretation." In *Objectivity, Relativism, and Truth*. Cambridge: Cambridge University Press.
———. 1991g. "Introduction: Pragmatism and Post-Nietzschean Philosophy." In *Essays on Heidegger and Others*. Cambridge: University of Cambridge Press.
———. 1991h. "Just One More Species Doing Its Best." *London Review of Books* 13 (14): 3–7.
———. 1991i. "Moral Identity and Private Autonomy: The Case of Foucault." In *Essays on Heidegger and Others*. Cambridge: Cambridge University Press.
———. 1991j. "Non-Reductive Physicalism." In *Objectivity, Relativism, and Truth*. Cambridge: Cambridge University Press.
———. 1991k. *Objectivity, Relativism, and Truth*. Cambridge: University of Cambridge Press.
———. 1991l. "On Ethnocentrism." In *Objectivity, Relativism, and Truth*. Cambridge: Cambridge University Press.
———. 1991m. "Philosophy as Science, as Metaphor, and as Politics." In *Essays on Heidegger and Others*. Cambridge: Cambridge University Press.
———. 1991n. "Postmodernist Bourgeois Liberalism." In *Objectivity, Relativism, and Truth*, 197–202. Cambridge: Cambridge University Press.
———. 1991o. "Pragmatism Without Method." In *Objectivity, Relativism, and Truth*. Cambridge: Cambridge University Press.
———. 1991p. "Pragmatism, Davidson, and Truth." In *Objectivity, Relativism, and Truth*. Cambridge: Cambridge University Press.
———. 1991q. "Representation, Social Practice, and Truth." In *Objectivity, Relativism, and Truth*. Cambridge: Cambridge University Press.
———. 1991r. "Solidarity or Objectivity." In *Objectivity, Relativism, and Truth*. Cambridge: Cambridge University Press.
———. 1991s. "Texts and Lumps." In *Objectivity, Relativism, and Truth*. Cambridge: Cambridge University Press.

———. 1991t. "The Priority of Democracy to Philosophy." In *Objectivity, Relativism, and Truth*. Cambridge: Cambridge University Press.

———. 1991u. "Unfamiliar Noises: Hesse and Davidson on Metaphor." In *Objectivity, Relativism, and Truth*. Cambridge: Cambridge University Press.

———. 1991v. "Wittgenstein, Heidegger, and the Reification of Language." In *Essays on Heidegger and Others*. Cambridge: Cambridge University Press.

———. 1994. "Taylor on Self-Celebration and Gratitude." *Philosophy and Phenomenological Research* 54 (1).

———. 1995a. "Philosophy and the Future." In *Rorty and Pragmatism: The Philosopher Responds to His Critics*, edited by Hermann J. Saatkamp. London: Vanderbilt University Press.

———. 1995b. "Response to Gouinlock." In *Rorty and Pragmatism: The Philosopher Responds to His Critics*, edited by Herman J. Saatkamp. London: Vanderbilt University Press.

———. 1995c. "Response to Lavine." In *Rorty and Pragmatism: The Philosopher Responds to His Critics*, edited by Herman J. Saatkamp. London: Vanderbilt University Press.

———. 1996a. "Idealizations, Foundations and Social Practices." In *Democracy and Difference: Contesting the Boundaries of the Political*, edited by Seyla Benhabib. Princeton, NJ: Princeton University Press.

———. 1996b. "Remarks on Deconstruction and Pragmatism." In *Deconstruction and Pragmatism*, edited by Chantal Mouffe. London: Routledge.

———. 1997. *Truth, Politics, and "Post-Modernism."* Assen: Van Gorcum.

———. 1998a. "A Defense of Minimalist Liberalism." In *Debating Democracy's Discontent*, edited by Anita L. Allen and Milton C. Regan. Oxford: Oxford University Press.

———. 1998b. *Achieving Our Country. Leftist Thought in Twentieth-Century America*. Cambridge, MA: Harvard University Press.

———. 1998c. "Feminism and Pragmatism." In *Truth and Progress*. Cambridge: Cambridge University Press.

———. 1998d. "Habermas, Derrida, and the Functions of Philosophy." In *Truth and Progress*. Cambridge: Cambridge University Press.

———. 1998e. "Hilary Putnam and the Relativist Menace." In *Truth and Progress*, 43–62. Cambridge: Cambridge University Press.

———. 1998f. "Human Rights, Rationality, Sentimentality." In *Truth and Progress*. Cambridge: Cambridge University Press.

———. 1998g. "Robert Brandom on Social Practices and Representations." In *Truth and Progress*. Cambridge: Cambridge University Press.

———. 1999a. "A World Without Substances or Essences." In *Philosophy and Social Hope*. London: Penguin.

———. 1999b. "Afterword: Pragmatism, Pluralism and Postmodernism." In *Philosophy and Social Hope*. London: Penguin.

———. 1999c. "Comment on Robert Pippen's 'Naturalness and Mindedness: Hegel's Compatibilism.'" *European Journal of Philosophy* 7 (2).

———. 1999d. *Philosophy and Social Hope*. London: Penguin.

———. 1999e. "Religion As Conversation-Stopper." In *Philosophy and Social Hope*. London: Penguin Books.

———. 1999f. "Trotsky and the Wild Orchids." In *Philosophy and Social Hope*. London: Penguin.
———. 1999g. *Truth and Progress*. Cambridge: Cambridge University Press.
———. 2000a. "Being That Can Be Understood Is Language." *London Review of Books* 22 (6): 23–25.
———. 2000b. "Dewey Between Hegel and Darwin." In *Truth and Progress*. Cambridge: Cambridge University Press.
———. 2000c. "Is 'Cultural Recognition' a Useful Concept for Leftist Politics?" *Critical Horizons* 1 (1): 7–20.
———. 2000d. "Response to Jürgen Habermas." In *Rorty and His Critics*, edited by Robert B. Brandom, 56–64. Oxford: Blackwell.
———. 2000e. "Response to Robert Brandom." In *Rorty and His Critics*, edited by Robert B. Brandom, 183–90. Oxford: Blackwell.
———. 2000f. "The Historiography of Philosophy: Four Genres." In *Truth and Progress*. Cambridge: Cambridge University Press.
———. 2000g. "Universality and Truth." In *Rorty and His Critics*, edited by Robert B. Brandom. Oxford: Blackwell.
———. 2001a. "Response to David Owen." In *Richard Rorty: Critical Dialogues*, edited by Matthew Festenstein and Simon Thompson. Cambridge: Polity.
———. 2001b. "Response to Shusterman." In *Richard Rorty: Critical Dialogues*, edited by Matthew Festenstein and Simon Thompson. Cambridge: Polity.
———. 2001c. "The Ambiguity of 'Rationality.'" In *Pluralism and the Pragmatic Turn: The Transformation of Critical Theory Essays in Honor of Thomas McCarthy*, edited by William Rehg and James Bohman. Cambridge, MA: MIT Press.
———. 2003. "Some American Uses of Hegel." In *Das Interesse des Denkens: Hegel aus heutiger Sicht*, edited by Wolfgang Welsch and Klaus Vieweg. Paderborn: Wilhelm Fink Verlag.
———. 2004. "Philosophy as a Transitional Genre." In *Pragmatism, Critique, Judgment: Essays for Richard J. Bernstein*, edited by Seyla Benhabib and Nancy Fraser. Cambridge, MA: MIT Press.
———. 2006a. "Pragmatism as Anti-Authoritarianism." In *A Companion to Pragmatism*, edited by John R. Shook and Joseph Margolis. Oxford: Blackwell.
———. 2006b. "Religious Faith, Intellectual Responsibility, and Romance." In *Cambridge Companion to William James*, edited by Ruth Anna Putnam, 84–102. Cambridge: Cambridge University Press.
———. 2006c. *When You Take Care of Freedom, Truth Will Take Care of Itself*. Edited by Eduardo Mendieta. Stanford, CA: Stanford University Press.
———. 2007a. "Analytic and Conversational Philosophy." In *Philosophy as Cultural Politics*. Cambridge: Cambridge University Press.
———. 2007b. "Cultural Politics and the Existence of God." In *Philosophy as Cultural Politics*. Cambridge: Cambridge University Press.
———. 2007c. "Grandeur, Profundity, and Finitude." In *Philosophy as Cultural Politics*. Cambridge: Cambridge University Press.

———. 2007d. "Holism and Historicism." In *Philosophy as Cultural Politics*. Cambridge: Cambridge University Press.
———. 2007e. "Justice as Larger Loyalty." In *Philosophy as Cultural Politics*. Cambridge: Cambridge University Press.
———. 2007f. "Kant vs. Dewey: The Current Situation of Moral Philosophy." In *Philosophy as Cultural Politics*. Cambridge: Cambridge University Press.
———. 2007g. "Naturalism and Quietism." In *Philosophy as Cultural Politics*. Cambridge: Cambridge University Press.
———. 2007h. *Philosophy as Cultural Politics*. Cambridge: Cambridge University Press.
———. 2007i. "Pragmatism and Romanticism." In *Philosophy as Cultural Politics*. Cambridge: Cambridge University Press.
———. 2007j. "Pragmatism as Romantic Polytheism." In *Philosophy as Cultural Politics*. Cambridge: Cambridge University Press.
———. 2007k. "Preface." In *Philosophy as Cultural Politics*. Cambridge: Cambridge University Press.
———. 2007l. "Wittgenstein and the Linguistic Turn." In *Philosophy as Cultural Politics*. Cambridge: Cambridge University Press.
———. [1979] 2009. *Philosophy and the Mirror of Nature*. 30th anniv. ed. Princeton, NJ: Princeton University Press.
———. 2010. "Intellectual Autobiography." In *The Philosophy of Richard Rorty*, edited by Randall E. Auxier and Lewis Edwin Hahn. Chicago: Open Court.

GENERAL REFERENCES

Allen, Barry. 2004. "What Knowledge? What Hope? What New Pragmatism?" In *The Pragmatic Turn in Philosophy*, edited by William Egginton and Mike Sandbothe. Albany: State University of New York Press.
———. 2009. "After Knowledge and Liberty: Foucault and the New Pragmatism." In *Foucault's Legacy*, edited by C. G. Prado. London: Continuum.
Allen, Jonathan. 1998. "The Situated Critic or the Loyal Critic? Rorty and Walzer on Social Criticism." *Philosophy and Social Criticism* 25 (6).
Ansell-Pearson, Keith. 1994. *An Introduction to Nietzsche as Political Thinker: The Perfect Nihilist*. Cambridge: Cambridge University Press.
Ashenden, Samantha, and David Owen, eds. 1999. *Foucault Contra Habermas: Recasting the Dialogue Between Genealogy and Critical Theory*. London: Sage.
Bacon, Michael. 2003. "Liberal Universalism: On Brian Barry and Richard Rorty." *Critical Review of International Social and Political Philosophy* 6 (2).
———. 2006. "Rorty and Pragmatic Social Criticism." *Philosophy and Social Criticism* 32 (7).
———. 2007. *Richard Rorty: Pragmatism and Political Liberalism*. London: Lexington.
Bennett, Jane. 2010. *Vibrant Matter*. London: Duke University Press.
Berlin, Isaiah. 1969. *Four Essays on Liberty*. Oxford: Oxford University Press.

———. 1999. "Does Political Theory Still Exist?" In *Concepts and Categories: Philosophical Essays*, edited by Henry Hardy. Princeton, NJ: Princeton University Press.

Bernstein, Richard J. 1986. *Philosophico-Political Profiles: Essays in a Pragmatic Mode*. Philadelphia: University of Pennsylvania Press.

———. 1987. "One Step Forward, Two Steps Back: Richard Rorty on Liberal Democracy and Philosophy." *Political Theory* 15.

———. 1991. *The New Constellation: Ethical-Political Horizons of Modernity/Postmodernity*. Cambridge: Polity.

———. 1995. "American Pragmatism: The Conflict of Narratives." In *Rorty and Pragmatism: The Philosopher Responds to His Critics*. London: Vanderbilt University Press.

———. 2006. "The Pragmatic Century." In *The Pragmatic Century: Conversations with Richard J. Bernstein*, edited by Sheila Greeve Davaney and Warren G. Frisina. Albany: State University of New York Press.

———. 2010. *The Pragmatic Turn*. Cambridge: Polity.

———. 2014. "'So Much the Worse for Your Old Institutions; Start Working Up Some New Ones.'" *Contemporary Pragmatism* 11 (1): 5–14.

Bernstein, Richard J., and Christopher J. Voparil. 2010. "General Introduction." In *The Rorty Reader*. Chichester: Blackwell.

Blake, Michael. 2005. "Liberal Foundationalism and Agonistic Democracy." In *Political Exclusion and Domination NOMOS XLVI*, edited by Melissa S. Williams and Stephen Macedo, 230–43. New York: New York University Press.

Brandom, Robert B., ed. 2000a. *Rorty and His Critics*. Oxford: Blackwell.

———. 2000b. "Vocabularies of Pragmatism: Synthesizing Naturalism and Historicism." In *Rorty and His Critics*, edited by Robert B. Brandom. Oxford: Blackwell.

———. 2005. "Heidegger's Categories in Being and Time." In *A Companion to Heidegger*, edited by Hubert Dreyfus. Oxford: Blackwell.

———. 2013. "An Arc of Thought: From Rorty's Eliminative Materialism to His Pragmatism." In *Richard Rorty: From Pragmatist Philosophy to Cultural Politics*, edited by Alexander Gröschner, Colin Koopman, and Mike Sandbothe. London: Bloomsbury.

Brodsky, Garry. 1982. "Rorty's Interpretation of Pragmatism." *Transactions of the Charles S. Peirce Society: A Quarterly Journal in American Philosophy* 18 (4).

Bryant, Levi, Nick Srnicek, and Graham Harman, eds. 2010. *The Speculative Turn: Continental Materialism and Realism*. Melbourne.

Butler, Judith. 1992. "Contingent Foundations: Feminism and the Question of 'Postmodernism.'" In *Feminists Theorize the Political*, edited by Judith Butler and J. W. Scott. London: Routledge.

Campbell, David, and Morton Schoolman, eds. 2008. *The New Pluralism: William Connolly and the Contemporary Global Condition*. London: Duke University Press.

Campbell, James. 1984. "Rorty's Use of Dewey." *Southern Journal of Philosophy* 22 (2).

Caputo, John D. 1983. "The Thought of Being and the Conversation of Mankind: The Case of Heidegger and Rorty." *Review of Metaphysics* 36.

Chin, Clayton. 2015. "Engaging the Present: The Necessity of Reading Rorty." *Contemporary Pragmatism* 12 (1): 55–70.

———. 2016a. "Between Analytic and Continental in Contemporary Political Thought: Methodological Pluralism in Pragmatism and the Situated Turn." *European Journal of Political Theory* 15 (1): 205–22.

———. 2016b. "Challenging Political Theory: Pluralism and Method in the Work of Bernard Williams." *Public Reason* 9 (1–2): 35–52.

———. Forthcoming. "Normative Engagement Across Difference: Pragmatism, Dialogic Inclusion, and Social Practices." *Philosophy and Social Criticism*.

Chin, C., and M. Bacon, eds. 2015. "Pragmatism and Political Theory." *Political Studies Review* 13 (3).

Chin, C., and L. Thomassen, eds. 2015. "Continental and Analytical Political Theory: An Insurmountable Divide?" *European Journal of Political Theory*, 14 (3).

Colapietro, Vincent M. 1998. "American Evasions of Foucault." *Southern Journal of Philosophy* 36 (3).

Connolly, William E. 1985. "Taylor, Foucault, and Otherness." *Political Theory* 13 (3).

———. 1987. *Politics and Ambiguity*. London: University of Wisconsin Press.

———. 1990. "Review Symposium on Richard Rorty." *History of the Human Sciences* 3 (1): 104–8.

———. 1991. *Identity/Difference: Democratic Negotiations of Political Paradox*. London: Cornell University Press.

———. 1993a. "Beyond Good and Evil: The Ethical Sensibility of Michel Foucault." *Political Theory* 21 (3): 365–89.

———. 1993b. *Political Theory and Modernity*. Ithaca, NY: Cornell University Press.

———. 1994. *The Terms of Political Discourse*. 3rd ed. Oxford: Blackwell.

———. 1995a. *The Ethos of Pluralization*. London: University of Minnesota Press.

———. 1995b. "The Twilight of Idols." *Philosophy and Social Criticism* 21 (3): 127–37.

———. 1999a. "Brain Waves, Transcendental Fields, and Techniques of Thought." *Radical Philosophy* 94.

———. 1999b. *Why I Am Not a Secularist*. Minneapolis: University of Minnesota Press.

———. 2002. *Neuropolitics: Thinking, Culture, Speed*. Minneapolis: University of Minnesota Press.

———. 2004a. "Method, Problem, Faith." In *Problems and Methods in the Study of Politics*, edited by Ian Shapiro, Rogers M. Smith, and Tarek E. Masoud. Cambridge: Cambridge University Press.

———. 2004b. "The Ethos of Democratization." In *Laclau: A Critical Reader*, edited by Simon Critchley and Oliver Marchart, 167–81. London: Routledge.

———. 2005a. "Immanence, Abundance, Democracy." In *Radical Democracy: Politics Between Abundance and Lack*, edited by Lasse Thomassen and Lars Tonder. Manchester: Manchester University Press.

———. 2005b. *Pluralism*. London: Duke University Press.

———. 2008. *Capitalism and Christianity, American Style*. London: Duke University Press.

———. 2011. *A World of Becoming*. London: Duke University Press.

———. 2013. *The Fragility of Things*. London: Duke University Press.

Conway, Daniel. 2001. "Irony, State, and Utopia: Rorty's 'We' and the Problem of Transitional Praxis." In *Richard Rorty: Critical Dialogues*, edited by Matthew Festenstein and Simon Thompson, 55–88. Cambridge: Polity.

Cooke, Maeve. 2005. "Avoiding Authoritarianism: On the Problem of Justification in Contemporary Critical Social Theory." *International Journal of Philosophical Studies* 13 (3).
———. 2006. *Re-Presenting the Good Society*. Cambridge, MA: Cambridge University Press.
Coole, Diana. 2013. "Agentic Capacities and Capacious Historical Materialism: Thinking with New Materialisms in the Political Sciences." *Millennium: Journal of International Studies* 41 (3).
Coole, Diana, and Samantha Frost, eds. 2010. *New Materialisms: Ontology, Agency, and Politics*. Durham, NC: Duke University Press.
Couzens Hoy, David, and Thomas McCarthy, eds. 1994. *Critical Theory*. Oxford: Blackwell.
Critchley, Simon. 1996. "Deconstruction and Pragmatism—Is Derrida a Private Ironist or Public Liberal?" In *Deconstruction and Pragmatism*, edited by Chantal Mouffe. London: Routledge.
Curtis, William M. 2015. *Defending Rorty: Pragmatism and Liberal Virtue*. Cambridge: Cambridge University Press.
Derrida, Jacques. 1996. "Remarks on Deconstruction and Pragmatism." In *Deconstruction and Pragmatism*, edited by Chantal Mouffe. London: Routledge.
Dewey, John. 2008a. *Reconstruction in Philosophy*. In *The Middle Works of John Dewey*, vol. 12, edited by Jo Ann Boydston. Carbondale: Southern Illinois University Press.
———. 2008b. "The Need for a Recovery of Philosophy." In *The Middle Works of John Dewey*, vol. 10, edited by Jo Ann Boydston. Carbondale: Southern Illinois University Press.
———. 2012. *Unmodern Philosophy and Modern Philosophy*. Edited by Phillip Deen. Carbondale: Southern Illinois University Press.
Digeser, Peter. 1995. *Our Politics, Our Selves: Liberalism, Identity, and Harm*. Chichester: Princeton University Press.
Dooley, Mark. 1999. "Private Irony vs. Social Hope: Derrida, Rorty, and the Political." *Cultural Values* 3 (3).
Edel, Abraham. 1985. "A Missing Dimension in Rorty's Use of Pragmatism." *Transactions of the Charles S. Peirce Society: A Quarterly Journal in American Philosophy* 21 (2).
Elkins, Jeremy, and Andrew Norris, eds. 2012. *Truth and Democracy*. Philadelphia: University of Pennsylvania Press.
Fairlamb, Horace. 1994. *Critical Conditions. Postmodernity and the Question of Foundations*. Cambridge: Cambridge University Press.
Festenstein, Matthew. 1997. *Pragmatism and Political Theory*. Chicago: University of Chicago Press.
———. 2003. "Politics and Acquiescence in Rorty's Pragmatism." *Theoria: A Journal of Social and Political Theory* 101:1–24.
Festenstein, Matthew, and Simon Thompson, eds. 2001. *Richard Rorty: Critical Dialogues*. Cambridge: Polity.
Finlayson, Alan, ed. 2010. *Democracy and Pluralism: The Political Thought of William E. Connolly*. Oxford: Routledge.
Foucault, Michel. 1980. *Language, Counter-Memory, Practice: Selected Essays and Interviews*. Ithaca, NY: Cornell University Press.

Fraser, Nancy. 1990. "Solidarity or Singularity: Richard Rorty Between Romanticism and Technocracy." In *Reading Rorty*, edited by Alan Malachowski. Oxford: Blackwell.
———. 1995. "From Irony to Prophecy to Politics: A Response to Richard Rorty." In *Pragmatism: A Contemporary Reader*, edited by Russell B. Goodman. London: Routledge.
Gadamer, Hans-Georg. 2004. *Truth and Method*. Translated by Joel Weinsheimer and Donald G. Marshall. London: Bloomsbury.
Galston, William A. 2010. "Realism in Political Theory." *European Journal of Political Theory* 9:385–411.
Gascoigne, Neil. 2008. *Richard Rorty: Liberalism, Irony, and the Ends of Philosophy*. Cambridge: Polity.
Green, Judith M. 2008. *Pragmatism and Social Hope: Deepening Democracy in Global Contexts*. New York: Columbia University Press.
———., ed. 2013. *Richard J. Bernstein and the Pragmatic Turn in Contemporary Philosophy*. London: Palgrave Macmillan.
Gronda, Roberto, ed. 2013. "Symposium on Dewey's Unmodern Philosophy and Modern Philosophy." *European Journal of Pragmatism and American Philosophy* 5 (1).
Gross, Neil. 2008. *Richard Rorty: The Making of an American Philosopher*. London: University of Chicago Press.
Guignon, Charles. 1982. "Saving the Differences: Gadamer and Rorty." *PSA: Proceedings of the Biannual Meeting of the Philosophy of Science Association* 2.
———. 1986. "On Saving Heidegger from Rorty." *Philosophy and Phenomenological Research* 46 (3).
Guignon, Charles, and David R. Hiley, eds. 2003. *Richard Rorty*. Cambridge: Cambridge University Press.
Gutting, Gary. 1999. *Pragmatic Liberalism and the Critique of Modernity*. Cambridge: Cambridge University Press.
———. 2003. "Rorty's Critique of Epistemology." In *Richard Rorty*, edited by Charles Guignon and David R. Hiley. Cambridge: Cambridge University Press.
Habermas, Jürgen. 1987. *The Philosophical Discourses on Modernity: Twelve Lectures*. Cambridge: Basil Blackwell.
———. 1992. *Postmetaphysical Thinking*. Translated by William Mark Hohengarten. Oxford: Polity.
———. 2000. "Richard Rorty's Pragmatic Turn." In *Rorty and His Critics*, edited by Robert Brandom. Oxford: Blackwell.
Hegel, G. F. W. 1991. *Elements of the Philosophy of Right*. Edited by H. B. Nisbet. Cambridge: Cambridge University Press.
Heidegger, Martin. 1975. "Sketches for a History of Being as Metaphysics." In *The End of Philosophy*. London: Souvenir.
———. 1977a. "The Age of the World Picture." In *The Question Concerning Technology and Other Essays*, translated by William Lovitt. London: Harper and Row.
———. 1977b. "The Question Concerning Technology." In *The Question Concerning Technology and Other Essays*, translated by William Lovitt. London: Harper and Row.

———. 1998. "On the Essence of Truth." In *Pathmarks*, edited by William McNeil. Cambridge: Cambridge University Press.

Hildebrand, David L., ed. 2014. "Symposia on Language or Experience: Charting Pragmatism's Course for the 21st Century." *European Journal of Pragmatism and American Philosophy* 6 (2).

Hiley, David R. 2002. "Is Eliminative Materialism Materialistic?" In *Richard Rorty*, vol. 1, edited by Alan Malachowski. London: Sage.

Honig, Bonnie. 2014. "'[Un]Dazzled by the Ideal'—James Tully's New Realism." In *Freedom and Democracy in an Imperial Context: Dialogues with James Tully*, edited by Robert Nichols and Jakeet Singh. Oxon: Routledge.

Honneth, Axel, and John M. M. Farrell. 1998. "Democracy as Reflexive Cooperation: John Dewey and the Theory of Democracy Today." *Political Theory* 26 (6): 763–83.

Horton, John. 2001. "Irony and Commitment: An Irreconcilable Dualism of Modernity." In *Richard Rorty: Critical Dialogues*, edited by Matthew Festenstein and Simon Thompson. Cambridge: Polity.

Horwich, Paul. 2010. "Rorty's Wittgenstein." In *Wittgenstein's Philosophical Investigations: A Critical Guide*, edited by Arif Ahmed. Cambridge: Cambridge University Press.

Howarth, David. 2010. "Pluralizing Methods: Contingency, Ethics, and Critical Explanation." In *Democracy and Pluralism: The Political Thought of William E. Connolly*. Oxford: Routledge.

Khan, Gulshan. 2016. "Critical Republicanism: Habermas and Mouffe." *Contemporary Political Theory* 12:318–37.

Kolenda, Konstantin. 1986. "Rorty's Dewey." *Journal of Value Inquiry* 20 (1).

Kompridis, Nikolas. 2000. "So We Need Something Else for Reason to Mean." *International Journal of Philosophical Studies* 8 (3).

———. 2006. *Critique and Disclosure: Critical Theory Between Past and Future*. London: MIT Press.

Koopman, Colin. 2006. "Pragmatism as a Philosophy of Hope: Emerson, James, Dewey, Rorty." *Journal of Speculative Philosophy* 20 (2).

———. 2007. "Rorty's Moral Philosophy For a Liberal Democratic Culture." *Contemporary Pragmatism* 4 (2).

———. 2009. *Pragmatism as Transition: Historicity and Hope in James, Dewey, and Rorty*. New York: Columbia University Press.

———. 2011a. "Genealogical Pragmatism: How History Matters for Foucault and Dewey." *Journal of the Philosophy of History* 5.

———. 2011b. "Rorty's Linguistic Turn: Why (More Than) Language Matters to Philosophy." *Contemporary Pragmatism* 8 (1).

———, ed. 2011c. "Special Issue on 'Foucault and Pragmatism.'" *Foucault Studies* 11.

———. 2013a. "Challenging Philosophy: Rorty's Positive Conception of Philosophy as Cultural Criticism." In *Richard Rorty: From Pragmatist Philosophy to Cultural Politics*, edited by Alexander Gröschner, Colin Koopman, and Mike Sandbothe. London: Bloomsbury.

———. 2013b. *Genealogy as Critique: Foucault and the Problems of Modernity*. Bloomington: Indiana University Press.

———. 2014. "Conduct Pragmatism: Pressing Beyond Experientialism and Lingualism." *European Journal of Pragmatism and American Philosophy* 6 (2).
———. n.d. "Political Theory Without Philosophical Ontology: The Work of Critique Without Judgment in William James." Unpublished manuscript.
Kuhn, Thomas. 1962. *The Structure of Scientific Revolutions*. 3rd ed. London: University of Chicago Press.
Kymlicka, Will. 1989. *Liberalism, Community, and Culture*. Oxford: Clarendon.
Laclau, Ernesto. 1996a. "Deconstruction, Pragmatism, Hegemony." In *Deconstruction and Pragmatism*, edited by Chantal Mouffe. London: Routledge.
———. 1996b. *Emancipation(s)*. London: Verso.
Laden, Anthony Simon. 2014. "Engagement, Proposals, and the Key of Reasoning." In *Freedom and Democracy in an Imperial Context: Dialogues with James Tully*, edited by Robert Nichols and Jakeet Singh, 13–31. Oxon: Routledge.
Latour, Bruno. 1993. *We Have Never Been Modern*. Cambridge, MA: Harvard University Press.
Levine, Steven. 2010. "Rehabilitating Objectivity: Rorty, Brandom, and the New Pragmatism." *Canadian Journal of Philosophy* 40 (4): 567–90.
Livingston, Alexander. 2012. "Avoiding Deliberative Democracy? Micropolitics, Manipulation, and the Public Sphere." *Philosophy and Rhetoric* 45 (3): 12.
Lukes, Steven. 2003. *Liberals and Cannibals: The Implications of Diversity*. London: Verso.
Macarthur, David, and Mario De Caro. 2010. "Introduction: Science, Naturalism, and the Problem of Normativity." In *Naturalism and Normativity*, edited by Mario De Caro and David Macarthur. New York: Columbia University Press.
Macedo, Stephen. 1990. *Liberal Virtues: Citizenship, Virtue, and Community in Liberal Constitutionalism*. Oxford: Clarendon.
MacGilvray, Eric A. 2000. "Five Myths About Pragmatism; Or, Against a Second Pragmatic Acquiescence." *Political Theory* 28 (4): 480–508.
MacIntyre, Alasdair. 1985. "Moral Arguments and Social Contexts: A Response to Richard Rorty." In *Hermeneutics and Praxis*, edited by Robert Hollinger. Notre Dame, IN: Notre Dame University Press.
Malachowski, Alan, ed. 1990. *Reading Rorty: Critical Responses to Philosophy and the Mirror of Nature (and Beyond)*. Oxford: Blackwell.
———, ed. 2002. *Richard Rorty*. 4 vols. London: Sage.
———. 2011. "Making a Difference in Cultural Politics: Rorty's Interventions." *Contemporary Pragmatism* 8 (1).
Malecki, Wojciech. 2011. "If Happiness Is Not the Aim of Politics, Then What Is?: Rorty Versus Foucault." *Foucault Studies* 11.
Marchart, Oliver. 2007. *Post-Foundational Political Thought: Political Difference in Nancy, Lefort, Badiou, and Laclau*. Edinburgh: Edinburgh University Press.
Marwah, Inder S. 2015. "A Dangerous Turn: Manipulation and the Politics of Ethos." *Constellations*.
Matarrese, Craig B. 2006. "Satisfaction or Supersession? Expression, Rationality, and Irony in Hegel and Rorty." *Clio* 36 (1).

McCarthy, Thomas. 1990. "Private Irony and Public Decency: Richard Rorty's New Pragmatism." *Critical Inquiry* 16 (2): 355–70.
———. 1991. *Ideals and Illusions: On Reconstruction and Deconstruction in Contemporary Critical Theory*. Cambridge, MA: MIT Press.
———. 1996. "Philosophy and Critical Theory: A Reply to Richard Rorty and Seyla Benhabib." *Constellations* 3 (1): 95–103.
McNay, Lois. 2008. "Recognition as Fact and Norm: The Method of Critique." In *Political Theory: Methods and Approaches*, edited by David Leopold and Marc Stears. Oxford: Oxford University Press.
———. 2014. *The Misguided Search For the Political*. Cambridge: Polity.
Meillassoux, Quentin. 2008. *After Finitude: An Essay on the Necessity of Contingency*. London: Continuum.
Mendieta, Eduardo. 2014. "Freedom as Practice and Civic Genius: On James Tully's Public Philosophy." In *Freedom and Democracy in an Imperial Context: Dialogues with James Tully*, edited by Robert Nichols and Jakeet Singh, 32–47. Oxon: Routledge.
Misak, Cheryl. 2000. *Truth, Politics, Morality: Pragmatism and Deliberation*. London: Routledge.
———, ed. 2007. *New Pragmatists*. Oxford: Oxford University Press.
Moon, Donald. 2004. "The Current State of Political Theory: Pluralism and Reconciliation." In *What Is Political Theory?*, edited by Stephen K. White and Donald Moon, 12–29. London: Sage.
Mouffe, Chantal, ed. 1996a. *Deconstruction and Pragmatism*. London: Routledge.
———. 1996b. "Deconstruction, Pragmatism, and the Politics of Democracy." In *Deconstruction and Pragmatism*, edited by Chantal Mouffe. London: Routledge.
———. 2000. *The Democratic Paradox*. London: Verso.
———. 2005. *On the Political*. London: Routledge.
Mounce, Howard. 1997. *The Two Pragmatisms: From Peirce to Rorty*. London: Routledge.
Newey, Glen. 2000. *After Politics*. Basingstoke: Macmillan.
Nietzsche, Friedrich. 2003. *Twilight of the Idols and The Anti-Christ*. Translated by R. J. Hollingdale. London: Penguin.
Norris, Christopher. 1989. "Philosophy as Not Just a 'Kind of Writing': Derrida and the Claim of Reason." In *Redrawing the Lines: Analytic Philosophy, Deconstruction, and Literary Theory*, edited by Reed Way Dasenbrook. Minneapolis: University of Minnesota Press.
Okrent, Mark. 1988. *Heidegger's Pragmatism: Understanding, Being, and the Critique of Metaphysics*. London: Cornell University Press.
Owen, David. 2001. "The Avoidance of Cruelty: Joshing Rorty on Liberalism, Scepticism, Irony." In *Richard Rorty: Critical Dialogues*, edited by Matthew Festenstein and Simon Thompson, 93–110. Cambridge: Polity.
———. 2016. "Reasons and Practices of Reasoning: On the Analytic/Continental Distinction in Political Philosophy." *European Journal of Political Theory* 15 (2): 172–88.
Peters, Michael A., and Paulo Ghiraldelli, eds. 2001. *Richard Rorty: Education, Philosophy, and Politics*. Lanham, MD: Rowman & Littlefield.

Pettegrew, John, ed. 2000. *A Pragmatist's Progress: Richard Rorty and American Intellectual History*. Lanham, MD: Rowman & Littlefield.

Pippin, Robert B. 1991. *Modernism as a Philosophical Problem*. Oxford: Blackwell.

Rabinow, Paul, ed. 1984. *The Foucault Reader*. New York: Pantheon.

Rajchman, John. 1985. "Philosophy in America." In *Post-Analytic Philosophy*, edited by John Rajchman and Cornel West. New York: Columbia University Press.

Ralston, Shane. 2011. "The Linguistic-Pragmatic Turn in the History of Philosophy." *Human Affairs* 21.

Ramberg, Bjorn. 2002. "Rorty and the Instruments of Philosophy." In *Richard Rorty: Philosophy, Culture, and Education*, edited by Michael Peters and Paulo Ghiraldelli. Lanham, MD: Rowman & Littlefield.

———. 2004. "Naturalizing Idealizations: Pragmatism and the Interpretivist Strategy." *Contemporary Pragmatism* 1 (2).

———. 2013. "For the Sake of His Own Generation: Rorty on Destruction and Edification." In *Richard Rorty: From Pragmatist Philosophy to Cultural Politics*, edited by Colin Koopman, Mike Sandbothe, and Alexander Gröschner, 49–75. London: Bloomsbury.

Rawls, John. 1971. *A Theory of Justice*. Cambridge, MA: Harvard University Press.

———. 1999. *The Law of Peoples*. Cambridge, MA: Harvard University Press.

———. 2005. *Political Liberalism*. Expanded ed. New York: Columbia University Press.

Redding, Paul. 2002. "History as Celebration or Justification? Rorty Versus the Non-Metaphysical Hegelians." *Clio* 31 (4).

Rehg, William, and James Bohman, eds. 2001. *Pluralism and the Pragmatic Turn: The Transformation of Critical Theory*. London: MIT Press.

Rescher, Nicholas. 2000. *Realistic Pragmatism: An Introduction to Pragmatic Philosophy*. Albany: State University of New York Press.

Rogers, Melvin L. 2009a. 'Democracy, Elites, and Power: John Dewey Reconsidered." *Contemporary Political Theory* 8 (1): 68–89.

———. 2009b. *The Undiscovered Dewey: Religion, Morality, and the Ethos of Democracy*. New York: Columbia University Press.

Rondel, David. 2011. "Anti-Authoritarianism, Meliorism, and Cultural Politics: On the Deweyean Deposit in Rorty's Thought." *Pragmatism Today* 2 (1): 56–67.

Rotenstreich, Nathan. 1985. "Rorty's Interpretation of Hegel." *Review of Metaphysics* 39 (2).

Rumana, Richard. 2002. *Richard Rorty: An Annotated Bibliography of Secondary Literature*. Amsterdam: Rodopi.

Schoolman, Morton. 2008. "A Pluralist Mind." In *The New Pluralism: William Connolly and the Contemporary Global Condition*, edited by David Campbell and Morton Schoolman. London: Duke University Press.

Sellars, Wilfrid. 1963a. "Philosophy and the Scientific Image of Man." In *Empiricism and the Philosophy of Mind*. London: Routledge and Kegan.

———. 1963b. *Science, Perception, Reality*. London: Routledge.

———. 1997. *Empiricism and the Philosophy of Mind*. Cambridge, MA: Harvard University Press.

Shapiro, Ian. 1990. *Political Criticism*. Oxford: University of California Press.

Shapiro, Ian, Rogers M. Smith, and Tarek E. Masoud, eds. 2004. *Problems and Methods in the Study of Politics*. Cambridge: Cambridge University Press.

Shusterman, Richard. 1994. "Pragmatism and Liberalism Between Dewey and Rorty." *Political Theory* 22 (3): 391–413.

Silverman, Hugh, ed. 1993. *Questioning Foundations: Truth/Subjectivity/Culture*. London: Routledge.

Sleat, Matt. 2007. "On the Relationship Between Truth and Liberal Politics." *Inquiry* 50 (3).

Stuhr, John. 1997. *Genealogical Pragmatism: Philosophy, Experience, and Community*. Albany: State University of New York Press.

Symposium. 2008. "Symposium on Pluralism and Democracy: The 'Radical Pluralism' of William E. Connolly." *British Journal of Politics and International Relations* 10 (2).

Talisse, Robert B. 2007. *A Pragmatist Philosophy of Democracy*. London: Routledge.

Taylor, Charles. 1989. *Sources of the Self*. Cambridge, MA: Harvard University Press.

———. 1990. "Rorty in the Epistemological Tradition." In *Reading Rorty*, edited by Alan Malachowski. Oxford: Basil Blackwell.

———. 2003. "Rorty and Philosophy." In *Richard Rorty*, edited by Charles Guignon and David R. Hiley. Cambridge: Cambridge University Press.

Tonder, Lars, and Lasse Thomassen, eds. 2005. *Radical Democracy: Politics Between Abundance and Lack*. Manchester: Manchester University Press.

Topper, Keith. 1995. "Richard Rorty, Liberalism, and the Politics of Redescription." *American Political Science Review* 89 (4): 945–75.

Tully, James. 2005. "Reply to Michael Blake and Leif Wenar." In *Political Exclusion and Domination NOMOS XLVI*, edited by Melissa S. Williams and Stephen Macedo, 250–58. New York: New York University Press.

———. 2008. *Public Philosophy in a New Key*. Vol. 1: *Democracy and Civic Freedom*. Cambridge: Cambridge University Press.

Volbers, Jörg. 2014. "Language or Experience?—That's Not the Question: A Case for Reflexivity." *European Journal of Pragmatism and American Philosophy* 6 (2): 175–99.

Voparil, Christopher J. 2006. *Richard Rorty: Politics and Vision*. Oxford: Rowman and Littlefield.

———. 2011a. "On Rorty and Brandom: Pragmatism and the Ontological Priority of the Social." *Pragmatism Today* 2 (1).

———. 2011b. "Rortyan Cultural Politics and the Problem of Speaking for Others." *Contemporary Pragmatism* 8 (1).

———. 2013. "Pragmatist Philosophy and Enlarging Human Freedom: Rorty's Deweyan Pragmatism." In *Richard Rorty: From Pragmatist Philosophy to Cultural Politics*, edited by Alexander Gröschner, Colin Koopman, and Mike Sandbothe. London: Bloomsbury.

———. 2014a. "Rorty and Dewey Revisited: Towards a Fruitful Conversation." *Transactions of the Charles S. Peirce Society: A Quarterly Journal in American Philosophy* 50 (3): 373–404.

———. 2014b. "Taking Other Human Beings Seriously: Rorty's Ethics." *Contemporary Pragmatism* 11 (1): 83–102.

Warnke, Georgia. 2003. "Rorty's Democratic Hermeneutics." In *Richard Rorty*, edited by Charles Guignon and David R. Hiley. Cambridge: Cambridge University Press.

Wenman, Mark. 2013. *Agonistic Democracy: Constituent Power in the Era of Globalisation.* Cambridge: Cambridge University Press.
——. 2015. "William E. Connolly: Resuming the Pluralist Tradition in American Political Science." *Political Theory* 43 (1): 54–79.
West, Cornel. 1989. *The American Evasion of Philosophy: A Genealogy of Pragmatism.* London: University of Wisconsin Press.
White, Stephen K. 2000. *Sustaining Affirmation: The Strengths of Weak Ontology in Political Theory.* Oxford: Princeton University Press.
——. 2004. "The Very Idea of a Critical Social Science: A Pragmatist Turn." In *The Cambridge Companion to Critical Theory,* edited by Fred Leland Rush, 310–35. Cambridge: Cambridge University Press.
——. 2011. "Contemporary Continental Political Thought." In *The Oxford Handbook of the History of Political Philosophy,* edited by George Klosko. Oxford: Oxford University Press.
——. 2016. "Continental and Analytic Lenses in Relation to the Communicative Action Paradigm: Reconstructive Thoughts." *European Journal of Political Theory* 15 (2): 189–204.
Widder, Nathan. 2000. "On Abuses in the Use of History: Blumenberg on Nietzsche; Nietzsche on Genealogy." *History of Political Thought* 21 (2).
——. 2012. *Political Theory After Deleuze.* London: Continuum.
Williams, Bernard. 2005a. *In the Beginning Was the Deed: Realism and Moralism in Political Argument.* Edited by Geoffrey Hawthorn. Princeton, NJ: Princeton University Press.
——. 2005b. "Pluralism, Community, and Left Wittgensteinianism." In *In the Beginning Was the Deed: Realism and Moralism in Political Argument,* edited by Geoffrey Hawthorn. Princeton, NJ: Princeton University Press.
Wingenbach, Ed. 2011. *Institutionalizing Agonistic Democracy.* Farnham: Ashgate.
Wolin, Sheldon. 1992. "What Revolutionary Action Means Today." In *Dimensions of Radical Democracy.* London: Verso.
Yack, Bernard. 1986. *The Longing for Total Revolution.* Guildford: Princeton University Press.
Zabala, Santiago, ed. 2005. *The Future of Religion.* New York: Columbia University Press.

INDEX

acquiescence: charge of, 18 248n11; ontological version of criticism of, 39
"actants," 117
agency, human, 7; contingency and, 85; distributive sense of, 117; limitations of, 117; in posthumanism, 111
"agentic capacities," 117
agonism, 224; and agonistic respect, 228; Connolly's, 237–243, 239; in democratic theory, 113, 225–237, 241; general features of, 226, 228; and intervocabulary engagement, 244; nonontological, social-practice-based, 225; ontological variant of, 227–228; and prioritization of conflict, 228; and question of political, 227; in Western tradition, 225
"agonistic dimension of games," 234
agreement: intersubjective 184, 185; in political life, 241; universalizing, 198–200
"Ambiguity of 'Rationality', The" (Rorty), 185
American society: contemporary, 176
analytical thought, and pragmatism, 224
analytic-continental divide, 224; and pragmatic naturalism, 93

anthropocentrism: danger of, 119; narcissistic, 112
antiauthoritarian, defined, 214
antiauthoritarianism, 102, 233; across critical social theory, 170–182; in critique of epistemology, 29; metaphilosophical, 55; metatheoretical, 172; Rorty's, 107, 211; in Rorty's hermeneutics, 44; and Rorty's liberalism, 157; and Rorty's positive ethicopolitical moral project, 218; tied to ethicopolitical project, 56
anticonvergence, Rorty's, 198
antiessentialism, Rorty's, 106, 107
antifoundationalism, 91, 98, 99; aim of, 121; antiauthoritarianism and, 212; and concept of contestability, 96; focus on social practices of, 10; in pragmatism, 10; radical thought of, 178; Rorty's, 38; and Rorty's linguistic turn, 77, 96
antiotherness, Rorty's, 198
antirelativism, 38, 92, 98, 99; and concept of contestability, 96; and Rorty's linguistic turn, 77, 96
antirepresentationalism, metatheoretical, 176

antiskepticism: aim of, 121; antiauthoritarianism and, 212
antitheoretical positions, Rorty's negative, 203
Apel, Karl-Otto, 8
Appearance and Reality (Connolly), 85
appearance-reality distinction, 74, 136; authoritarianism of, 179; failure to address modernity of, 139; in linguistic practice, 174; nature of knowledge without, 140; and truth of tradition/community, 176
attachment, strategy of, 73
authoritarianism, authority without, 135
authority, 205; without authoritarianism, 121, 135; claims to, 229; and contemporary social theory, 168–170; in contemporary sociopolitical criticism, 182; continued desire for, 35; forms of, 175; grandeur and profundity, 183; of knowledge claims, 33; and larger group loyalties, 177; nonhuman, 107; normative, 160, 184, 200; and objectivity, 36; ontological category of social, 26–27; radical questioning of, 144; reflexive, 233; Rorty's explanatory and normative, 119; social origin of, 39, 242; and social practices, 36, 216–217; vs. truth, 150; in universal ontological conditions, 151; in Western philosophy, 29
autonomy: from present, 196; quest for, 187, 190

beauty, and neopragmatism, 7
beauty, philosophical, and sociopolitical progress, 160
becoming: new ontologies of, 110–111; ontocosmology of, 113–114, 118
behavioralism, in political science, 249n9
behaviorism, in epistemology, 33
being: contingency of, 123; frameworks of authority for, 212
Being: concealments of, 89; Heidegger's understanding of, 87; nature of, 118, 123; primacy of, 76; revelation of, 91; understanding of, 82–83
"belatedness," Rorty's view of, 136
Bennett, Jane, 111–112
Berlin, Isaiah, 161–162
Bernstein, Richard, 10, 159
Bloom, Harold, 162
Blumenberg, Hans, 135–136, 136–137
Brandom, Robert, 35, 36, 37, 68, 94, 108, 188–190

canon reformation, 131
causality, emergent vs. efficient, 117
causation, as key element of justification, 30
causes: cause-justification conflation, 249n8; distinguished from justifications, 101
certainty: and authority, 67; continued desire for, 35; and epistemological behaviorism, 32; and "Platonic Principle," 30; Platonic quest for, 33–34; in Western thought, 29
certainty, philosophical, in Western thought, 81
certainty, quests for, 211
coherence, truth as, 72
commensurability: assumption in hermeneutics of, 40; of discourses, 67
communication: enabling productive, 49; undistorted, 181. *See also* language; languages
communitarian political theories, 13, 158, 160–161
communities: of identification, 177–178; in modern societies, 175; normative ideal of, 175; and ontological reality, 67; in social criticism, 176
community, 205; and conditions of Being, 74; ideal, 205
comparison, and injunction to holism, 214–215
compensation, ontological disposition of, 73
"complacent liberalism," Rorty's, 35
compulsion, continued desire for, 35

concept change, 67; in Rorty's *PMN*, 27; Rorty's understanding of, 28, 79; vocabulary for, 97
concepts: as "essentially contestable," 87; reconstructing, 129–130
conceptual systems: limitations of, 115; as systems of linguistic behavior, 103
conflict: and agonism, 226; contemporary democratic, 239; moral, 177; in pluralist democracies, 14; theorization of, 227; about values, 11
Connolly, William E., 18, 65, 99, 100, 103, 111, 139, 145, 170, 227, 228, 242, 243; agonism of, 237–243; concepts for, 87; continentalism of, 85–89; critical engagement with Rorty of, 90–96; critique of modernity of, 138; democratic ethos of, 225; on existing matrix of democratic discourse, 238; and inevitability of ontology, 70–73; logic of world-picture for, 147; modern values for, 139; naturalism of, 103, 122–123; on naturalized Hegelianism, 139–140; on Nietzsche, 150; ontological account of Foucault of, 196–197; ontological approach of, 15–16, 20, 70–73, 76, 86, 146, 147; ontological assumptions in politics for, 115–116; ontological critique of Rorty of, 85; ontological thinking of, 117–118, 123–124; ontology of, 117–118; and ontology of politics, 67; ontology of resistance of, 141; ontopolitical approach of, 66, 109, 113; on the political, 241; politics of, 19; positive ontopolitical account of, 113; and question of grounds, 226; recent political thought of, 112–113; Rorty critiqued by, 14; and Rorty on critique within political theorizing, 132; and social-scientific method, 115; and standard of truth, 139
consensual language: of deliberative democracy, 176
consensus: and community norms, 176; democratic practice restricted to, 226;

normatively justified, 178–179; in political life, 241; true *vs.* false, 178; truth as, 72
Consequences of Pragmatism (Rorty, *CP*), 128
consequentialism, 256n3
conservatism, Rorty's theoretical, 252n15
constitution, notion of: deflationary view of, 193; language of, 45
contestability, 85; claim of, 17; Connolly's mechanism of, 123 Connolly's onto-ethical-political concept of, 95–96; and critical reflexivity, 118; and ontological approaches, 145; priority of, 123, 125; relativizing effects of, 124
continental political theory, 19, 23; Connolly's, 85–89; and crisis in foundations, 66; emphasis on critique of, 169; language as tool in, 80; naturalism in, 83; ontological approach to, 145; postfoundational, 70; post-Heideggerian, 85; and pragmatism, 8, 93, 224; and problem of justification, 83; Rorty's engagement with, 5, 47, 74, 96, 152, 156, 223, 245, 251n9; trends in, 211; "weak ontology" from, 4
contingency, 89; and continental philosophy, 76; determination as limitation within, 88; fidelity to radical, 118; freedom as recognition of, 166; general reality of, 88–89; Heideggerian, 93; language of, 78; of life and, 113; of linguistic practices, 132; necessity of, 89, 91, 113, 141, 170; and new materialism, 109; as recalcitrance, 117; recognizing, 144; for Rorty, 66, 80
Contingency, Irony, and Solidarity (Rorty; *CIS*), 79, 160, 162, 177, 183, 199
conversation: activity of reasoning, 235; bringing philosophy down into, 229; democratic, 235; Rorty fomenting of, 246
conversational philosophy, 224
conversation partners, expanding realms of, 208

Cooke, Maeve, 170, 175, 181–182, 186
correctness, normative, 38
correspondence, truth as, 72
cosmopolitanism, 177; ideal, 175; inclusive, 184; nonauthoritarian pursuit of, 166; romantic framing of, 183
creativity, in emergent causality, 117
critical clarification, second-order, 152
critical detachment, 231; normativity and, 118
critical social theory, 167, 168; antiauthoritarianism of, 170; continental, 246; debates in, 169; disagreements within, 169; ethically oriented modes of reflection in, 168–169; liberalism in, 156; public-private divide in, 171; and radical thought, 167–168
critical theory, 5, 6, 23, 170; antiauthoritarian, 181; Habermasian, 155; normative meaninglessness in, 181; and pragmatism, 8, 247n3; and radical thought, 178; Rorty's rejection of, 179
critical theory-radical thought, and analytic-continental typology, 255n14
criticism: and citizen activity, 233; nature of, 191
critique, 205
critique, practice of, 197; common prioritization of, 222
cultural-critical conception, of philosophy, 128
cultural criticism: and Dewey, 54; role for theory in, 55
cultural critique, "transformational," 222
cultural evolution: as continuous, 103; narratives of, 104
cultural freedom, Rorty on, 134
"Cultural Left," the, 195
cultural naturalism, 250n22
cultural politics, 19, 165; aim of, 167; analysis of, 69; capacity to engage in, 210; conception of, 204; contest of narratives in, 136; and critical reconstruction, 204; critical reflexivity within Rorty's conception of, 97; defined, 68; democracy in, 94; developing frameworks for, 213; and linguistic interventions, 205; logical spaces in, 208; normative foundation of, 208–209; philosophy as, 49, 94, 156, 200; privileged center to, 229–230; as public dialogue, 204–208; Rorty's, 9, 58, 94, 207, 241; Rorty's use of language of, 219; in sociopolitical-cultural matrix, 206; status of languages in, 221; vocabulary of, 97, 205
"Cultural Politics and the Existence of God" (Rorty), 68
culture: flourishing of, 167; growing point of, 69; in political theory, 173–174; public, 130

Darwin, Charles, 51, 120, 148
"Darwinian naturalism," 104
Davidson, Donald, 77, 78, 79, 104, 147
deconstructionism, American, 193
dedivinization, and modernity, 172–173
Deleuze, Gilles, 114
deliberation, model of democratic dialogue opposed to, 234
deliberative theory, political maxim in, 236
democracies, 243; agonistic, 113, 116, 145, 226–227; antiauthoritarian conception of inclusive, 217; background condition of possibility for, 229; competing normative standards in, 144; conflict in agonistic, 224; diverse-vocabulary-using groups in, 234; diversity of pluralistic, 141; ethos of engagement in, 116–117; at heart of pragmatism, 209–210; linguistic social practices of, 23; normative core of, 238; pluralistic, 204; as political method, 158; ' radical utopia,' 14; reasons in context of, 235–236; sense of belonging in, 236; theories of, 202
democracy, 242, 245; ethics and, 186; ethos of, 211

democratic politics: conditions associated with, 180; difference among, 203–204; ethical dimension of, 238; ethical sensibility for contemporary, 197; justification in, 213; modern, 178; pragmatic, 164–165; and relevant community of justification, 177
demos, and political theory, 243
Derrida, Jacques, 193, 248n12, 251n9
Descartes, René, 25, 29
descriptions: in historical development, 131; in human inquiry, 45; "reasonable re-descriptions," 233; relation of critique to, 133; second-order task of describing, 129
determination as limitation, 113, 117, 138
Dewey, John, 7, 11, 18, 42, 147, 148, 159, 218; antiauthoritarianism of, 54; critical intelligence of, 56; divided thought of, 52–60; reconstructive disposition from, 93; Rorty's contested relationship to, 50–51; Rorty's interpretation of, 52–53, 61; and Rorty's pragmatism, 50–51; Rorty's specific use of, 23
dialogue: enabling productive, 49; model of democratic, 234; prolonged intercultural, 181; public, 204–208
difference: democratic engagement among, 175; democratic politics among, 203–204; normative value of, 168; radical ontological reification of, 219; reifying, 198–200
differentiation, romantic, 210
disagreement: ontological, 241; in practical democratic politics, 227
disciplinary matrix, T. Kuhn's concept of, 43
discourse: commensurability of, 67; democratizing of, 95; Foucault on, 197; pluralizing, 95
diversity: agonistic democratic engagement in, 228; at level of theoretical difference, 246

double-entry orientation: Connolly's, 124; to interpretation, 73, 75, 115; to political theorizing, 115
dualisms, philosophical: Dewey's opposition to, 53, 54; Dewey's overcoming of, 54–55

eliminative materialism, 25; Rorty's, 24, 101; vocabularies in, 26
emancipation, and radical thought, 190
empiricism, and inquiry, 46
engagement: Connolly's ethos of, 239–240; in democracy, 116–117; as ontological exposition, 242
enlarging human freedom, project of, 205
Enlightenment: continental homogenization of, 144; and political ideals of modernity, 171; in understanding of modernity, 135, 137
Enlightenment rationalism, Rorty's critique of, 13
epistemic norms, behavioral explanations of, 32–33
epistemological behaviorism, 28–35; explanations of knowledge in, 33; in *PMN*, 32
epistemology: behaviorism in, 33; Dewey's critique of, 56–57; primacy of, 71–72; Rorty's critique of, 24, 56–57, 66–67; sociopolitical criticism linked to, 90
Essays on Heidegger and Others (Rorty; *EHO*), 80
essence, question of, 93
essentialism: critique of, 145; Rorty's, 198–199
ethical judgment, and antiauthoritarianism, 170
ethicization, Rorty's, 57–58
ethicopolitical moral project, in sociopolitical strategy, 49
ethnocentric manner, of Rorty's liberalism, 158

ethos: hermeneutics as, 40; metatheoretical hermeneutical, 41; in political strategy, 239–240; Rorty's, 46, 48–50
ethos building, 241
Ethos of Pluralization, The (Connolly), 119
European philosophy: radical social transformation in, 187–188
"evangelico-capitalist resonance machine," 240, 252n14
evolution, as continuous, 103
evolutionary theory, language of, 104
"existential faiths," 116, 124

faith: language of, 146; ontological, 151
fallibilism, 212, 213; pragmatist, 230; and Tully's uses of language, 231
fallibilistic virtues, 56
"false consciousness," 179
"Feminism and Pragmatism" (Rorty), 199
feminists, and public-private divide, 159
Festenstein, Matthew, 132–133, 175
field linguist, 77, 78
finitude, 96; acknowledgment of, 221; desirable sense of, 98; and language and Being, 84–85; nonabsolutistic philosophy of, 84; Rorty's interpretation of, 85
force, distinguished from persuasion, 191
Foucault, Michel, 5, 19, 86, 90, 156, 198, 251n9; in Connolly's critique, 91; critique of, 222, 223; and desire for sublimity, 195; on freeing of difference, 198; as "ironist," 187; normative reluctance of, 197; on oppressive nature of liberal-democratic power relations, 194; Rorty compared with, 192–198; Rorty's interpretations of, 20; on status of social criticism, 192, 193, 196
foundationalism: Connolly's criticism of, 149; critique of, 44; defined, 6; moribund, 37; and naturalism, 100; possibility of social, 99; rejection of, 6; for Rorty, 245–246; Rorty's critique of, 13, 66–67, 163;

social, 90–91, 97; undermining, 92. *See also* antifoundationalism
foundations: crisis of, 8, 65; and "Heideggerianism of Left," 8–9; vs. idealizations, 164; pathways away from problem of, 74–75; role of ontology after, 75
fragility, ontocosmology of, 113–114
Fraser, Nancy, 13, 162
freedom: and comprehensive doctrines, 166; contingency as recognition of, 166; defining human, 188; Foucault on, 197; negative, 162; recording of, 234; unparalleled positive, 189
future: of politics, 211; Rorty's view of, 132; shift from eternity to, 209

Gadamer, Hans-Georg, 44, 47, 249n14
Geistesgeschichte, 131, 136
genealogy, 231; pragmatism and, 222–223
God: existence of, 68; Nietzsche's death of, 150
goodness: and neopragmatism, 7; and political freedom, 180
"good society," 168–169, 175–176
grandeur, in Rorty's sociopolitial criticism, 182–183
Gross, Neil, 12
grounding, logic of, 138
"guidance problem," 169

Habermas, Jürgen, 8, 13, 94, 170, 179, 186, 190, 198, 221; critical theory of, 171, 221; on democratic dialogue, 180; "discourse ethics" of, 175, 177; ideal of universal validity of, 176; on justification in modernity, 200; as liberal, 187; liberalism of, 158; notions of rationality of, 181; and political thinking, 156; and public liberalism, 171; on Rorty, 172–173; Rorty's critique of, 14, 20; social criticism of, 178; universal validity of, 204

Hegel, Georg Wilhelm Friedrich, 5, 19, 137, 152, 188, 251n9; conception of philosophy of, 130–132; and critical conception of rationality, 134; idealism of, 148; "pattern of insistence" of, 140; and Rorty's criticism of Dewey, 51; theory of sociality of reasons of, 134
Hegelianism: amenable to modern sensibilities, 140; naturalized, 139–140
Heidegger, Martin, 5, 19, 52, 136, 146–147, 162, 250n4, 251n9; critique of pragmatism of, 142; on epistemology and modernity, 86; and "eventing" of Being, 87; and figuration of Being as becoming, 114; historicity of, 82; and language as social practice, 92–93; and language of contingency, 78; notion of ontological difference of, 9; ontic-ontological distinction of, 227; on pragmatism, 32; questioning Being of, 86; Rorty's reading of, 83; sense of historicity and contingency of, 80–81; structure of Being of, 113; on Western thought, 81, 90
"Heideggerianism of Left," 8–9
Heideggerian model, reflexivity in, 215
Heideggerians, as Rorty's target, 136
Heideggerian theory, Rorty's critique of, 213
Herculine Barbin (Foucault), 195
hermeneutics, 23; as attitude, 39–44; and continental thought, 212; and ethos of tolerance, 218; Gadamerian, 44; in *PMN*, 39; and question of inquiry, 39, 46; Rorty's pragmatist view of, 47; Rorty's rejection of, 44–47; Rorty's turn to, 23; and vocabulary change or debate, 43–44
historical contingency, Heidegger's theory of, 76
historical perspective, languages in, 132
historicism, 66, 98, 152; and focus on intermethodological exchange, 102; of Hegel, 130; and holism, 214; and human inquiry, 43; and T. Kuhn's scientific paradigms, 42–43; and language, 149 and

naturalism, 99, 215; naturalistic, 142–152; and nominalism, 213; and normative change, 132–135; relation of naturalism with, 147; Rorty's, 20, 131, 133, 134, 135, 149, 150, 152, 215; in Rorty's articulation of philosophical practice, 98–99; in Rorty's hermeneutics, 44; in Rorty's pragmatic approach, 99
history, 126; functions of, 131; language and, 80; and prioritization of culture, 128; Rorty's holistic use of, 147; and sociopolitical criticism in, 128
holism, 106, 231; historical, 129; and human inquiry, 43; linguistic practices in, 133; methodological imperative to, 122, 214; and normative political practices, 102; Rorty's, 215; in Rorty's hermeneutics, 44; sociopolitical, 56; theoretical, 32
Honig, Bonnie, 230, 254
Honneth, Axel, 8
hope: ethos of melioristic, 209; history and narrative as source of, 135; politics of social, 209
humanity: in modernity, 137; new self-image for, 181; in political theory, 166; as sole object of normative value, 119
humility, undesirable sense of, 98

identification, moral communities of, 208
identity, 205; existing thick *vs.* inclusivist, 165; moral, 176–177; and normativity, 175; rationality in moral, 185; in Rorty's approach to social criticism, 176
ideologiekritik, category of, 179
ideology, rational argument *vs.*, 178
imagination: in normative change, 184; political, 185; reason and, 181, 182; social creative, 210; value of, 184
immanence, radical, 124
inclusion, as such, 219
inclusivism, cosmopolitan, 183
inclusivity, in. Rorty's politics, 20

inquiry, 43, 67, 220; ambiguous nature of, 115; antirevolutionary conception of, 34; and commensurability, 40; conditions of possibility of, 60; constraints on, 167; ethical approach to, 165; ethicized, 186; governing metatheoretical frame for, 43; hard and soft varieties of, 42; hermeneutics and question of, 39, 40–41; languages of, 59; on metaphilosophical level of vocabularies, 39; and the mind, 29; process of, 59; rationally reflexive approach to, 244; redescription in, 129; Rorty's politicization of, 219; Rorty's reconstruction of notion of, 58–59; Rorty's reframing of, 216
intellectual history, 131
intellectual history, Rorty's view of, 79
intelligence, "critical," 56
intercultural engagements, rationality in, 186
intergroup engagement, 237
intermethodologies, 203, 224; discussion, 116; disputes, 116; horizontal engagement, 224; languages as basis for, 124–125; pluralistic exchange in, 118; Rorty's model of, 236
internormative engagement, 212, 213, 217
interpretation: double-entry orientation to, 73, 75, 115; language as process of, 77–78
interpretive critique, Tully's theory as, 231–232
intervocabulary engagement, agonistic approach to, 244
intervocabulary normative exchange, metavocabulary of, 208
intervocabulary relations, 149, 221
"ironists," radical thinkers as, 187

James, William, 7, 18, 51, 114, 147, 148
Jefferson, Thomas, 164
Joas, Hans, 8
justice: and authority, 166; insufficiency of established, 239; for Rorty, 165; and self-creation, 163; solidarity vs., 161; vocabulary of, 160
justification: authoritarian forms of social, 183; for building cosmopolitan inclusive community, 174–175; causation as key element of, 30; coherentist model of, 34; communities of, 186; distinguished from cause, 101; Forty's reconceptualization of, 35; impossibility of absolute, 65; and intervocabulary exchange, 206; and language-using humans, 92; linguistic, 213; in linguistic practices, 132; and radical thinking, 189; rational, 186, 219–220; relation to truth of, 173; relevant community of, 177; Rorty's theory of, 160, 162–163; social, 69; of social change, 195; social mode of, 165; social norms of, 32; as social practice, 128; social practice of, 34, 49; as social relation between language-using subjects, 101; sociologizing, 179; sociolpolitical process of, 206; in sociopolitical contexts, 186; sociopragmatic conception of, 37; in Western public culture, 173
justification, problem of, 6, 16, 21, 203; and antiauthoritarianism, 170; and commonality among difference, 167; in contemporary political thought, 75; and continental contingency, 83; and diversity of languages, 122; and double-entry interpretation, 115; and eliminative materialism, 33; and language, 101; and normative transformation, 244; ontological approach to, 245; for Rorty, 76–77; and Rorty's liberalism, 157; in Rorty's *PMN*, 31–32; Rorty's pragmatic account of, 23

Kant, Immanuel, 249n7
knowledge: figurations of limits of, 151; and neopragmatism, 7; Rorty's examination of, 28; and social justification of belief, 32
knowledge-as-power: Baconian, 144

knowledges: insurrection of subjugated, 197
Kompridis, Nicolas, 181–182, 186
Koopman, Colin, 15, 31, 38, 183, 222, 223, 243, 249n15; normativity without foundations for, 77
Kuhn, Thomas, 41, 42–43, 184

Laclau, Ernesto, 13
Laden, Anthony, 234, 235
language: and Being, 83, 84; Connolly on theories of, 87–89; constitutive role of, 47; and continental philosophy, 76; as epistemological standard, 77; as essential to human existence, 46 of existential faith, 124; fortunes of, 200–201; as fundamentally poetic, 88; and hermeneutics, 45; meanings constituted in, 45–46; and methods of inquiry, 45; naturalization of, 102; nonfoundational priority of, 77; of nonpurposive contingency, 104; normative authority shifted to, 92; in pragmatic, social terms, 96; and problem of justification, 101; of qualified affirmation, 169; for Rorty, 66, 87, 90, 93; Rorty's anticommensuration view of, 58; in Rorty's articulation of philosophical practice, 98–99; in Rorty's naturalism, 101; Rorty's vocabulary of vocabularies in, 37; as social practice, 78, 92, 103–104; sociopolitical importance of, 92; strategic *vs.* nonstrategic use of, 178; technical interpretation of, 84; theory of, 25; as tool, 77, 91; of unmasking, 74; world-disclosive function of, 13. See also eliminative materialism
language of games, 233
languages: analyses of, 152; constitutive space of freedom within, 133–134; contingency of, 125; as critical political resources, 152; in cultural politics, 70; engagement of plural, 204; focusing political theorizing on, 125; in imaginative redescription, 206; of inquiry, 59; for intervocabulary relations, 133; invention of new, 35; of liberal-democratic politics, 230; lived consequences of, 212; and naturalism, 102; ontological, 67, 94–95, 120; philosophy for intervening in, 132; of purpose, 221; in Rorty's recontextualization, 59; in Rorty's reflexivity, 216; Rorty's tool-based accounts of, 143; as social practice, 220–221; as social practices, 121, 128, 147; status of, 221; as tools, 80, 102; as vocabularies, 95–96; Wittgensteinian account of, 232
language use: and fallibilism, 231; holistic nature of, 205; of humans, 120; naturalistic account of, 104; normative diversity within, 218; in political critique, 189; social sphere of, 101; standards for validity within, 174; and universality, 171–172
Legitimacy of the Modern Age, The (Blumenberg), 135–136
liberal-democratic politics, language of, 207, 230
liberalism: assumptions of, 225; commitment to, 164; in critical social theory, 156; "ethnocentric," 165; historicist justification of, 164; minimalist articulation of, 165 and postmodernism, 230; reconstruction of, 167; Rorty's engagements with, 6; Rorty's identification with, 157; Rorty's vision of pragmatic, 253n9; during 1990s, 158
liberalism, Rorty's postmodern bourgeois, 159
"liberal naturalist" alternative, to scientific inquiry, 102–103
liberal political theories, and Rorty's foundationalism, 160–161
liberal proceduralism, 219
liberal theory, Rorty on, 5–6
liberal utopia, Rorty's notion of, 13–14
linguistic change, process of, 26

linguistic diversity, 163, 201
linguistic innovation, 199
linguistic norms: applying and transforming, 133; social origin of, 26
linguistic practice, 56, 186; analysis of, 72; appearance-reality divide in, 174; contingency of, 132; criticizing, 214; defined, 233; and democratic justification, 232–233; Foucault on, 197; and identity, 177; and justification, 173; justification in, 132; and new vocabularies, 207; and political forms of life, 221–222; in radical thinking, 189, 190, 192; sociocultural criticism of, 23; theory as, 205
linguistic relations: desirability of reciprocal, 240; transformation of norms through expansion of, 199
linguistic turn: authority and contingency, 76–78; for foundationalism, 6
linguistic turn, Rorty's, 24–25, 91–92, 128; to antifoundationalism and antirelativism, 96; impact of antiauthoritarianism on, 76
literacy, and free discussion, 179
literary criticism, 162
Locke, John, on sensations, 29–30
logic: *vs.* litter, 114; of the political, 242
logical spaces: language of, 208; Rorty's conception of, 207–208
Longing for Total Revolution, The (Yack), 187
Lyotard, J. F., 178

MacIntyre, Alasdair, 13
macropolitical project, Rorty's, 165–166
Malachowski, Alan, 12
Marx, Karl, 188; Connolly's critique of, 140; critique of Hegel's ontology of Spirit of, 140; "pattern of insistence" of, 140
Marxists: on "false consciousness," 179; as Rorty's target, 136
mastery, 119, 148, 215; ethics of, 142; implicit human-centered, 127; and modern malignancies, 138–142; ontology of, 18–19, 120, 143; and priority of social, 150–151; self-assertion *vs.*, 135; "technological," 137, 144
materialism, new, 108–118; mastery and, 119; and naturalism, 126; normative motivation in, 122–123; ontological actants in, 111–112
materiality: "agentic capacities" of nonhuman, 111; Connolly's assumptions about, 123–124; consequences of, 111; dynamic nature of, 110–111; and politics, 109; reconsidering, 109, 111
maxims, of Rorty's theoretical model, 211
McCarthy, Thomas, 91, 171, 172, 173
McNay, Lois, 151, 227, 236
meaning: compared with language, 46; in language, 45–46; and methods of inquiry, 45; phenomenon of, 44
means, Rorty-Habermas debate over, 178
meliorism, pragmatist, 209
mental states: as normative phenomena, 26; reporting of, 25, 26
metaphor: at center of history of human languages, 79; in linguistic development, 143
metaphysics: crisis in, 65; and language and Being, 84–85; Rorty's interpretation of, 85
methodological diversity, 24
methodological imperative, to holism, 122, 214
methods, philosophical: interpretive *vs.* empirical, 41; post-Nietzschean, 47
micropolitics, 239, 241
Mill, John Stuart, 158, 162
mind: analytic philosophy of, 22; and mind-body problem, 24, 25; Rorty's essays on philosophy of, 25; as standard of philosophical knowledge, 28
minimalism, ontological, 148
minority rights, 230
modernity, 126; Anglo-American, 118; central flaw of, 89; common rejection of, 136–137; for Connolly, 138, 141, 142, 146; continental critiques of, 136; as continual

process of critique, 139; and cosmopolitan project of the Enlightenment, 217; critical reflexivity within, 104; critique of, 138; critique of postmodernity, 171; Heidegger's understanding of, 82, 83, 86–87; humanity in, 137; insufficiency of moral motivation in, 210, 211; justification of, 152; models of, 135; ontological analysis of, 144; and ontology, 71; paradox of, 141–142; and problem of justification, 172; rational developments of, 178; reconstructing, 142; for Rorty, 135–138; and Rorty's reflexivity, 216; significance of, 137; and theory of critical reflexivity, 135; ultimate concern of, 138; and weak ontology, 145–146
modernity/postmodernity, 168
moral obligations, universal, 174
morals: in Kuhn's remapping of human culture, 42; social-practice-based approach to, 49
Mouffe, Chantal, 14, 227
multiculturalists, and public-private divide, 159
mutual protection, logic of, 162
mutual respect, relations built around, 235
myopias, liberal, 230

narratives: contest of, 136; in cultural practices, 129; in human inquiry, 43; reconstructing, 129–130; role of, 185; of smaller, more intimate groups, 177; upward, 132
naturalism, 66, 98, 115; alternative reconstruction of, 108; Connolly vs. Rorty on, 125–126; in continental thought, 83; as contingent language, 216; cultural, 250n22; Darwinian, 214; defined, 214; and historicism, 99, 215; immanent, 115, 117; and language, 149; linguistic form of, 122; and mastery, 121; and new materialism, 126; ontological, 141; pragmatic, 92 as process of naturalization, 122; reconstructing, 108–118; relation of historicism with, 147; scientific, 102; as set of mutually limiting and enabling injunctions, 148; social foundationalism of, 142–143; social-practice-based, 100; and strategic priority of language as social practice, 100
naturalism, Connolly's, 115; and materialist ontology of *immanent*, 114; ontological, 100, 112–113, 114, 115; ontological framework of immanent, 112–113; reading of Rorty's, 100
naturalism, Rorty's, 20, 102, 103, 120, 121, 122, 148, 150, 215, 216; antiessentialist, 120; articulation of philosophical practice in, 98–99; pragmatic approach to, 100–108
naturalization, process of, 103
natural sciences, Rorty's alteration of, 104
nature: distinction between man and, 45; and nature-culture divide, 120
negative methodological injunction, 214
neopragmatism, 7–8, 12, 50
"New Realism," 257n10
Nietzsche, Friedrich, 5, 19, 80, 114, 151, 188, 249n12; Connolly's reading of, 139; critique of metaphysics of, 150; on knowledge as mode of power, 140; and language as social practice, 92–93; and language of contingency, 78; and primacy of Being, 83; on truth within Western thought, 139; Western philosophy critique of, 90
Nietzscheanism, Foucault's, 193
Nietzscheans, as Rorty's target, 136
nominalism, 212, 213
nonauthoritarian theory, as sociopolitical criticism, 167
normative/analytical political theory, 168
normative authority, 120; antiauthoritarian leveling of, 111; of languages, 121; sociopragmaic conception of, 37
normative transformation, 226, 242, 244

normativity, 205; Dewey's, 53; and Foucault, 192–198; without foundations, 15–19, 77, 172; as human issue, 119; human responsiblity for, 38–39; intrinsic, 112; and justification of vocabulary, 107; and language, 122; linguistic approach to, 121; linguistic practices of, 138; politicization of, 175; question of, 214; rationally reflexive approach to, 244; relation between critique and, 168; Rorty's practice-based view of, 175; Rorty's social conception of, 209, 217

norms: antiauthoritarian, 233; criticism of liberal, 221; generated by critical theories, 169–170; and normativity, 175; Rorty's pragmatism about, 255n7; of smaller, more intimate groups, 177; spectrum of, 215–216; using, 108; vocabularies and, 107

objectivity: as-accurate-representation, 155; and authority, 36; and normative authority of social, 27; and standards of inquiry, 59
ontocosmology, Connolly's, 118
ontological analysis: Connolly's, 75; contestability in, 17
ontological detachment, strategy of, 73
ontological difference, Heidegger's notion of, 9
ontological minimalisms, 94, 148
ontological thought, 19, 97; and cultural-critical method, 19; to material world, 109; and metatheoretical difference, 18; in political theory, 15–17, 67, 250n1; postfoundational, 5; Rorty's criticizing of, 99
ontology, 71; and agonism, 227; analytic sense of, 250n4; as arbiter of human culture, 28; contestability of, 72, 123; defined, 127; and Foucault, 192–198; limits of, 72; materialist, 114; as method, 99; and necessity of contingency, 91;

new-materialist, 110, 112; political, 170; priority of, 123, 125; problem of status of, 146; for sociopolitical criticism, 4. *See also* weak ontology
ontology, Connolly's, 117; pluralistic, 239; theorization of, 70; use of, 20
ontology, Rorty's, 120–121; critique of, 24; opposition to, 67; rejection of, 15
ontopolitical assumptions, mastery and attunement of, 72–73
ontopolitical interpretation, 71
ontopolitical method, Connolly's, 70
oppressive norms, critiques of, 202
otherness, as abstracted generalization, 197
overlap, continuum of degrees of, 217
Owen, David, 169, 255n8

panpsychism, Rorty's, 147–148
paradigm: change, 184; intersubjective, 171; Kuhn's concept of, 43
Peirce, Charles Sanders, 7, 18
performative contradiction, 172
persuasion, distinguished from force, 191
philosophical antiauthoritarianism, and Rorty's liberalism, 157
Philosophical Discourses of Modernity, The (Habermas), 172
philosophy: analytic and conversational, 224; as-criticism-of-culture, 128; as cultural politics, 94, 200; and foundations of knowledge, 28; as metadiscipline, 32–33; public model of, 23; relation between politics and, 171; sociological critique of, 28–35; task of, 107–108; in Western thought, 29
philosophy, history of, Rorty's reading of, 105
philosophy, practice of, Rorty's "internal critical challenge" of, 60
Philosophy and the Mirror of Nature (PMN; Rorty), 23, 29, 30, 31, 34, 128, 205
Philosophy as Cultural Politics (Rorty; PCP), 67, 205

Plato, 44, 248n2; on certainty, 81; "Platonic Principle," 30; and "society as Man writ large," 194–195
pluralism: and agonism, 226; and commonality among difference, 167; Connolly's view of, 114, 139; as constitutive of democratic politics, 162; democratic, 126, 225–237; in Kuhn's scientific paradigms, 42–43; of logical spaces, 207–208; methodological, 220; multifaceted, 220; as ontology dynamic, 99; political, 7, 16, 21, 167; problem of, 148, 203; questions of, 220; Rorty's defense of, 161; Rorty's early, 48–50
pluralistic, in cultural politics, 94
pluralistic authority, social conditions of, 212
pluralistic democracy, in Rorty's politics, 20–21
PMN. See *Philosophy and the Mirror of Nature*
political, the: ontologization of, 227, 228; question of, 242; reification of category of; social basis of, 191
political culture, liberalism as, 158
political exchange, as interpretive intervention, 206
political interpretation, in social scientific method, 115
political liberalism, agonism in, 225
political life, Tully's view of, 241
political methodology, critical, 223
political orders, justification of, 202
political practices, human, 129
political theorizing, 129, 132
political theory, 129, 132; analytical, 5; approaches to, 125; basis of, 6'; built-in ontological presuppositions in, 240–241; and citizen activity, 229; contemporary, 143, 144, 220, 244–245; cultural-political difference in, 116; distinction for reflexive, 243; focus of, 228; as form of sociopolitical criticism, 244; horizontal conception of, 231; justification of normative claims in, 6; metapolitical trends in, 5–15; multiple purposes served by, 3; and new materialism, 109, 112; normative, 152; normative/analytical, 168; normative project of, 229; ontological, 5, 71, 109, 111, 156, 161, 243, 250n1; pluralistic, 220–224; Rorty's connections to and insights for, 155; social-practice-based, 244; Tully's contributions to, 234–235; turns in contemporary, 22; weak-ontological turns in, 70
political theory, Rorty's, cultural engagement in, 173
Political Theory and Modernity (Connolly), 138, 146, 151
political thinking, "socially weightless" form of, 151
political thought: external standards dominating, 213; metatheoretical frame for, 203; ontopolitical method of interpretation in, 74–75; pragmatic, 7, 11 (*see also* pragmatism); and problem of political pluralism, 7 (*see also* pluralism)
politics: abnormal, 206; agreement and disagreement in, 241; approaches to theorizing, 99; democratic, 177; dialogical, 240; diversity, 242; double-entry orientation to, 73; foundations of, 160; identity, 237; inclusive ethos for, 167; and modernity's tensions, 210; Mouffe's definition of, 227; ontological assumptions in, 115; ontological conditions behind, 96; ontological limitations on, 75; philosophical validation of, 171; relation between philosophy and, 171; of social hope, 209
Politics and Ambiguity (Connolly), 85, 87, 119
positive attachment, normativity and, 118
possibility, noncausal condition of, 106
postfoundationalism, 6, 8; agonism in, 225; and ontological political theories, 16; weak ontology distinguished from, 17

postfoundationalists, Rorty's democratic politics rejected by, 14–15
post-Marxists, 158
postmodernism: American, 193; and liberalism, 230
postmodernity, critique of, 171. *See also* modernity
poststructuralists, and public-private divide, 159
power: and neopragmatism, 7; use of term, 194
power politics, contemporary, 230
practical reasoning, historically situated practices of, 233
pragmatism, 5, 6; antifoundationalism in, 10; R. Bernstein on, 10–11; and conflict about values, 11–12; contemporary, 7–8; and continental thought, 212; dominant narrative of, 10; and ethos of tolerance, 218; "genealogical," 222–223; Heidegger on, 82, 142; and idealism-realism argument, 104; inclusive ethos of, 245; and mastery, 119; metaphilosophical, 48; neopragmatism, 7–8, 12, 50; Nietzschean, 81; about norms, 35–36; question of, 22–24; and rationality, 8; Rorty's, 10, 23, 44–45, 48–50; and Rorty's antiauthoritarian, 191; and Rorty's liberalism, 157; situated approaches of, 17–18; social-scientific analysis of, 245; third wave of, 17, 18; Tully's, 230; and weak ontology, 17, 18, 86
prediction, in natural *vs.* social sciences, 43
prima philosophia, 170
"Priority of Democracy to Philosophy, The" (Rorty), 163–164
"privileged representations," claims for, 32
profundity, in Rorty's sociopolitcal criticism, 182–183
public, ontological articulation of moral sources in, 238
public ethics, 238
public ethos, critical responsiveness to, 239

public grandeur, and external authority, 183
public philosophy, 231, 233; and comparative dimension of critique, 231; and Connolly's agonism, 237–243; intellectual history of, 228; Tully's, 229
public-private divide, 183; as heuristic distinction of emphasis in language, 189; radical thought in, 187; in Rorty's politics, 159–160; vocabularies in, 182
public reason, criterion of, 164
purpose, notion of: category as horizontal, 221; focuses on diverging, 223; and normativity, 175; and public-private divide, 160; in tension, 163

Quine, W. V. O., 30, 31, 32

"radical critique," Rorty's use of term, 251n9
"radical democracy," 14
radical thought, 155, 170, 186; coerced discourse in, 190; contemporary difference for, 199; in critical theory, 168, 169, 178; critique of, 171; and democratic engagement among difference, 175; general weakness of, 187; problem with, 191; in public-private divide, 187; and radical thinkers, 192; Rorty's critique of, 187; weak ontology as subset of, 255n15
rationalism, theories of foundational, 233
rationality: criteria for, 130; critical approach to, 186; as critical reflexivity, 216; as ethical relation among groups, 217; in intercultural engagements, 186; in intersubjective construction, 186; modern claim to, 146; in moral identity, 185; and new vocabularies, 186; pragmatic, 8, 182–186; reconstruction of, 38, 178; Rorty's reconstruction of, 134, 138, 179, 181, 182, 185, 219, 234; theory of communicative, 180
rational progress, and cultural-political possibilities, 131

Rawls, John, 5, 163–164, 166, 185, 221; liberalism of, 158; reflective equilibrium of, 191; Rorty's essay on, 165
reading, reconstructive, 224
reason: critical, 178; as intersubjective disposition, 185; naturalizing, 179; in normative change, 184; Rorty's understanding of, 182–183; sociality of, 178; and transformation, 182
reasonableness: criterion of, 164, 165; of engagement, 236
reason giving, activity of, 124
reason-imagination dichotomy, 168
reasoning: activity of, 235; democratic, 234
reciprocity: and ontological political theory, 243; relations built around, 235; rule of, 235
recognition, relations built around, 235
reconstruction, defined, 59
recontextualization, Rortian, 59
redescription, conflictual and inclusive, 224
reflexive agency, at metatheoretical level, 245
reflexive development, in pragmatic social criticism, 190
reflexive growth, 217
reflexive theory, 244
reflexivity, 91, 92; and contingency, 95 democratic pluralistic, 99; encouragement of critical, 61; and ethic of tolerance, 217–218; as goal of social theory, 215; methodological, 90–96; and ontological political theory, 243; operativity of, 123; in political theory, 15–19; possibility of, 217; rationality as, 134; Rorty's view of, 61, 66, 135, 215; self-assertion as, 135–138
relating, frameworks of authority for, 212
relations with others, problem of, 199
relativism: charge of, 134; and naturalism, 100
relativity, language of, 149
religion, in public discussion, 68

representationalism: logic of, 55; as vocabulary, 101
resistance: counterontology of, 143; ontology of, 141
responsibility, ontological category of social, 26–27
responsiveness, critical, 238
romantic depth, and external authority, 182
romantic novelty, privatization of, 188
Rorty, Richard, 237; agonistic readings of, 228; alternative readings of, 157; antiauthoritarianism of, 10, 29; antiepistemological and antiontological turn of, 35; Connolly compared with, 124; Connolly's critical engagement with, 90–96, 97; Connolly's criticism of, 149, 197–198; continental critiques of, 66; critical receptions for, 12–15; critical role of, 12; critique of epistemology of, 29; cultural-political method of, 9, 19; disposition to justification of, 69; early metaphilosophy of, 19–20; early strategic elimination of, 24–28; end of inquiry for, 41; hermeneutics rejected by, 46; Koopman's reinterpretation of, 15; on language as tool, 80; language for, 92, 93; liberalism of, 6; linguistic turn of, 102, 149; metaphilosophical context for, 37; metatheoretical political thinking of, 203; metatheoretical reading of, 21; method and model of, 4; methodological project of, 46; and modern claim to rationality, 146; naturalism of, 105–106; on necessity of contingency, 89; 1990's attacks on, 157; normative authority of, 36; and normative correctness of critical and political discourses, 34; ontological analysis rejected by, 97; ontological critique of, 120–121; ontological method rejected by, 20; on pilosophy of mind, 28–29; and political consequences, 202–203; political reading of, 157–167; political theory of, 4, 12–13; pragmatic turn of, 22–23, 47; and

Rorty, Richard (*cont.*)
  problem of metatheoretical difference, 18; reading strategy of, 51–52; reconstructing, 3; relation to Hegel of, 130; second "Enlightenment" of, 38; skepticism about theory of, 252n15; sociological circumvention of, 60; and sociopolitical criticism, 12–15; strategic prioritization of social of, 42; theoretical holism of, 32; in third-wave scholarship, 20
Rorty-Dewey criticism, three waves of, 50–51
Rorty-Habermas debate, 178
Rousseau, Jean Jacques, 188, 194
Russell, Bertrand, 184

Said, Edward, 199
scheme-content distinction, 147
science: normal *vs.* revolutionary, 41–42
sciences: correct shape and status of human, 46; model of nature in, 115; new theoretical models in, 114
scientific inquiry, 102
scientific paradigms, 41
scientific revolutions, 79
scientism, nineteenth century, 130
secularization, and modernity, 172–173
self-assertion: as critical reflexivity, 135–138; defined, 137; Rorty's narrative of, 143–144
"self-awareness," in Rorty, 131
self-consciousness, "historical," 137
self-creation: ideas of, 162; and justice, 163; vocabulary of, 160
self-foundation, defined, 137
self-image, replacement of human, 209
"self-justification," in Rorty, 131
self-reliance, Rorty on, 134
Sellars, Wilfrid, 30, 31, 32, 37, 38, 107, 213
sensations, language of, 25–26
social, the: in conceptual-linguistic change, 27; messiness of sphere of, 242; ontological category of, 26–27; ontological priority of, 67–73, 90, 97, 150, 212; priority of, 23
social activist, philosopher as, 53
social change: contingent nature of, 79; cultural-political conception of, 74; justification of, 195; linguistic, 130–131; and ontological analyses, 74; pursuit of, 209; and vocabularies, 188
social constructivism: anthropocentrism of, 111; for new materialism, 110
social critic: philosopher as, 54; Rorty's image of, 58
social criticism: alternative social world in, 191; nonessentialist criteria for, 134; philosophy as form of, 55; pragmatic, 190; proceeding includsively with, 157; social conception of, 178
social criticism, Rorty's, 176, 198
social foundationalism, 90–91, 142–143
social interaction, and human freedom, 188
socialization: and levels of awareness, 163; in radical thinking, 189
social justification, and public-private divide, 163
social life, normative transformation of, 242
social mobility, and free discussion, 179
social practice: ethicopolitical, 211; language as, 122; linguistic, 232; in Rorty's naturalism, 101; in Rorty's view of contingent, 104
social-practice-based approach, 49
social-practice-based tool, and contingency of language, 213
social practices: to address foundationalism, 8; and antiauthoritarianism, 100–108; and authority, 26, 36; concept of purpose in, 58; Dewey's account of, 52, 56; external vindication for, 175; and freedom, 166; languages as, 92, 147; linguistic, 55, 56; and ontological reality, 67; political thought situated in, 152; and radical thought, 191–192; rational, 134; Rorty's pragmatic vocabulary of, 106; Rorty's

understanding of, 79; sharing of normative, 10
social relationships, and reflexive theory, 244
social sciences: Connolly's methodological criticisms of, 70–71; horizontal differences in, 43; object of inquiry in, 58; ontological reflection in, 71
social-scientific analysis, of pragmatism, 245
social theory: continental critical, 246; radical, 191
sociolinguistic process, justification as, 94
sociological circumvention, strategy of, 23
sociopolitical change, 208; forms of, 134; reduced to linguistic development, 90; Rorty's model of, 93–94
sociopolitical criticism, 128; from analytic thought to, 23; authority in contemporary, 182; as conflict between linguistic practices, 181; contemporary, 167–168, 170; embedded, 156; engaging in, 214; framing of task of, 127; in languages, 102; and ontology, 67; philosophical resources for, 142–152; philosophy as, 134; pluralistic, 204; political theory as form of, 244; problem of justification in, 6–7; recognizing others in, 186; reconceiving model of, 109–110; Rorty's, 48, 60, 61, 132, 200; Rorty's conception of, 20, 70; Rorty's model of, 108, 142; Rorty's theory of, 214–215, 232; situated, 119; theoretical political practice as form of, 205; theoretical practice as, 213; theory in, 156; vocabulary for, 97
sociopolitical inquiry: and concept of purpose, 53; and development if pragmatist theory in, 126; metatheoretical role for, 55–56; metatheories in, 233; model of theoretical praxis in, 55; ontology in, 143; resources for, 134; Rorty's democratic ethos for, 219; theoretical justification in, 195; weak-ontological response to, 125

sociopolitical life, 123; contemporary, 187; moral progress in, 149; role of theory in, 201; standards for judging, 148
sociopolitical progress, Rorty's view of, 127
sociopolitical reality, distortions of, 178
solidarity: among democratic community, 160; demands of human, 163; and inquiry, 216; moral ideal of, 185; oppositional, 162; purpose of achieving, 161; and standards of inquiry, 59
Sources of the Self (Taylor), 210
space and time, for Rorty, 149–150
speaking: diverse ways of, 208; frameworks of authority for, 212; new ways of, 201; obsolete ways of, 147. see also language
Spinoza, 114
spirit-histories, Rorty on, 131–132
Spivak, 199
standards, context-independent, 173
strategic elimination, Rorty's, 24–28
subjectivity, and normative authority of social, 27

talking, various ways of, 55. See also speaking
Taylor, Charles, 210
Terms of Political Discourse (Connolly), 87
theory: politicization of, 205; reality as proper subject of, 68; unproductive absolutist conceptions of, 223. See also political theory
time, Heidegger's sense of, 81
tolerance, 165; agonistic respect compared with, 238; vs. emancipation, 219; and radical thought, 190; Rorty's ethic of, 217–218; as theoretical disposition to normative change, 190–191
tool metaphor, Rorty's, 133
tools: criterion for betterness of, 179; in Rorty's naturalism, 120
Total Revolution: longing for, 188; of radical thinkers, 187

transcendence: Connolly's opposition to, 115; and immanence, 124
transcendental explanation, 105
"transitionalism," in reconstruction of Rorty, 15
"Trotsky and the Wild Orchids" (Rorty), 159
truth: approaches to, 33; authority of, 142; for Connolly, 140; Heidegger's understanding of, 86–87; and neopragmatism, 7; and political freedom, 180; Rorty on, 79; in social criticism, 172; solidarity vs., 161; theories of, 139; of tradition/community, 176; universal nature of, 173
Tully, James, 202, 225, 226, 227, 229, 230, 231, 237, 240, 241, 243, 244; on agonistic engagements, 236; contributions to contemporary political theory of, 234–235; debate with liberalism of, 230; on existing matrix of democratic discourse, 238; framing of linguistic engagement by, 233; nonontological agonism of, 228; on Rorty's "revolutionary insight," 228; theory of democracy of, 232

uncertainty: in Connolly's naturalism, 123; in Connolly's view, 117; in emergent causality, 117
universalism, moral, 210
universality: approach of, 207; commitment to, 171; Rorty's rejection of, 172
universe: James's model of pluralistic, 114; pluralistic, 125
unmasking, notion of, 74; critique of Rorty's, 142; language of, 74; logic of, 136, 137–138
utility, category of, 69

validity, universal, 171, 173, 174
values: conflict about, 11; scientific, 42
Vattimo, Gianni, 248n12
violences, of contemporary norms/institutions, 244

virtues: civic, 167; finding democratic, 180–181
vitalism: Darwin's, 148; Deleuze's inorganic, 114; Rorty's, 147–148
vocabularies, 122, 163; achieved with new stability, 130; adopting new, 191; alternative, 26; attractiveness of, 215; and authority, 201; and category of utility, 69; concepts within, 36; creation of new, 79; of cultural politics, 68, 205; and Darwinian naturalism, 214; ethicopolitical ontology of, 212; and freedom, 166; idiom of, 35; impermanence of, 130; in inquiry process, 59; languages as, 95–96; of liberal democracies, 158; for naturalism, 215; new, 205, 206; and normative authority, 200; outward pointing, 161; and political forms of life, 222; political theory and other, 228–229; practices of reasoning within, 181–182; public, 174, 204; and public-private divide, 160; and relating to Being, 95; role in philosophy of, 127; for Rorty, 106–107, 121; Rorty's hostility to, 121; Rorty's vocabulary of, 133; and social change, 188; social justification as measure between, 91; subvocabularies, 207; as tools, 77, 133; various uses of, 101; "vocabulary of," 94, 95, 134, 203, 212.220
vocabulary: naturalistic, 252n16; ontological, 242; Rorty's sociological, 105; Rorty's understanding of, 100
Voparil, Christopher, 3, 49, 51, 56, 162, 186, 199

"we-accusation," Rorty's, 196
weak ontology, 16–17, 72, 100; and agonism, 225; and Anglo-American forms of continental thought, 169; and Connolly, 112; within critical social theory, 169; failure of postmetaphysical thought in, 141; mastery and, 119; and modernity, 145–146; and necessity of

contingency, 170; in political theory, 70; pragmatism and, 86; Rorty's criticism for, 97; as subset of radical thought, 255n15
we-belonging (community), 240
"we-focus," criticisms of Rorty's, 219
"we liberals" label, 176
West, Cornel, 7–8
West, rationalistic rhetoric of, 175
Western democracies, 164; inclusion and, 219; public vocabularies of, 187
Western philosophy: desire for authority in, 29; foundationalist project of, 9; Heideggerian critique of, 90; Nietzschean critique of, 90
Western theory, central division of, 224
Western thought, 159; centrality of self-foundation to, 172; Connolly's critique of, 250n1; criterion of reasonableness in, 165; history of, 172, 229; language in, 230; pragmatism in, 11; rationalism in, 207; Rorty's accounts of development of, 135; universal validity in, 172
White, Stephen K., 14, 16, 97, 144–145, 240, 245
Wittgenstein, Ludwig, 52, 93, 232–233
Wolin, Sheldon, 227
"world, the": limits of human ability to organize, 150; synoptic view of, 147
world-picturing, visual metaphors of, 146

Yack, Bernard, 187–188

Zuhanden, primordiality of, 80

NEW DIRECTIONS IN CRITICAL THEORY

Amy Allen, General Editor

The Wrath of Capital: Neoliberalism and Climate Change Politics, Adrian Parr

Media of Reason: A Theory of Rationality, Matthias Vogel

Social Acceleration: A New Theory of Modernity, Hartmut Rosa

The Disclosure of Politics: Struggles Over the Semantics of Secularization, María Pía Lara

Radical Cosmopolitics: The Ethics and Politics of Democratic Universalism, James Ingram

Freedom's Right: The Social Foundations of Democratic Life, Axel Honneth

Imaginal Politics: Images Beyond Imagination and the Imaginary, Chiara Bottici

Alienation, Rahel Jaeggi

The Power of Tolerance: A Debate, Wendy Brown and Rainer Forst, edited by Luca Di Blasi and Christoph F. E. Holzhey

Radical History and the Politics of Art, Gabriel Rockhill

Starve and Immolate: The Politics of Human Weapons, Banu Bargu

The Highway of Despair: Critical Theory After Hegel, Robyn Marasco

A Political Economy of the Senses: Neoliberalism, Reification, Critique, Anita Chari

The End of Progress: Decolonizing the Normative Foundations of Critical Theory, Amy Allen

Recognition or Disagreement: A Critical Encounter on the Politics of Freedom, Equality, and Identity, Axel Honneth and Jacques Rancière, edited by Katia Genel and Jean-Philippe Deranty

What Is a People?, Alain Badiou, Pierre Bourdieu, Judith Butler, Georges Didi-Huberman, Sadri Khiari, and Jacques Rancière

Death and Mastery: Psychoanalytic Drive Theory and the Subject of Late Capitalism, Benjamin Y. Fong

Left-Wing Melancholia: Marxism, History, and Memory, Enzo Traverso

Foucault/Derrida Fifty Years Later: The Futures of Genealogy, Deconstruction, and Politics, edited by Olivia Custer, Penelope Deutscher, and Samir Haddad

The Habermas Handbook edited by Hauke Brunkhorst, Regina Kreide, and Cristina Lafont

Birth of a New Earth: The Radical Politics of Environmentalism, Adrian Parr

GPSR Authorized Representative: Easy Access System Europe, Mustamäe tee 50, 10621 Tallinn, Estonia, gpsr.requests@easproject.com